C. H. DODD

Also by F. W. Dillistone

CHARLES RAVEN

C. H. DODD

Interpreter of the New Testament

by

F. W. Dillistone

HODDER AND STOUGHTON
LONDON SYDNEY AUCKLAND TORONTO

The author and publishers are grateful to Faber and Faber Ltd. for permission to quote extracts from Four Quartets by T. S. Eliot in chapter 19.

Preface

IN THE COURSE OF WRITING THE BIOGRAPHY OF C. H. DODD I HAVE
sought the help of many who at one time or another were his companions
on his journey through life. I am specially grateful to the members of his
immediate family circle who shared their memories with me and allowed
me to see diaries and papers which he had preserved. His literary
executor, Professor C. F. D. Moule, has assisted me in every possible way,
as have two distinguished Mansfield men who were his students and then
his friends for roughly half a century—Dr. Norman Goodall and Dr. J. S.
Whale. Their comments on first drafts of the manuscript, in part or as a
whole, have been invaluable.

I have also been privileged to draw upon the memories of other Mansfield
men—in particular, Nathaniel Micklem and John Marsh, each a former
principal of the college, Professor H. Cunliffe-Jones, Dr. Geoffrey Nuttall,
and Dr. Gordon Robinson. Dr. Edward Hardy, formerly Dean of Jesus
College, Cambridge, kindly enabled me to meet Fellows of that college
who had been contemporaries with Dodd, and the Rev. W. F. Flemington,
formerly Principal of Wesley House, gave me much information about
the period during which Dodd occupied the Norris-Hulse Chair of
Divinity. From across the Atlantic came ready assistance from Professor
Amos N. Wilder of Harvard, Professor Paul Minear of Yale, Professor
Langdon Gilkey of Chicago and Professor W. R. Farmer of the Perkins
School of Theology in Dallas. For details of Dodd's outstanding contribution to the production of the New English Bible I am indebted to
the Archbishop of Canterbury (Dr. F. D. Coggan), Bishop J. A. T.
Robinson and Professor J. K. S. Reid.

To many others who have provided me with information through
interviews or correspondence I tender my sincere thanks. Furthermore it is
pleasant to record my indebtedness to three fine memoirs of Dodd written

5

respectively by Dr. George Caird (for the British Academy), Professor
F. F. Bruce of Manchester University and Professor W. D. Davies of
Duke University, North Carolina. The last-named was joint editor of
the Dodd Festschrift in 1954 and he has spared no pains in correspondence
to enable me to gain a true picture of a great scholar and generous teacher.

I have regarded it as my main task to write the story of Dodd's life
rather than to attempt a detailed critique of his historical reconstructions
and theological interpretations. Doctoral theses have been written on his
attitude to history and on his distinctive approach to eschatology.
Moreover, in recent literature many references may be found to Dodd's
handling of New Testament problems. On my part I have tried to give
an account of a man who was not only one of the leading New Testament
scholars of this century but also a devoted son and husband and father, a
brilliant lecturer and writer, a man deeply sensitive to human needs and
passionately concerned to bear witness to that gospel which he believed
to be the power of God unto salvation.

June 1976   F. W. D.

Contents

Introduction

ONE SUNDAY IN 1921, DURING MY FIRST YEAR AS AN UNDERGRADUATE
at Oxford, I found my way to Mansfield College to attend morning
service. I cannot now remember what drew me there—I presume that I
had spotted the name of some well-known preacher on the terminal list
which hung on college notice-boards. A good many people were walking
along the quiet Mansfield Road which passes the college, whose setting
is as pleasant as any in Oxford. Its chapel is a fine late-nineteenth-
century building, lofty, rectangular, with windows depicting a catholic
range of famous figures—particularly scholars—in the history of
Christianity. At that time the large congregation sat in chairs facing the
raised sanctuary where, behind a communion table, the Principal and Staff
had their stalls. The pulpit was on the right, a lectern on the left.

Immediately before the beginning of the service a procession entered
from the south door. The Chaplain who led the way was followed by a
remarkable trio whose image still remains vividly in my memory.
Walking side by side came two of the college tutors: behind them the
Principal, either alone or escorting the visiting preacher—normally a man
holding high office in one of the Free Churches, or a distinguished
ecclesiastic from Scotland.

The Principal, Dr. W. B. Selbie, was short though substantially built,
with closely-cropped beard, and eyes which looked out with a steady
intensity from a somewhat impassive face. He came to be known as the
'inspired mouse' for, although when walking with head slightly bent
forward he seemed to suggest a certain shyness and inoffensiveness, when
he mounted the pulpit he became more like what one imagines an Old
Testament prophet to have been—eloquent, outspoken in his moral
judgments, passionate in his summons to Christian action.

But if Selbie was the mouse, the two who walked ahead of him in the

9

procession might have been compared to the giraffe and the robin. One, Dr. Vernon Bartlet, was very tall, with large head and long flowing beard, an eminent Church historian, a grave representative of that Puritan divinity which was part of Mansfield's tradition. (He was referred to by his students as the 'elongated saint'.) The other, the Rev. C. H. Dodd, was tiny in comparison, quick in his movements, a face alert but without strain, a well-proportioned head with dark slightly wavy hair—he seemed almost to hop and dance by the side of his venerable colleague. This was my first introduction to a man whose books were to exercise a dynamic influence on my own understanding of the New Testament and whom I was to be privileged to know through personal acquaintance at a later time. His own association with Mansfield College began when he came to Oxford as an undergraduate nearly twenty years before my own time. He remained devoted to the college until his death in 1973. Probably no other institution provided him with comparable opportunities for the development of his outstanding gifts as teacher, preacher, writer, interpreter, and finally director of the translation of the New English Bible.

PART 1

Wrexham

I

Father and Mother

CHARLES HAROLD DODD WAS BORN AT WREXHAM ON APRIL 7TH, 1884. In the late nineteenth century Wrexham was the largest town in North Wales, an important market centre and a link between the dominantly Welsh-speaking villages on its westward side and the Shropshire plain of rural England which stretched eastwards from the Border a few miles distant. Settled as early as the twelfth century, its chief glory was the parish church, a building almost cathedral-like in its architectural splendour, dating from the early sixteenth century. Under the patronage of Henry VII a magnificent tower, 136 feet in height with hexagonal turrets, had been erected, and eastwards from this there extended a lengthy nave with a fine perpendicular roof. The church was imaginatively sited and until late in the seventeenth century was the focus of the town's religious and social life.

The Toleration Act of 1689, however, became the Magna Carta of Protestant Dissent and small congregations of Dissenters began to establish themselves in Wrexham. By 1857, when the population of the town was about 7,500, five places of worship existed besides the Parish Church and within a decade this number had increased to ten, seven for English-speaking and three for Welsh-speaking Nonconformists. Even this number almost doubled within the next thirty years, partly through the increase of population, partly through secessions. Figures show that just before Charles Harold was born, thirty-seven per cent of the town's population were regular attendants at church or chapel.

The chapel to which his family belonged was named Pen-y-bryn. It had been opened in 1789 and flourished during the nineteenth century to such an extent that in 1897 the foundation stone of a new complex of buildings, including sanctuary and schoolroom, was laid. Salisbury Park Congregational Church replaced Pen-y-bryn, which was sold to a congregation of Welsh Baptists. But Pen-y-bryn was a name of sacred memory to the members of the Dodd household. They lived near the chapel and engaged wholeheartedly in its many activities.

In the general life of the town one major division was that which existed between church and chapel folk. The other was between those who spoke English and those whose regular language was Welsh. Ordinarily English predominated, but on market day or on the occasion of an annual fair Welsh came into its own. The inn-yards would be crowded with gigs and traps from the country. The Welsh woman's hat would occasionally be seen and Welsh voices would be heard everywhere on the streets. Again, with the developing prosperity of coal-pits and steel works on the Welsh side of Wrexham, Saturday evenings brought in crowds of weekly shoppers different in character from the agricultural workers but often sharing with them the use of a common language. A small boy in this border town could not fail to be aware of the phenomenon of bilingualism, and although in the Dodd home English was always spoken, the boys found ways and means of picking up enough Welsh to enable them to converse with those whose native tongue it was. Maids for example who helped Mrs. Dodd in household duties would often speak to the boys in their own language and the oldest was able to teach his younger brothers their numbers in Welsh almost before they knew them in English. Dodd's early fascination with words and language equivalences was to continue with him throughout his life.

II

At his ordination in 1912 Dodd declared publicly, 'To the influence of home and church (I can scarcely separate them) I owe everything in early days.' It was not long after he was born that his parents took possession of Clovelly Cottage, their family home until his father's death in 1928. The church was Pen-y-bryn, of which his father was deacon, choir-leader and Bible-class teacher. Except during the annual two weeks' holiday, these were the two geographical foci around which his life during its first eighteen years revolved.

But if these were the two geographical foci of influence, even more influential were the two parents the story of whose lives together must surely constitute one of the most romantic records of educational achievement in North Wales, or indeed in any other area, in the late nineteenth century. Mrs. Dodd (née Sarah Parsonage, born in 1854) had lost her own mother in infancy and her father died when she was still very young. Brought up by her stepmother in the most straitened circumstances, she nevertheless succeeded in gaining a Queen's scholarship and became one of the earliest of women students to be trained as a teacher in London. Her two years spent at Stockwell College were blissfully happy and provided her with memories which gave pleasure throughout her life. Her first post was in a school at a small town in Shropshire, from which after a short time she moved to become headmistress of an infant school in the Welsh village of Penygelly. In 1882, however, she relinquished her formal teaching when she married Mr. Charles Dodd, the assistant master at the Brookside School in Wrexham. (He was appointed headmaster two years later.) Between 1884 and 1891 she bore four sons and, behind the scenes, took no small part in their education. In due course she guided their homework, shared their wakening interests in literature and music, and created the peaceful and orderly environment within which scholarly gifts could grow to maturity.

A gentle woman, regarded as delicate in her early years, she lived to the age of eighty-six, continuing her regular daily walks until within a fortnight of her death. After her husband died, she returned to the neighbourhood where she had been headmistress, and delighted in the welcome she received from many she had taught in the infant school. 'In stature,' her eldest son once wrote, 'she was unusually short and she was always proud of her tiny hands and feet, with good reason. Her nose and mouth were somewhat too large for beauty but she had fine brown eyes and a mass of curly dark-brown hair, which she wore, after the fashion of the time, in ringlets falling to her shoulders. She did not "put up her hair" until my infant fingers found the ringlets irresistible playthings.' Supporting her husband in every aspect of his public service, devoted to the welfare and advancement of her sons, she willingly gave precedence to her duties in the home over the educational career that she might have achieved.

Whereas little is known of the Parsonage family background, in the case of the Dodds much valuable information about their early history in North Wales was collected by their youngest son Professor A. H. Dodd, who also wrote a fascinating booklet for the Denbighshire Historical Society giving details of his father's career as teacher and schoolmaster in the Brookside School from 1867 to 1919.[1]

It appears that there were Dodds living in the Gresford district in the seventeenth century, and a certain Robert Dodd (the name was spelt sometimes with one and sometimes with two d's), who was married to Mary Roberts in 1786 and lived on a small farm at Gwersyllt, was the direct ancestor of Charles Dodd the schoolmaster. The latter's father, Edward Dodd, grew up on the family farm but, being a younger son, was apprenticed to a whitesmith in Wrexham and duly qualified as a craftsman. Within a few years, however, his health collapsed and he became incapable of pursuing his trade. He returned to his father's farm and worked as a labourer, being paid at the rate of six shillings a week. In 1846 he married Frances Griffiths, and their son Charles was born in 1855. After his marriage Edward left the farm and for the remainder of his life engaged in a variety of jobs depending on the state of his health. His grandson Charles Harold remembered him in the late eighties as a gentle, kindly and rather silent man who worked at that time as a salesman for German yeast, which was then beginning to displace the native barm in the baking of bread. He travelled round the villages of the area, driving a horse and trap and sometimes taking his grandson with him. But in 1891 he died and the boy's memories were more of his grandmother, who was a woman of ability and forceful character, bearing the burden of a semi-invalid husband and a young family with energy and resourcefulness. There were five children, of whom one died in early childhood and one was adopted by an aunt who had no children of her own. But the conditions under which the others grew up were grim in the extreme. They were vividly described many years later by the grandson himself.

> The house in which they lived stood at the entrance to a court built by the brook-side. As I knew it, the court was a squalid slum. Thirty or forty years before it had probably not descended quite so low but it must always have been a place of mean poverty-stricken dwellings. My grandmother made a little money by taking in lodgers, who shared the living-room with the family. My father seldom spoke of those days. The lodgers were often rough men of coarse speech and disgusting habits, frequently drinking to excess. One day when he was about seven, they made him drunk for sport. Such experiences lay behind his fanatical teetotalism in later years. He once told me how on one occasion as a small boy he made up his mind to help the family income, unbeknown to his parents, by selling newspapers in the streets as the neighbours' boys did. But on setting out with his papers under his arm, he met a gentleman to whom he was known, one of the deacons of the chapel. He felt so utterly ashamed of being caught at his job that he turned back and never dared to sell papers again. The incident is illuminating. It shows at once how needy the family was and at the same time how tenaciously they held to a certain arbitrary standard of 'respectability'; to be seen selling papers in the street was to let the standard down. It is easy to call it petty snobbery; but to those who

stood upon the very verge of the 'morass of destitution' and degradation, everything, however trivial, which stood for standards of life which they were resolved not to give up, was a source of strength, hope and courage in the grim struggle.

At school he early showed ability. At the age of twelve he was accepted as a pupil teacher and began a career of fifty years, without interruption, in the service of the same school. In due course he took the examination by which in that period the 'Queen's Scholars' were selected to receive two years' training in a Normal College at the expense of the State. He came out very near the head of the list and was offered a scholarship. It was a notable opportunity for fitting him to advance in his profession. But poverty stood in the way. The headmaster was prepared to offer him at once a position as an assistant teacher and the salary he earned would enable him to ease the burden of his mother and to improve the family's standard of living. He did not, I think hesitate in his choice nor did he regret it. But all his life he felt deeply that his one great opportunity had been missed. Above all when he became headmaster he was sensitive to his lack of qualifications which belonged to his professional colleagues and even to the assistant masters whom he employed on his staff. It was not only a sense of personal inferiority: it was a feeling that he was letting the school down and it drove him to overtax his strength in acquiring, quite unnecessarily, other qualifications to compensate for the lack.

During those early years he worked desperately hard under serious disabilities. In that crowded little home it was difficult indeed to find privacy and quiet for study. It became his practice to rise at 5 o'clock in the morning and get most of his study done before starting his day's work in school. During the summer he would go out of doors. In a park about a mile and a half from the town there stood an old oak whose gnarled bole formed a convenient seat: he called it 'the armchair'. Here as a youth he would sit for hours of a summer morning at his books. He must however have spent a good deal of time during those years on his grandfather's farm, I suppose on Saturdays and during the school holidays, for when he spoke of the farm he spoke as of something which was part of his own life. He was versed in most of the arts of farming including that of threshing with a flail and he had a stock of farming lore at his fingers' ends. When he taught agriculture at school it was not altogether out of text books. When his uncle decided to give up the farm the question was who should succeed him. The farm had always been in the family and the landlord wanted it to continue so. It was offered to my father.

I believe the offer had some attraction for him. But by this time he

C.H.D.—2

was becoming established in his profession. He was the senior assistant master of the school with the promise of succession to the head-mastership. The existing headmaster was nearing the time when he must retire. So the farm went to a distant cousin and my father stood by the school becoming headmaster in the year in which his eldest son was born. He always kept, however, in some undefinable way, the sense of belonging to the land, and even succeeded in transmitting something of it to me at a remove of two generations.

III

The record of Charles Dodd's self-education is an extraordinary story. When he was fourteen he began his five years' apprenticeship as pupil teacher, teaching basic subjects all day and receiving instruction from the headmaster in the evening. Then, as assistant master, he became re-sponsible for more advanced studies. He proceeded therefore to teach himself Latin and higher mathematics and in 1879 had the satisfaction of knowing that the Brookside School stood first in Denbigh and Flint in these subjects. Soon he was studying French and chemistry, finding special interest in the latter and establishing a makeshift laboratory in his own home. In addition, partly as a hobby, he took up the study of geology and archaeology and was in time elected a fellow of the Geological Society. His eldest son Charles Harold shared these latter interests and made many an expedition with his father to examine rocks and ancient building sites. To him we owe a striking portrait of his father as he knew him in the years of his own boyhood:

My father was slightly under middle height, small-boned, lean and wiry. His features conformed to a very common Welsh type: face short, nose short and straight, high cheek bones, small but firm chin, deep-set blue eyes, his hair reddish-brown, very thick and curly. As a young man, to judge from early photographs, he wore it long, brushed into a high waving crest, and he cultivated luxuriant side-whiskers as well as a moustache. Whiskers and moustache, as well as the beard which he wore for a few years in middle life, were bright golden-red. He was rapid in his movements, a fast walker, impetuous in utterance, quick-tempered. He had more than his mother's restless energy and none, so far as I could see, of his father's placidity. His health was never robust (how could it be?) but his constitution must have been remarkably tough for he worked terrifically all his life and until he was well on in middle life he had scarcely ever spent a day in bed. During all the years from my earliest recollection until his retirement he observed an invariable routine. He rose at 6.45, made early morning tea and took a cup to my mother in bed, then completed his toilet and retired to the drawing-room for half-an-hour's meditation. This was his one spell of complete privacy in the day and no one ever thought of breaking into it. At 7.45 he sallied forth for a walk upon which all his boys accompanied him as they grew old enough. He always attributed his good health to this morning walk. Breakfast was at 8. At 8.30 he left for school which opened at 9 and closed at 12.30. At 1 he was back for dinner and after this he invariably slept in his chair for 10 minutes, my mother watchful meanwhile to keep us quiet. He left for school at 1.45 and was back for tea at 5. Several evenings in the week he had a class for pupil teachers from 6 to 8 or 8.30: the other evenings he would spend correcting papers or the like. On Saturday he usually had employment at school in the morning; and in the afternoon took his only spell of recreation in the week. Sunday was different but equally strenuous. If he was spending the Sunday at home, he attended a prayer-meeting at 10.15 followed by service at 10.45. In the afternoon he taught a bible-class for young men. In the evening he attended service again and usually conducted a choir-practice after it for, like his grandfather, he 'led the singing' at Chapel. But very frequently he took services at one of the village chapels in the neighbourhood—most frequently at one which had been built by a congregation originally gathered in the kitchen of my great-grandfather's farmhouse. On such Sundays he would walk there and back twice, morning and evening, and be with his class in the afternoon: a 'busman's holiday' indeed. School and chapel were the two focal points of his existence and he served both with complete devotion. Personal ambition in the ordinary sense he lacked entirely: but he was intensely ambitious for the success of the school and its scholars and touchy over anything that affected its credit. As time wore on he was almost inordinately ambitious for the advancement of his sons. He was proud and sensitive. He was generous to a fault; and I mean that literally, for I believe generosity did become a fault when the benefaction which gratified his generous impulses increased the burden of economizing which pressed hardly upon my mother. To us, most unjustly, she appeared stingy and he openhanded. Yet the impulse was a truly generous one. Not only did he contribute beyond his means to the support of the chapel and its various enterprises and activities: he had also a retinue of pensioners. They were mostly companions or acquaintances of his poverty-stricken boyhood, men who had fallen on evil days: and it was a point of pride in him never to disown the associations of his early days. My mother who knew how easily Father was imposed upon, would sometimes try to intercept the attack but she rarely succeeded.

It was within this remarkably stable and patterned environment that the boys grew up. Home, church and school were together at the hub of the wheel: Erddig Park, the magnificent estate on the edge of the town was a favourite place for rambling and games, and virtually every country-spot within walking distance became familiar, as the boys accompanied their father or later went on their own. There were the annual holidays— at Towyn, at Beaumaris, at Rhos-on-Sea—confined it seems to Welsh resorts. When Dodd was twelve years old there was a memorable visit to London, primarily for singing at the Crystal Palace but including visits to the Houses of Parliament, St. Paul's Cathedral and the City Temple. But Wrexham and its immediate neighbourhood was the virtually unchanging scene within which he was born, nurtured, educated, firmly rooted, until the critical transplantation to Oxford took place in 1902. Some memories of the pattern of school-routine and Sunday observance, which he put on record in the 1920s, provide a fascinating description of what he called 'The Vanished Order', an order which so largely moulded his own development.

Note

1. In 1897 Brookside (Independent) School became Victoria Boys' Board School.

2

Schooldays

I

DODD'S RECOLLECTIONS OF SCHOOLDAYS COVERED ONLY THE PERIOD during which he was a pupil at the Brookside School—in the Infants' Department from five till seven and then in the Boys' School until he was twelve years of age. At that time he won a scholarship to Grove Park Secondary School, but was not allowed by his father to take it up lest it be thought that some special privilege had been accorded to the headmaster's son. Here is his own record of his earliest formal education:

My education was begun at a school of a type which no longer exists. It was one of the schools fostered by the British and Foreign School Society. These schools were the counterpart of the 'National' schools which were designed to educate the children of the poor in the principles of the Church of England. The 'British' schools were supported mainly by non-conformists and the religious teaching given in them had the colour of an undenominational protestantism. They were organized upon what was called the 'Lancastrian' system, the governing principle of which was that the expenses of a teaching staff were retrenched by employing the older boys to teach the younger. . . .

The school of which I speak had been founded in the thirties of the last century. It was housed in a substantial stone building of the period, with a red-brick extension added shortly before I became a pupil. This building had been placed on the bank of a stream which ran through a deep gully dividing the town into two parts. In my time the grey gable-end of the school buildings, plain but not without dignity, looked out over a wide thoroughfare covering the bed of the stream. The name Brookside (Bruckside), however, clung to the school to the end.

The entire block contained eight rooms, large and small, and in them over six hundred children were accommodated, distributed into three departments, boys, girls and infants. Large classes were inevitable and two or three classes would work in the same large room, separated by green baize curtains hung on metal rods.

When each class was engaged in learning its lesson, as the custom was by repeating it in unison until it was known by rote, the noise can hardly be imagined by those who did not go through this kind of thing in their youth. I have always suspected that the necessity from earliest days of working against a hubbub has something to do with a fortunate knack in later life of ignoring noise and stir when I am concentrating upon reading or writing. Not that I always concentrated on the task in hand. I recall that at the age of eight I was expected to learn Wordsworth's poem *The Pet Lamb* which I thought (and still think) a very silly piece. But meanwhile from the other side of the baize curtains came the stirring [sounds] of Macaulay's *Horatius* from the sturdy throats of ten year olds. That was how I learned the *Lay of Horatius*, much of which I can still repeat. It was my first love in English poetry.

I still see vividly in the mind's eye the rather low schoolroom; deep window embrasures in the thick walls and diamond paned windows; in the middle a big stove which in winter roasted those who were nearest to it and diffused a faint sense of warmth to the distant benches. About half the room was occupied by a stepped stage or gallery, which accommodated the benches or desks for two classes: the remaining floor-space was occupied by a third class. The master's desk stood at the foot of the gallery, near the door. At nine in the morning we trooped into school, hung up our caps on the hooks along the wall and marched to our places. The master conducted prayers and then the curtains were drawn and the classes began work, the three masters making themselves heard simultaneously as best they could.

The school was maintained largely by voluntary subscriptions, supplemented by grants from the Board of Education. A local educational charity of the 18th. century provided free tuition for a certain number of poor boys. The rest paid weekly fees . . . The majority of the pupils, I suppose, were the children of artisans, small shopkeepers, etc. There were the children of N.C.O.'s and men of the regiment quartered in the local barracks; there was a group of farmers' children who came in daily from the country and there was a sprinkling of children of tradesmen and small professional men and partners in a firm manufacturing agricultural implements. Thus the school, though primarily intended for the 'poor', did in fact draw upon a large part of the population of the borough. It represented pretty accurately the social world in which I was brought up. We knew that there was another social world lying beyond our province and inhabited by the gentry who had their own speech, manners and customs all different from ours. But with them we had no concern. Our own world had its well-marked class divisions but at school we mixed pretty indiscriminately and (apart from the real 'poor', the foundation boys) an outsider would perhaps have seen little difference among us in speech, dress or manners.

My father's predecessor as headmaster who held the position for thirty or forty years, was a Scot. I figure him to myself as the type of the old-fashioned Scots 'dominie': a dour man, free in the use of the tawse but with a great zeal for education, a deep faith in 'the mathematics' as a regimen for supplying and fortifying the mind . . . My father who was with him as pupil, as pupil teacher, and as assistant without any intermission from the day he entered the school as a child to the day when he succeeded to the headmastership, certainly owed much to his influence and perpetuated the essentials of his tradition while he embarked on adventurous developments at which the old dominie would doubtless have shaken a disapproving head.

In my time the hard core of popular education was still the three subjects which were commonly described in a fossilized witticism, as 'the three R's', reading, writing and arithmetic. Of the thoroughness and efficiency of the training we received in these basic subjects I can speak with emphasis. We did learn to spell—and I have never been able to understand why it is considered a mark of superior education to be uncertain about English orthography—and we were drilled into the art of writing 'copperplate' from the day when we began writing 'pothooks' in the Infants' Department to our last day at school. I have long lost the art but I am not prepared to say that the time given to a scrupulous striving for neatness and precision of line and clearness of form was wasted time. The art of reading we practised out of 'readers' which contained a collection of passages deemed suitable for the young. They were mostly of little value. Even then I rather despised their attempts to convey information or a moral in a factitiously bright and simple style. At the same time I am still grateful that there was impressed upon me at so early an age the practice of clear, deliberate and audible reading with correct emphasis. In the upper standards we learned some history. We also read portions of Shakespeare's plays with a minimum of explanatory notes and committed long passages to memory. Since it seems to be common form to say that English literature lessons in school permanently kill any interest in the texts that were read, I think it worthwhile to affirm that the plays which I read at school before I was twelve—*Julius Caesar* and *The Merchant of Venice*—are among those which I understand best and to which I go back with most pleasure. I might further observe at this point that in my experience the much decried practice of learning by rote has been of quite incalculable value to me. I learned not only passages of English poetry and portions of the Bible in English and Welsh but later on long screeds of Virgil, Livy, Thucydides, Demosthenes, Euripides and other classical authors. Such memorized passages, in my experience, as they lodge in the mind, insensibly shape one's own thought and its expression. It is thus that literature exerts its deepest influence: I do not believe there is any other way which is comparably effective . . .

I was introduced to maps at the age of six and from that time to this they have fascinated me. An introduction to maps was by way of an accurate plan of the school buildings and playground which, properly explained, left us in no doubt what a map was and how it was to be understood. We then passed on to maps of England and other countries. We also learned to draw maps. There, as in the writing lesson, immense emphasis was laid upon precision of form, fineness of line and the neat printing of names. [He comments on drawing and copying models.] Fidelity, accuracy, clearness of line and general neatness were the qualities desired. Imagination did not enter into the matter.

Beyond the routine subjects my father always kept two or three special subjects going in the upper standards. For many years he taught Latin. Mathematics included not only arithmetic but algebra, Euclidean geometry and a subject known as mensuration. Another subject was Physiography, a kind of compound of physical geography, geology and elementary astronomy. From time to time there was a class in the theory of Agriculture intended to appeal to the farmers who sent their sons to the school. It fell to my lot to learn mensuration, book-keeping and Euclid. That I had my schooling before the reformers decided that Euclid was outmoded I shall never cease to be thankful. Euclid is not so much mathematics (in which I was never interested) as applied logic. The pleasure of it (and to me it was acute pleasure) was that of following step by step an argument conducted according to strict rules and ending with the triumphant Q.E.D. Since Euclid has gone without anything to take its place, most people leave school with no conception of what a logical argument is. Latin had unfortunately been dropped from the school curriculum shortly before I reached the grade at which I might have begun it. But from the age of 9 I attended the Latin class which my father had for the pupil teachers in evenings and before I left the school at the age of 12 I was reading Caesar.

These various divagations were possible because it was a 'voluntary' school and the managers appointed by the subscribers left the headmaster a good deal of freedom and initiative. The special subjects were in many cases taught in accordance with the syllabus put out in the department of Science and Art at South Kensington and the department's inspector examined us in them as they did also in drawing. In what I have called the routine subjects Government kept control of the standard of teaching by means of examinations conducted by H.M. Inspectors of Schools. Upon the results of these examinations depended the government grant which supplied the school with a substantial part of its income. The annual examination in November was an event of the school year to which both teachers and pupils looked forward with a good deal of nervous expectancy. For two or three days H.M.I. was in command. The chief inspector I remember as a strutting, cock-sparrow of a man, in check tweeds, with a red face and an elegant pair of blond 'Dundreary' whiskers. He had written an historical treatise which we were obliged to use as a text-book. It was curiously unsuitable for the purpose. Yet I found it most interesting. It was, in fact, my first introduction to critical history. The author examined various popular stories in the light of the evidence and often drew sceptical conclusions. I remember in particular his treatment of the story of King Edgar's tribute of wolves' heads and of the same King's river-trip at Chester in a barge rowed by six subject princes. Original sources were cited verbally and references were given. Before I was twelve I had at least so much acquaintance with the Anglo-Saxon Chronicle, Flormer of Worcyla, William of Huntingdon and others and, above all, I already knew that if the truth was to be known about past events you must go back to sources as nearly as possible contemporary and apply such critical tests as are appropriate. So I owe H.M.I. a substantial debt though I thought of him at the time as a sort of tiresome, pernickety, Grand Inquisitor.

Apart from examinations, there were two great occasions in the school year. One was the breaking-up at the end of term in preparation for the month's holiday in July. The other school occasion was the Annual Entertainment held about Christmas time. For this we prepared for weeks beforehand. My father took great pride in training the school choir which, always assisted on these occasions by 'old boys' who supplied the tenor and bass parts, performed part songs and choruses. The *pièce de resistance* was one of Handel's oratorios. He was ingenious in devising slight dramatic sketches of a topical or amusing character. For these compositions he often supplied the incidental music, unless some popular traditional melody could be adapted for the purpose. An ever popular item was the 'musical medley' in which current songs were strung together on the thread of a tenuous plot and given an amusing turn. The surprising thing was that he, whose puritan principles branded the music-hall as a 'haunt' of sin, seemed always to be well *au fait* with the music-hall songs of the moment—with the tunes at least and enough of the words to provide basis for an adaptation.

II

In 1896 Dodd entered Grove Park Secondary School. Founded as a private school in 1823, The Groves occupied a substantial residence, built in 1765, and maintained an honourable record of secondary teaching throughout the nineteenth century. The only comparable institution in Wrexham was the Grammar School. This however declined in numbers during the second half of the century and ultimately, under the provisions of the Welsh Intermediate Act, The Groves was converted into a public intermediate School and granted the endowments of the Grammar School. This was in 1895. Known now as Grove Park School it began to expand both by widening the range of subjects taught (hitherto classical studies had been dominant) and by erecting new buildings. These were opened in 1902 and in the academic year 1902–3 the school gained premier places in the Central Welsh Board examinations both in classics and in science.

Dodd was fortunate therefore to have entered the school at a time when it was advancing in prestige and in educational standards. But above all it was his good fortune to come under the direct charge of a master, A. E. Leckenby, who was a brilliant teacher of the classics and had the satisfaction of sending a succession of his pupils as scholars to Oxford or Cambridge. In 1903 a Cambridge professor who was an examiner for the Welsh Board called attention to the 'brilliant classical teaching' at Grove Park. 'I have never,' he reported, 'met with better teaching in any school or university in Great Britain.' Dodd undoubtedly possessed a flair for languages from his earliest years (picking up Welsh, for example, without home encouragement) but it was to Leckenby that he owed the basic discipline in Latin and Greek, particularly the latter, which sent him forward to achieve outstanding distinction in the whole realm of classical studies.

Yet his studies were not narrowly confined to classical languages. He gained reasonable proficiency in mathematics and French, read Shakespeare and acted Portia in the school play, enjoyed Jane Austen but could not abide Dickens, maintained a keen interest in history, especially of the ancient world. He enjoyed cricket but had no special athletic gifts (except that he was a good sprinter: when he was nearly fifty, he easily won the fathers' race at his son's prep-school sports). He had some interest in gardening but without question his two major recreations were walking and music.

Walking became almost a fetish in the Dodd family. Father walked, mother walked, and their son made the daily walk a normal rule of life. Although slight modifications of his regular programme naturally were accepted when his own home and family had to be considered, he never lost his zest for walking or his conviction that good health depended on strict observance of this daily exercise. He walked quickly and purpose-fully—acting out symbolically, perhaps, the essential character of his total life-story.

In addition he loved to sit at the piano and play and sing. Singing was in his blood. When he was twelve he was given a place in the chapel choir and remained a devoted member of it until his visits home became less frequent. He delighted to join in sacred cantatas and folk songs. Though he never became a distinguished pianist he was a good accom-panist and refreshed himself by improvising or playing over familiar tunes. Unlike his father he was not an early riser in the home but when he finally appeared he would often go straight to the piano for a brief exercise before breakfast. His brothers never forgot one April 1st when they got ahead of him and removed the inner mechanism of the piano before he came down. Perhaps because he was not easily upset, his chagrin and anger on this occasion remained a vivid family memory.

For holiday he was happy to go with the family and enjoy ordinary seaside recreations. Sometimes the holiday was at a resort where a seaside mission under the auspices of the Children's Special Service Mission was in progress and he appears to have attended the beach services and other activities naturally and happily. He always had a concern for his younger brothers, joining in their pursuits and settling their quarrels, telling them Bible stories and dramatic episodes from history. He loved charades, and on special family occasions was the inspiring genius in the production of good tableaux. It seems to have been an exceptionally untroubled up-bringing within the warm affection of the home. Beyond its boundaries there was the supportive community of Pen-y-bryn to which he became deeply attached and to which he returned in retrospect in a remarkable paper which he once gave to a university society in Oxford. It gives so lively an account of the religious atmosphere of his early days that to attempt to summarise it would be to spoil it. Apart from a brief postscript, I shall tell this story of Sunday observance in Wrexham in his own words.

3

Pen-y-bryn Chapel

I

'IN THE GOOD QUEEN'S DAYS WE WERE VERY RELIGIOUS. IT WAS ASSUMED that everybody went to church or chapel. If you "went nowhere", it was a discreditable fact to be concealed. At least you did not show yourself abroad too boldly on Sunday. On that day the whole normal life of the town was at a standstill, and except during the times before and after divine service the streets were deserted. After the early morning milk-carts had ceased to rattle there was a dead calm until, from ten o'clock onwards, front doors opened to let out family parties starting for church. Paterfamilias, in silk hat and frock coat, led the way. Mamma shepherded the children, big and little, in their stiff and unaccustomed Sunday best. And with what decorum they advanced! As group met group grave and distant greetings were exchanged. Boys, who might be boon companions (or sworn enemies) from Monday to Saturday, eyed one another sheepishly over unnaturally spotless Sunday collars. Not until after service would we unbend. Gradually the family groups merged into little processions making for their several places of worship.

'The number of these was astonishing. The usual sects of Christianity were all represented, and practically every one of them by at least two distinct congregations, English and Welsh. But among the multiplicity of religious divisions there was only one which marked a real cleavage: the division between "church" and "chapel". The Roman Catholics hardly came into the picture; they were understood to be Irish, and alien to the town. The bulk of the population was divided between the Established Church and Dissent. The two communities lived side by side, but apart. I do not remember that there was any active animosity, except perhaps at election time; for with us it was certainly true that the Church of England was "the Tory party at its prayers", and Dissent was solidly Liberal. Social distinctions too were involved. The Dissenters, who almost certainly outnumbered the "church people", included most of the shopkeepers, large and small, and the respectable artisans, with a fair quota of minor professional people. The Church held the gentry and the superior professional class and, at the other end of the scale, their immediate dependants and the "poor", who were more or less objects of charity.

'My family were Dissenters, belonging to the body to which in Wales that term was especially applied, the Independents. All my relations on both sides were of the same persuasion. As a matter of course we bought our food from a dissenting grocer, our clothes from a dissenting clothier; we employed a dissenting milkman, carpenter, jobbing gardener, and chimney-sweep. To do otherwise would have been felt as disloyalty. In social life there was little intercourse between the two communities. Intermarriage was thought undesirable; it "took you away from your own place". Either the family was divided ecclesiastically, and that was barely respectable, or else one partner or the other deserted the ancestral fold. It was generally felt that if such mixed marriages did take place, it was right that the wife should follow her husband's religion, even if it meant "going to church". The necessity was deplored. No other excuse for such a change of denomination was accepted. It was tacitly assumed that a Dissenter who conformed was either Laodicean or moved by worldly motives; for we were not unaware that the Establishment conferred social prestige. There was a common saying, "Mae wedi gadael crefydd, wedi mynd i'r eglwys" ("he has left religion and gone to church"). My father, who was, I believe, exceptionally tolerant and broadminded, did not countenance such a saying. I remember him often expressing the opinion that a man might find salvation in any church, if he lived up to his lights. But I am sure the implication was that the Episcopalian light was a dim one! The thought of any one of his family falling away would have grieved him. As for my formidable old grandmother, I have heard her declare that while she lived no descendant of hers should be seen on Sunday anywhere but in Salem Chapel.

II

'Of life in the Episcopal community, therefore, I can say nothing. Among ourselves the most rigid Puritan traditions were maintained. Sunday was the high festival of our religion. Work and play alike were taboo. You might walk in the garden and admire the flowers, but to pull up a casual weed was reprehensible. If in dressing on Sunday morning I had the misfortune to detach a responsible button, I had to prove beyond doubt that its absence was an affront to decency before my mother could feel justified in stitching it on. To take a bath on Sunday was not thought of. To shave was a misdemeanour. Shortly before my time a minister of our chapel had, so my grandmother told me, been arraigned by his deacons for this crime. He found indulgence on the plea that his beard was exceptionally dark and of strong growth. My father, until well on in middle life, shaved on Saturday night in preparation. When in due course I myself started to shave, I was rebuked for my untimely zeal to show a shining Sabbath face. To write a letter on Sunday was a secular occupation, which could be justified only by genuine necessity. No books might be opened but "Sunday books", and that category was rigidly defined. No music but "sacred music" might be sung or played. It is true that the problem of classifying instrumental music as sacred or secular was never quite satisfactorily solved. I remember being pulled up for playing on the piano a "piece" which my music teacher had certified as suitable for Sunday, because, apparently, my father associated its melody with some secular words. No toys of any kind were permitted. I recall a very curious exception. One of our mild indoor amusements was the mounting of "scraps" in an album. One year Christmas fell on a Sunday. This was a depressing conjunction, for we might only look at our presents and then put them aside "till to-morrow". But among them we found an assortment of "scraps" in the form of Bible pictures, and these we were allowed to cut out and mount even though the day was a Sabbath. My vivid recollection of this early episode shows how exceptional the indulgence appeared. I have no doubt that it cost my parents much anxious casuistry, and represented a very imaginative and sympathetic thought for us.

'The activities of Sunday were practically restricted (apart from an exception which I shall mention presently) to going to chapel twice and to Sunday School in the afternoon. A short walk after service was permitted, but it must not exceed half-an-hour or so. I well remember head-shaking over some young person of our communion who had been seen "going for a walk on Sunday afternoon". The gravity with which the formula was pronounced left no doubt that this was a first step in the *facilis descensus Averno*.

'The "Puritan Sunday" has often been described, and caricatured. The examples that I have given are, so far as my memory serves, strictly accurate, and typical. It will no doubt be inferred that our Sunday was a day of unmitigated gloom and misery. I gather from literature that this was the effect of the institution upon many of my contemporaries. I can only say that it was not so for me. I suspect that the difference lies largely in the simple fact that I grew up in an environment in which the Puritan tradition was not only dominant but unquestioned. It might no doubt be irksome to be parted from some new plaything, or to interrupt the reading of an exciting book, but after all one did not expect to play cricket at Christmas or to go skating at midsummer. The Sabbath was as firmly fixed in the order of things as the weather and the seasons. Both rested on the immutable fiat of the Creator. And it must be remembered that this view was taken by the *whole* of that narrow community within which we lived. Those who did not "go to chapel" were nothing to us; those who did took our view. Consequently as a small boy I was not exposed to the mortification of being prevented by the religious scruples of the family from doing what my companions were allowed to do. They were under the like unquestioned discipline. In my later boyhood change was in the air. The younger members of my own generation grew up already in a climate of restlessness and incipient revolt. It was then that the Sabbath restrictions began to be irksome. In my early years they were simply accepted without a thought that things could be otherwise.

'That being so, Sunday had many alleviations. In fact, at the risk of being disbelieved, I will go so far as to say that I rather liked Sunday. When I ask myself why it should have been so, I do not think it was in any way a sign of precocious piety. The reasons why I liked it might be summed up in the simple fact that it was different from other days, and there was little enough variety in our lives. Even the Sabbath quiet was not unappreciated. Sunday clothes, though in some ways a nuisance, gave an agreeable sense of being handsomely dressed. Then there was the food: sausage with the breakfast bacon, a hot joint and fruit pie for dinner, home-made cakes for tea. Such delicacies were rare on weekdays. Over and above these carnal delights Sunday was in a special way a *family* day. During the week my father was scarcely visible to us except during hurried meals. On Sunday, though he was still much occupied at chapel, he was relatively at leisure and often in a less unbending mood, and took his place at the centre of family life. This I found a pleasant thing. My mother too, immersed all the week in the household affairs of a large family, with only one maid, somehow found spare time on Sunday. How she managed it I do not quite know. Sunday meals can hardly have allowed, strictly, a day of rest, and curiously enough the prohibition of work and play did not preclude the entertainment of friends to tea. After tea there would often be hymn-singing round the piano, and this I enjoyed. Again, the hour after evening service was the time when friends "dropped in". For us boys, moreover, Sunday brought the pleasure of meeting a particular circle of companions. Most of them, it is true, were schoolfellows during the week, but they formed an inner, confidential group, and we met under different conditions. We might not play together, but boys at the gregarious age find some queer satisfaction merely from rubbing shoulders and wagging tongues.

'There is little here that will seem to a modern reader to give any grounds at all for the statement that a small boy liked the Puritan Sunday. Yet so it was. These sedate Sunday teas, with hymns round the piano, these mildly gossiping Sunday evening calls, made up almost the whole of our social round, apart from Christmas parties and an occasional "chapel tea" or similar function. And of outside amusements we had few. Chapel was, in fact, our social world, to a degree to which I know no modern parallel.

'In that world my father was a person of importance. He "led the singing", as his grandfather had done before him. He conducted a bible class for young men. He was also a deacon, the diaconate being the executive organ of government in our community. It met monthly at the houses of its members in turn. "Deacons' Meeting" was a function we looked forward to; it meant a specially good tea, with the best china and hot cakes, of which we partook in awed silence. After tea the bearded senators retired to the parlour, where the newly installed gas-fire had been lighted in advance, the curtains drawn, and everything arranged in apple-pie order for their august deliberations.

III

'I should now attempt to give some account of the kind of piety that was nurtured in this little community and others like it. The attempt can hardly succeed. It means that a man is trying to form a judgment on a boy's impressions of his elders. Of the deeper motives of their lives it is impossible to speak. I can only say that I thought then, and looking back I see no reason to think otherwise, that for the most part, however narrow their outlook may have been, they were simply sincere in their faith and conscientious in trying to live up to it. Their private lives were austere and self-controlled. They were almost inhumanly laborious in their callings, suspicious of almost all forms of pleasure or relaxation. The Dissenter of fiction is a vulgar money-grubber. My people thought no shame of making all the money they could by means they judged strictly honest. To wealth they did not aspire, but a modest competence was a good gift of God. To be in debt or beholden to anyone was the last disgrace. But they spent little on personal ends. They gave to the "cause" with a prodigality that often meant real denial to themselves and their families. My father, out of his straitened means, sent his sons to the university at the cost of years of wearing anxiety, but he let us go short there rather than reduce by a penny his comparatively large subscriptions to chapel or any of its subsidiary activities.

'If these men were desperately conscientious in the ordering of their own lives, they felt justified in applying a severe criticism to the conduct of others. Their religion certainly fostered a rare faculty for disapproval. I am not thinking of light gossip with a touch of malice. That existed among us, as in all narrow communities, but it was strongly reprehended. I am thinking of the weighing of moral conduct and the assigning of praise or blame with the gravest sense of responsibility. The matter involved might seem trivial, and the standard imposed impossibly narrow, but all was as serious as if it were the Last Judgment. These men can seldom have remembered the evangelical precept, "Judge not that ye be not judged". If they had, I suspect that in their hearts they would have said that they did not shrink from the corollary, "With what judgment ye judge ye shall be judged". They asked nothing else than to be judged by the standards they applied. Self-righteous? No doubt. Its opposite is the modern tolerance that lays its finger along its nose and says, "We are all rascals together".

'What of the religion that lay behind this rigorous moralism? I cannot tell. These men, in spite of their devotion to the community, were individualists at heart and reserved about their inner life. Certainly they would never have taken kindly to the "confessional-in-commission" of the Methodist class-meeting or its modern analogues. They might pray aloud in prayer-meeting, but their prayers remained, fundamentally, impersonal; they did not give themselves away. How far the more mystical and sacramental aspects of the Christian religion entered into their experience was their own secret. I have reason to think there was more of it than might appear. But so far as the overt and corporate expression of religion is concerned, mysticism and sacraments had little or no place. We found the emotionalism of the "Ranters" as distasteful as the formality of the Established Church. Our religion was certainly not fanatical, not even very enthusiastic. It was sober, prosaic, even rationalistic, strange as the epithet would have sounded to the chapel leaders.

IV

'Its theoretical basis I can only describe as an etiolated Calvinism, Calvinism drained of the good red blood of its dogmatic theology. It is

C.H.D.—3

strange to think on how small an allowance of positive dogma a religious system could maintain itself, which owed its existence to the massive theology of Geneva. What the preaching in our chapel was like in my early days I have not the faintest recollection, but I am sure it had no very profound doctrinal content. Nor can I remember that I ever received any definite dogmatic instruction (except indeed on *Congregational Church Principles*, in which we were well grounded). The great watchwords of Calvinism, predestination, election, eternal damnation, and the rest were not unfamiliar, but the ideas they stood for were seldom expounded or discussed. They were mysteries lying in the background of faith. Even the doctrines of the Incarnation and the Atonement were implied rather than expounded. The doctrine of the Trinity, so far as I remember, I felt to be rather "churchy". Yet if any question was raised, we were rigidly orthodox in these articles. When I came later to read the old Puritan divines I felt instinctively at home with them. Here I found a clue to the piety in which I had been brought up. They gave form to our unexpressed assumptions. We were certainly never told that we were of the "Elect"; if anyone had said so it would have been embarrassing. But it was in fact the presupposition of our attitude to religion, and to life. It justified the strict discipline under which we lived, and the sharp distinction drawn between "professing Christians" and the worldly. It no doubt accounted for the fact that (in contrast to the Methodists) no "conversion" was expected of us as we grew up. The children of believers were "within the covenant", and it was assumed that as they came to years of discretion they would wish to "join the church", and so to become fully enfranchised members of that close community whose traditions and institutions governed our lives. The procedure by which we were admitted to membership was designed to impress upon us the moral responsibilities of the status we were assuming. Little stress was laid on "religious experience", and belief was almost taken for granted.

'The one distinctive dogma, if dogma it should be called, which had effective force with us was that of the authority of the Scriptures. The Bible was the Word of God, the "lawbook of the Church"; it was our textbook of morals, and it took the place of creeds and confessions whose use as standards of faith was deprecated. The Bible, it was assumed, would lead a diligent reader into true belief, without any need for these "man-made" guides. It was read daily and systematically at family prayers. We were expected to study it privately and to commit passages to memory. Its truth and "verbal inspiration" were taken for granted, in theory at least; in practice, like all sensible persons, we took liberty to make reservations. I know that at a very early age I found some of the stories hard to swallow; but I made no great difficulty about them. In our ordinary reading, fiction was looked upon with suspicion, but there was an approved class of story which announced itself as "founded upon fact". I remember that I placed many of the Bible stories in that category, and was quite content. I do not suppose the theory was suggested to me; I believe it would have passed muster. But in other ways the literal acceptance of the Bible was being shaken.

'The doctrine of evolution, after a long time-lag, began to penetrate into our circle. I can recall clearly what may have been the first time I heard it discussed. I was perhaps about twelve at the time. I was with my father on a walk over the moors, in which he was accompanied by two or three of his friends. It was, I remember, Good Friday. We did not observe the ecclesiastical festivals (taking perhaps over-literally the Apostle's strictures on those who "observe days and months and seasons"), and Good Friday, being a public holiday, was commonly taken as an opportunity for a jaunt into the country. It was not because of the day that the talk turned upon theological, or rather biblical, topics; they were ordinary subjects of conversation. Someone mentioned "this evolution that they talk about"; could it be reconciled with the teaching of Holy Writ? The Bible said plainly, "God created great whales." Was it legitimate to follow the scientists so far as to admit that He caused them to evolve out of other forms of life? My father, who was a geologist, had an ingenious theory, drawn, I believe, from the works of one Hugh Miller, whose book on the Old Red Sandstone was at that time regarded as a geological classic. (Whether it still commands respect I cannot say.) The theory, if I have got it rightly, was to the effect that Moses was divinely granted in vision six glimpses of the universe as it was in various geological epochs. He faithfully recorded what he had seen at each stage. How the successive stages came about was not revealed to him, and upon this science could have its say. This was obviously a compromise position. "The impregnable rock of Holy Scripture" was undergoing some grouting.

'The beginnings of biblical criticism too reached our ears. I was about seven when a young student, destined to become one of the leading biblical scholars of his generation, came to preach at our chapel. In later years he told me of an incident that occurred at that time. He had preached on the Book of Daniel, assigning to it a date much later than the traditional. After service a deputation of young men waited on him. They had always understood, they explained, that it was from data in the Book of Daniel that the time of the End of the World was calculated. If that book was now to be dated some four hundred years later than was supposed, was the End of the World postponed correspondingly? Here were the first mutterings of the storm that was to overwhelm so many of our ancient landmarks. But the examples I have given will show how slightly, for the time, we were affected by them.

V

'If I were to characterize briefly our religious situation, I should say that it represented a very late survival of a tradition which had been immensely living and powerful. Its forms lingered among us, and still held significance, when they had almost vanished over most of the country—or at any rate most of England. But the ideas and experiences which had originally given life to the forms were scarcely present. A deep and even passionate loyalty to the tradition itself, to the community in which it was embodied, and to family associations of many generations was, I believe, the most effective motive. When once hereditary loyalties were disturbed, by movements of population, by the dispersal of families and the incursion of new elements, especially from over the border, and by the general broadening of interests which cut across our narrow and intense way of life, there was nothing to keep the inherited scheme of things in being. There was behind us no great ecclesiastical organization and no clearly understood theology. Everything now depended on the individual. It was upon the basis of religious individualism that modern Congregationalism was formed out of the elements of the older Independency, and it is a different thing. I believe I lived in the last days when the great tradition of Calvinistic Dissent was still a force in the daily lives of men and women, and in the shaping of a society, and before I was grown up its power was gone.'

So Dodd grew up within a tightly-knit, firmly disciplined, interdependent society of Independents. Its social activities—the Chapel tea, the annual Sunday School treat, the Christmas party, an occasional magic-lantern show—constituted the only diversions from the regular round of education during the week and worship on Sunday. The circus and the theatre were regarded as 'worldly' amusements. Yet there is no sign that he chafed against these restrictions. In the personal testimony given at his ordination he declared with great simplicity:

I was born into a Christian home and in my earliest years prayer became a natural and a real thing to me. It was during a time when trouble because of serious illness at home had taught me to pray with a deeper sense of need. But I recall, in quite a simple and childish way, giving myself to Christ and some years later, with fuller knowledge, I registered my faith in Him and purpose to serve Him by joining the fellowship of Pen-y-bryn Congregational Church, in which I had grown up from childhood. I left home for Oxford with the consciousness of being in faith and purpose a disciple of Jesus Christ.

This consciousness, broadened indeed and deepened by later experiences, remained the guiding and determining influence throughout his life.

PART 2

Oxford

4

A Double First

I

AMONGST THE PAPERS WHICH DODD PRESERVED WAS A TINY DIARY BEGUN in January 1896. Over the following thirty years he kept similar diaries, small in size and confined in the main to brief entries. The major concern was the weather. Day after day changes were faithfully recorded. 'Mild and damp', 'drizzling', 'quite springlike', 'splendid sunrise', 'white frost', 'frosty all day'—these are entries for January in his twelfth year. 'Weather wretched, thickish fog in evening', 'exceedingly heavy rain and sleet in night and early morning, ceasing gradually: very high wind'— such are the more sophisticated comments in the diary for 1906. One of his often-quoted remarks in his book on *Apostolic Preaching* written many years later was to the effect that when Paul went up to Jerusalem and stayed with Peter for a fortnight it was to be presumed that they did not spend all of their time talking about the weather. But weather observation had obviously been a duty seldom neglected in his own life.

The second feature of the diaries is the faithful logging of the daily walk. Sickness, the occasional substitution of the bicycle, impossible weather might sometimes break the sequence, but the walk became virtually a ritual of obligation. There could have been scarcely a road or bypath around Wrexham and later around Oxford and Warwick that was not traversed scores of times by Dodd and his friends.

In addition to the weather and the walk, the chief matters noted were the younger brothers' ailments, parties or celebrations in church and home, and Sunday activities. Normally these included attendance at divine service morning and evening (the preacher's texts were usually recorded) and Sunday School or Bible Class in the afternoon. The summer holiday gained rather more detailed attention and very occasionally some outside event was mentioned—a journey to Hawarden to watch Mr. Gladstone's funeral procession, the dramatic news of the end of the Boer War, a lecture on the Education Act of 1902. But the general impression gained from the diaries is that from his early school days until his ordination in 1912 life moved within strictly circumscribed limits—'swotting' (as he called it), walking, religious activities. The most unpredictable variant was the weather.

Yet there can be no doubt that a change of enormous consequence took place in October 1902 when the youth, whose world had hitherto revolved around the family home in Wrexham, found himself alone in his own rooms at University College, Oxford. For nearly thirty years Oxford was to become increasingly his place of work and the major influence moulding his career.

The diary entry of December 9, 1901, tells of his journey from Wrexham, in company with a schoolfellow, R. I. Hopwood, to take the scholarship examination at Oxford. For some undefined reason he made University College his first choice: Hopwood had chosen the more customary objective for a boy from Wales, Jesus College. In the event both were successful and the beginnings of university life were probably made the easier by the fact that Dodd could share them with a close friend from the same school. Certainly in his first year at Oxford his constant companions on his walks and at tea in the afternoon were Hopwood and a Wrexhamian, Neddy Roberts, from another college.

No reference is made in his diary to the scholarship award, which was clearly a notable event for himself, his family and his school. Something of its significance in North Wales was recalled in a letter written many years later by Sir Goronwy Edwards, the eminent historian. 'I came,' he wrote, 'from the neighbouring county of Flintshire and in my schooldays the four Dodd brothers were regarded by the rest of us as the most menacing competitors for University emoluments particularly in Oxford.' Charles Harold led the way. Two of his brothers followed him with scholarships to Oxford, the third to the University of Wales. It was an astonishing record.

II

Dodd once remarked, 'When I first came to Oxford I thought I was in heaven' and, in a scrap book, he kept and treasured a quotation from the Earl of Birkenhead's life of Lord Halifax describing Oxford in 1899:

It was his good fortune that his first taste of the *douceur de vivre* occurred in an Oxford as yet unviolated, and for a few precarious years still a haven of cloistral peace. There were already signs of these changes which have since reduced her to an industrial shambles, but they were small and scarcely noticed. 'It was one of those boundary periods, the meaning of which is missed at the time, but is plain in retrospect. The place was still monastic, but the clamour of the outer world was at its gates.'

These gates were still barred, and behind them Oxford lay in the hush of the Middle Ages. Only a few horse-drawn vehicles were to be seen where the sweep of the High disclosed its successive beauties. Even the ugly Victorian houses to the north, with forsythia, lilac and syringa in their gardens, seemed part of the peace of the University. The other entries to the city were almost unblemished, and it could be seen from afar by the traveller like some beckoning oasis in the desert. This was an Oxford still redolent of the past, whose tranquillity proclaimed the purpose of her founders, a place dedicated to study and meditation. A man who was born at a time when he could drink deep of this cup before it became contaminated was granted a rich experience never to return.

University College, to which Dodd came, has no pretensions to splendour of grounds and buildings like Magdalen and Christ Church, but it occupies a commanding position on High Street and lays claim to being the oldest foundation in the university. Though Mark Pattison described it in the nineteenth century as 'a college generally filled with commonplace men', it was in fact, at the turn of the century, a remarkably well-balanced society, proficient academically and pre-eminent athletically with its first Eight Head of the River, and with two of its members captains respectively of University Rugby and Association Football teams. In the period 1901–2 it boasted two Presidents of the Union, one being A. D. Lindsay, a future Master of Balliol. There were roughly 140 undergraduates and of the ten dons on the governing body seven were involved in classical studies, historical, philological and philosophical. It was a tolerant and open college community, without cliques or ecclesiastical dogmatisms. The years at the dawn of the century have been called the 'Golden Age of Univ' and one who was contemporary with Dodd has written that 'we commoners were incubating a Prime Minister (Clement Attlee), a Cabinet Minister, a Bishop, a Judge, an Ambassador, an Air-Marshal and a best-selling novelist'.

Many of these, indeed, took their studies very lightly and read pass degrees. It was the scholars and exhibitioners who were expected to uphold the college honour in the Examination Schools, and at the beginning of his career Dodd was taken in hand by the Classics Tutor, A. B. Poynton. Poynton published little but was a born teacher and regarded the team which he sent into the Schools each Hilary Term much as a coach would regard his men on the football field or on the river. The glory of the college depended on their performance. Besides giving regular tutorials, he entertained his pupils in his rooms each Friday evening in term when they sat around the fire and translated Pindar without previous preparation. His specialism, on which he lectured for the university, was Cicero's Orations.

Poynton was a shy but friendly man, devoted to the college, greatly valued by all serious pupils, and ultimately elected by the Fellows to be Master. One of his most brilliant pupils was E. R. Dodds, later Regius Professor of Greek, who came to Univ nine years after Dodd. His comment on Poynton reveals the kind of guidance that any pupil would have received in the early stage of his wrestling with the meaning of ancient texts: 'He saw the task of scholarship not as the reinterpretation of ancient masterpieces or the rediscovery of ancient modes of thought but simply as the transmission of the most exact possible mastery of two ancient languages.' Rigorous exactitude in matters of grammar, syntax and vocabulary was the ideal and indeed the demand set before Dodd at the very beginning of his university career.

At the end of five terms he was examined in Honour Moderations and achieved the hoped-for First Class. He failed, however, to gain either of the coveted university prizes—the Ireland or the Gaisford. It is significant that in the Ireland examination his translation papers from Latin and Greek were of a very high standard: it was in the rendering of English into ancient prose and verse, Latin in particular, that his marks brought him down to fourteenth place on the final list. His tutor advised, 'I should keep reading in odd moments at Greek Prose and Latin Poetry', which doubtless he did, but the art of translation was to remain his major skill.

In Trinity Term 1904 he began the second part of the regular Oxford course—Greek and Roman history coupled with the study of philosophy grounded in the works of Plato and Aristotle. He had two tutors, each demanding a weekly essay. In ancient history he worked with R. W. Macan, an exact historian who had been teaching in the college since 1884 and who was an authority on Herodotus. He was a large-minded man who had welcomed the establishment of a college (Mansfield) representing Dissent in Oxford. Before Dodd had completed his course, Macan had been elected Master, succeeding J. F. Bright, a strong but rather forbidding character whose sermons in Chapel became noted for their rolling phrases and grand style. Preaching once on behalf of a collection to be made for famine relief in Calcutta he called up 'the grim spectre stalking the purlieus of the Oriental Metropolis', and, in his farewell sermon before retiring to Norfolk, exclaimed, 'I go to my ancestral home in Norfolk, the antechamber to the tomb.' Macan, more genial, was in turn meticulous about precise forms and ceremonies. He liked to be announced on any suitable occasion as the Master of 'the College of the Great Hall of the University', which is the official designation of the society commonly called University College. His pupils gained a thorough knowledge of the recorded events of the ancient world under his guidance: problems concerned with the *interpretation* of history had scarcely begun to be seriously debated in the Oxford school.

In philosophy there were two tutors who shared the work at Univ— A. S. L. Farquharson who was an expert on Aristotle and E. F. Carritt who lectured on problems of moral and political philosophy and, in course of time, developed a special interest in aesthetics. Dodd's closer relationship seems to have been with Carritt, and it is likely that he would have found the latter's concern with moral issues particularly congenial. He was never deeply troubled by theories of knowledge or by problems of metaphysics. His concern for as long as he could remember had been with the question of how to live in such a way as to be furthering rather than hindering God's purpose in and for the world. Carritt's stress on moral obligations being grounded in objective reality must have seemed compatible with the emphasis of his own father on duty and moral responsibility being grounded in the constraint of the living God. Carritt emphasised that obligations arise out of the relations of persons: it was not difficult for his pupil to go further and to identify the sense of ultimate obligation as evidence of the presence and pressure of the personal God.

Outside the college he attended lectures on numismatics and archaeology —two of his future special interests; on Greek religion by L. R. Farnell; on Roman municipal law and inscriptions. He was thus becoming familiar with facets of the world into which Christianity came and he was to continue exploring this world throughout his life. He shared the conviction, then assumed almost without question at Oxford, that the same kind of philosophical and theological problems with which that world was concerned had still to be wrestled with today and that modern man's mental equipment for tackling those problems was roughly the same as it had been in the time of Plato. Though there was an intense study of the details of history there was an extraordinary confidence that the all-important matters in life—the quest for truth, beauty and goodness—had remained constant since European civilisation began. In so far as Dodd developed a philosophical position of his own it was 'realistic' rather than 'idealistic'. God, man and the world were there to be known: the individual had a mind to apprehend these realities and if he was prepared to labour honestly and put himself in a position to apprehend that which was to be known (pre-eminently by the study of literature) he could be confident of success in the search for the ultimate meaning of the universe. There was no call to worry unduly about the questions of how we know, how we select, how we interpret, how we change. There was a vast range of material to be mastered and the urgent task was to go ahead and bring it under control and into an acceptable order. Once such an order had begun to emerge, man could go forward confidently to shape his own plans and purposes in conformity with what appeared to be the pattern belonging to the ultimate nature of things.

In due course he gained his first in Greats[1], and as a 'double first' was well equipped to pursue further academic studies if he so wished. The college encouraged him to stay on at Oxford and from 1906 to 1909, when he committed himself to training for the ministry at Mansfield College, he was engaged in research combined with certain minor teaching duties. These I shall describe in more detail later. Meanwhile the record of his undergraduate days would be incomplete without some reference to his activities beyond the purely academic. What were his other interests?

III

At the turn of the century athletics played a major part in undergraduate life and Univ was in the lead in most forms of sport. One can imagine that the Captain of Boats soon spotted the short and lean freshman from Wrexham as a potential cox and Dodd on his part was not averse to seeking some distinction in this role. However, his efforts on the river did not take him very far. An unfortunate collision with the Wadham boat (in which the future 'Red Dean' of Canterbury, Hewlett Johnson, was rowing) led to the sinking of the latter and to a change of the Univ cox a few days later. He never coxed the college boat in bumping races, though he evidently followed the fortunes of successive Eights with keen interest and attended at least one bump supper to celebrate success.[2]

Though he enjoyed debating in school and college societies, he did not join the Union, probably because he felt unable to afford it. Characteristically he paid for his brother Percy to become a member when he came to Jesus College as a freshman in 1905. For him, the altogether congenial way of relaxing and maintaining fitness was to walk. Over Shotover or through Mesopotamia, up to Boar's Hill or along the tow-path to

Godstow—day after day he walked, and even worked out a kind of discipline which included one longer walk each week and one very long walk each month. Many a question, ethical, philosophical, theological, gained an airing as he and a friend, who came to live on his own staircase in 1903, tramped together over the countryside around Oxford. This was L. W. Grensted, who was to become the second holder of the Chair of the Philosophy of the Christian Religion in the university. Coming from Lancashire with a mathematical scholarship, he found himself in rooms at the head of the kitchen staircase, opposite to those occupied by Dodd. Grensted was shy, short but thick-set, immensely knowledgeable in all branches of natural history, especially entomology, and soon to be captivated by the new psychological interests being aroused in Britain by the translation of some of Freud's writings into English. From mathematics he went on to study philosophy, the problems of which had already often figured in his discussions with his friend. 'We used,' he once wrote, 'to stand in our doorways at night, talking and discussing, almost too tired to stop and undress for bed.' In turn it is more than likely that Dodd, who became deeply interested in developments of modern psychology, first became aware of that subject's importance through his friendly discussions with his undergraduate neighbour.

IV

From first to last in his Oxford career Dodd gave priority to that which had been given priority in the Wrexham home—the observance of divine worship and the use of the appointed means for growth in the knowledge of God. And the physical centre, which quickly became his spiritual home, was Mansfield College, the focal point of Dissent in the university. On his first Sunday in residence it was the most natural thing in the world for him to set his sights in that direction. 'In morning went a short walk,' his diary records, 'and then to Mansfield College Chapel. Went to lunch with Prof Gray. In evening to College Chapel. Stayed out of hall. At 8.30 went to service conducted by Mr. Lenwood at Mansfield. Text Mark 10: 39.' A mid-week service on Wednesday evening was a regular feature at Mansfield and this also he normally attended. Sometimes too he dined at the college. He did not in any way neglect the opportunities offered by his own college but Mansfield provided the treasured link with his own religious tradition—an island of Dissent in the midst of the almost unquestioned dominance of Anglicanism within the life of the university.

It was only in 1871 that Oxford and Cambridge had opened their doors to those who could not in conscience subscribe to the Thirty-nine Articles of Religion. Even during Dodd's time as an undergraduate the move to allow non-Anglicans to examine for the Honour School of Theology was strenuously opposed and the higher degrees in divinity were still denied to Dissenters. (The barrier was removed in 1921.) Regulations about compulsory attendance at college chapel had been relaxed and he probably felt no embarrassment in being present at services in Univ, especially as the Chaplain was exceptionally liberal-minded. (A scholar was expected to wear a surplice and this may have caused some searchings of heart.) But at Mansfield he was amongst his own people, and in spite of developing friendships with Anglicans in his own college and happy associations with evangelical Anglicans at St. Aldate's Church and Wycliffe Hall, his loyalty to his own denomination and to Mansfield in particular seems never to have wavered.

The founding of Mansfield College was one of the most remarkable events to have happened in Oxford in the nineteenth century. In some respects the impulse to establish in the university area a college for the training of men for the Nonconformist ministry was comparable to that which had stirred devotees of particular traditions in the Church of England to found theological colleges such as Ridley Hall in Cambridge and St. Stephen's House in Oxford shortly before Mansfield came into being. But larger issues were involved. Hitherto Nonconformist colleges had been situated in great cities which served their surrounding regions— London, Manchester, Birmingham, Bradford, Leeds—and connections with universities had been slight. (Not until 1904 was a Faculty of Theology established in Manchester.) After 1871 however a steady stream of Nonconformists found their way to Oxford and Cambridge, and the question began to exercise the minds of leading dissenting ministers: Would these young men be either swallowed up into the pervading Anglicanism or lost to religion altogether if there were no representative institution to which they could feel some attachment? There were indeed churches of each of the leading denominations in both Oxford and Cambridge, but those were mainly concerned with ministry to towns-people. Could not the distinctive dissenting tradition be more adequately represented by a college which would primarily train men for the ministry but also serve as a rallying point for dissenting undergraduates in the university?

The desirability of such a college was felt even more keenly in the Oxford context than in Cambridge which had since the seventeenth century maintained a certain sympathy with the Puritan tradition. Moreover, there was no Congregational church in Oxford as influential as Emmanuel Church in Cambridge. To establish a college in Oxford which could give men the advantages of university teaching while preparing them for the ministry, and at the same time provide a kind of university pulpit for preachers of non-Anglican denominations, was an aim which gained increasing support in Congregationalist circles and led ultimately to the removal of their Springhill College from Birmingham to Oxford and to the appointment of Dr. A. M. Fairbairn to guide its destinies as first principal.

No choice could have been happier. A Scotsman born in Aberdeen and gaining his education through almost herculean efforts of his own, he had attained an eminent position in the field of historical theology and was equally conversant with Scottish, English and German divinity. He wanted the new college to be a school preparing men for the work of the ministry and a pulpit reaching out to and influencing members of the university. The school would need the physical amenities of library and lecture-rooms: the pulpit those of a chapel. In course of time the theological library became one of the best of its kind in Oxford, while the lecture rooms soon drew men of all denominations to hear the distinguished scholars who were appointed to the faculty of the college. Moreover for many years the chapel held an almost unrivalled place as a notable centre of preaching in the university. Dodd listened there to famous visitors from the Scottish universities and colleges as well as from Free Church English pulpits. He rarely missed a Sunday.

Gradually he became acquainted with a remarkable group of senior men. The Principal, Dr. Fairbairn, was nearing the end of his career—he retired in 1909 just before Dodd entered on his full ministerial training—but was still a powerful figure in college and highly respected in the university. While holding firmly to his Free Church principles he did everything possible to promote sound learning in biblical and historical theology and to make the college chapel a place of dignified worship and inspired proclamation. In furthering these aims he had the devoted co-operation of George Buchanan Gray, a man who, like Fairbairn, had striven through immense difficulties to acquire a higher education and who came to be regarded in the early years of this century as second only to S. R. Driver amongst Oxford Old Testament scholars. Indeed, it became known that Driver would have gladly designated him as his successor in the Regius Chair of Hebrew had this been possible: but the Chair was tied to a canonry of Christ Church until half a century later.

A second colleague was Vernon Bartlet, whose own education had been more traditional—Mill Hill and Oxford—and who became a worthy representative of his own university's eminence in patristic studies. Finally, from 1903–11, New Testament scholarship was in the hands of

C.H.D.—4

Alexander Souter, an acknowledged authority in the field of textual criticism, who produced a widely used lexicon of New Testament Greek. He left Mansfield in 1911 to become Regius Professor of Humanity in the University of Aberdeen but not before he had played some part in the training of the man who was to be within a few years his successor in the college. Dodd became deeply attached to Souter and spent many short vacations with him in his Aberdeen home.

In addition to these senior full-time teachers there was a young man who had joined the staff in 1901 as tutor in New Testament Greek but whose wider responsibility it was to act as pastor of Nonconformist undergraduates in the university. (There were Anglican pastors associated with St. Aldate's Church and Pusey House.) This was Frank Lenwood, one of the most remarkable men of his generation. A classical scholar of Corpus Christi College, he had not only gained a 'double first' but had also been President of the Union. Active in the Student Volunteer Missionary Union, he was also the pioneer in the organisation of Free Church Camps for schoolboys in 1898 and from his base in Mansfield he exercised an outstanding influence in Oxford from 1901–9 when he left for missionary service in India. Dodd came to regard him with admiration and affection, even though at a later stage he differed from him sharply on Christological interpretation. He was undoubtedly indebted to him for an awakened interest in Boys' Camp and Settlement activities and a concern for foreign missions which he never lost through the coming years.[3]

V

The undergraduate years were divided almost equally between Oxford and Wrexham, with no kind of difficulty, it seems, in moving to and fro from the one environment to the other. At Oxford he was reading ancient history and philosophy, walking and cycling with friends, attending services of worship, prayer meetings and Bible study circles. At home he was completely disciplined in his studies, retiring to an upstairs room, often with a hot-water bottle to keep himself warm, active in walking and cycling with his father and brothers, faithful in attendance at Pen-y-bryn chapel when he was not himself preaching in some small country charge, sharing still in choir and Christian Endeavour fellowship just as he had done before he left home.

Thus Greece and Rome, the Welsh and English countryside, Jerusalem and Galilee—all were moulding the developing consciousness of the young man who on his twenty-first birthday spent the morning in writing the sermon which was to be preached in a Methodist chapel on the following Sunday. To interpret the Christian faith to his contemporaries in the light of the history and language of the ancient world was already becoming a dominant ambition. He might have immersed himself more and more in classical studies and gradually dissociated himself from the family circle and school acquaintances and chapel fellowship at Wrexham. But these loyalties held him fast. And this enabled him, when the time came, to speak and write in such a way that even those with little formal education could understand his message. Scholarship never became an end in itself. He sought to equip himself with the best possible tools of historical and linguistic disciplines in order that he might use them efficiently for the better communicating of the Christian faith to the world of the twentieth century.

Notes

1. One of Dodd's distinctions was that he could stop in the middle of a three-hours written paper, put his head in his hands and sleep for five minutes. He seems to have left no record of how he managed to wake up again on time.
2. Once when the flood water was running strongly the coach 'easied' the crew too near the weir. Seized by the current, the boat was being carried swiftly past the line of fender posts across the river and towards the weir, while the crew desperately and ineffectually back-paddled. 'My God, cox,' cried the coach, 'you're lost!' Dodd leaped to his feet in the thwart and as the eight slipped by flung his arms round the post and clung on as he used to say 'for dear life'. Rescue was effected with the aid of the lock-keeper's barge and boat hook!
3. Lenwood, after a period of devoted service in India, became a leader on the headquarters staff of the London Missionary Society. He fell while climbing on the Aiguille d'Argentières in 1934 and was killed instantly.

5

Opportunities for Research

I

WITH A 'DOUBLE FIRST' SAFELY BEHIND HIM WHAT WOULD HE DO NEXT? His college tutors had been more than satisfied with his First in Greats and encouraged him to return to Oxford in September and to try for a Fellowship by examination at Magdalen. In addition he began work on a dissertation for the Craven Fellowship in the university. In neither case did he gain the award, but his performance in the Craven was so meritorious that the examiners made him a special grant for travel and research. At the end of October, however, a new prospect unexpectedly opened up. The classics department at Leeds University needed temporary assistance and Dodd accepted the post offered to him at very short notice. On 5 November he was beginning lectures on Latin and Greek literature and assuming responsibility for a production of Aristophanes' *The Clouds*, which was due to be performed at the end of the month.

The latter task was certainly formidable. The original producer, a member of the classics department, had been taken ill and a few days before the actual performance the stage manager followed suit. Preparations had been in progress for many months and, seeing that it was the first Greek play to be produced in Leeds, a great deal hung upon the success of the venture. In the crisis the newcomer took over the direction of the final rehearsals and in the last week acted also as stage manager. (A visit to a Palestine bazaar late on the night before the first performance enabled him to secure a badly needed Graeco-Roman lamp.) The result was a triumph. Cyril Bailey came up from Balliol and declared that he had never enjoyed an evening more. In the few weeks as a stopgap Dodd had proved himself to be not only a promising teacher but also a man with a strong dramatic sense which was destined to find expression in his later work.

A testimonial from Professor Rhys Roberts who was then head of the classics department shows how great an impression the young Oxford graduate had made in his first teaching assignment: it also provides a striking pen-portrait of him as he was in 1906:

Owing to the sudden illness of our Classical Lecturer, Mr. Dodd was called upon—in mid-term and almost at a moment's notice—to give some 13 lectures a week to Greek and Latin classes of all grades from the lowest to the most advanced.

It would have been no light task even for an experienced teacher to succeed, without any opportunity for special preparation, to the entire work of an able and attractive lecturer. But Mr. Dodd, young as he is, stood the test with complete success. Widely read and widely interested in classical history and philosophy as well as in classical literature and language generally, he was well equipped for the demands made upon him; and, working hard without any loss of his naturally buoyant spirits and winning manner, he gained at once the respect and the liking of his pupils. The classes he took contained some rather intractable elements, but not the slightest difficulty of discipline arose. Though pleasant, he is also firm; and it was no doubt speedily recognized that, in a conflict of wills, he would be able easily to make his own prevail. At the end of the term, he took his full share in the written examinations and I was much struck by the thoroughness and judgment which he showed as an examiner as well as by the marked progress made by the students he had taught. I ought to add that, heavy as were the strictly professional demands on his time, Mr. Dodd found leisure to see a good deal of the general life of the place, and also to give most valuable help in the management of two students' performances of *The Clouds* of Aristophanes. In the latter undertaking his interest in classical archaeology, and his considerable skill in music and drawing, proved highly useful.

Judging by the severe test I have described and speaking from many years' experience of classical lecturers, I wish to say that I have known no one who, at the same age, seemed more likely to have a career of unusual distinction as a scholar and as a teacher. The institution will be fortunate which secures the services of so promising and so interesting a man.

II

The Leeds engagement, however, proved to be only a brief interlude. In the New Year Dodd returned to Oxford and took on some teaching duties at Univ while working on his German. He seized the opportunity to attend lectures on a wide range of subjects and to make some acquaintance with the treasures of the British Museum in London. For his special research in ancient history he had chosen numismatics and in this field Berlin possessed unrivalled resources. In April, therefore, he left home to spend a term in that city. He quickly established himself, dividing his time between visiting museums where sculptures and coins from the Graeco-Roman world were on display, attending lectures such as were being given by Willamowitz-Moellendorf on Hellenistic culture, and availing himself of the opportunities of sitting in the lecture-rooms of great biblical scholars such as Harnack and Weiss in the faculty of theology. He also joined in the devotional and missionary activities of Christian student circles, making friends and inviting them to be his companions on the walks which continued as regularly in Germany as in Britain.

Lectures ended early in August but he continued work in the galleries and museums and made brief expeditions to mountain resorts. On 26 August he was home again in Wrexham, having gained invaluable first-hand knowledge of German classical and biblical scholarship and having greatly advanced his proficiency in the German language. He had been particularly impressed by Harnack and, in spite of all the criticisms of and reactions from this great historian's interpretation of Christianity which were soon to become fashionable in Germany and elsewhere, it is doubtful if Dodd ever deviated to any substantial degree from the attitude to history embodied in Harnack's work. From boyhood days he had listened to sermons and addresses and in Oxford had heard many lectures on ancient history. But now for the first time he spent a whole term in the lecture-room of an acknowledged master in the history of early Christianity. He admired Harnack's methods, he shared his deep religious concern. Statements made by Harnack could have been made later on by Dodd; statements made about Harnack could equally well have been made later on about Dodd.

For example Harnack declared, 'This I know: the theologians of every country only half discharge their duties if they think it enough to treat of the Gospel in the recondite language of learning and bury it in scholarly folios.' And again, 'The Christian religion is something simple and sublime: it means one thing and one thing only: Eternal Life in the midst of time, by the strength and under the eyes of God.'[1]

Such were Harnack's deep convictions to which Dodd must have given whole-hearted assent. Following Luther, he spoke of Christ as 'the mirror of God's paternal heart' and Dodd never abandoned the belief that this reflection can be discerned more and more in its concrete details if a student brings all his resources to the examination of the New Testament documents.

In a fine appreciation of Harnack the man, Wilhelm Pauck has said this:[2]

In a certain sense, every true teacher is an historian, and nobody can be a true historian unless he is willing to be also a teacher. For, in every present, men find that they must come to terms with the cultural legacy which they have inherited from their fathers. They must take possession of it and incorporate it in their own lives. They must fit it to the requirements of their own situation and thus transform it and then transmit it to their children and their children's children.

In this sense, Harnack was a supreme teacher-historian. His writings as well as his activities clearly prove that he believed it to be the highest task of the historian to prepare his fellow men for right action in the present. 'Only that history which is not yet past but which is and remains a living part of our present deserves to be known by all,' he wrote. Hence he regarded all history as mute as long as it is nothing but a display of an antiquarian interest or dealt with only in terms of archaeology, that is, as long as it is understood to be merely a record of past human life.

'A supreme teacher-historian'. Was not this to be the ideal to which Dodd would increasingly aspire? He might have become the dedicated antiquarian, concentrating his scholarly investigations upon coins and inscriptions. He might have become the eager archaeologist, for archaeology was an enterprise which had already captured his interest. But for too long already he had been concerned with the central task of communicating the Gospel to his fellow men living in the present for it ever to become possible for him to surrender himself to disciplines almost completely related to the past.

III

Harnack's influence may have been of great significance for Dodd's future in another respect. His book *What is Christianity?* achieved enormous popularity. He once told Paul Tillich that in the year 1900 the main railway station of Leipzig, one of the largest in Central Europe, had been blocked by freight cars filled with copies of his book for shipment all over the world. It was translated into more languages than had so far been the case for any other book except the Bible. And the reason for this popularity was not far to seek. It offered Christian believers freedom from the rigid doctrinal frameworks within which their faith had hitherto been enclosed. It set forth Christianity as the revelation of God's relation to mankind in terms of a particular career which men could apprehend as part of their own historical inheritance and to which they could respond in a way which made sense within their contemporary world. Harnack's *History of Dogma* had revealed his immense learning in the language and literature of the Hellenistic world. But he was convinced that the pure stream of original Christianity had become contaminated as it had flowed into the broad river of Hellenistic culture. It was necessary to rediscover its *essence* and to express it in terms which could gain a hearing in the modern world.

Now although Dodd had already devoted himself in school and university to gaining a mastery of Hellenistic language and literature, he had not yet explored its implications for the study of the Christian faith to which he had given his full allegiance. Within the Reformed tradition to which he belonged, early creeds and patristic formulations of doctrine were less the test of orthodoxy than was the case, for example, in Anglicanism. Might it be his own life's work to follow Harnack by examining with the utmost care the relation of the biblical records to the wider culture of the Graeco-Roman world within which the earliest Christians lived? Could he define the Gospel which was originally proclaimed within that world and then ask whether, in fact, that Gospel had been misinterpreted (as Harnack implied) by the very categories of the new language-system into which it was perforce translated? Such thoughts may have begun in only the most tentative way to exercise his mind as he sat in Harnack's lecture-room in Berlin. The fact remains that the continuity between the work of the great German liberal historian and that of the young Oxford student who was to become Britain's leading New Testament interpreter can easily be discerned.

IV

As has happened so often in Germany, one theological position, seemingly impregnably established, is suddenly subjected to an onslaught of such vehemence that it appears before long to be on the verge of collapse. The year before Dodd arrived in Berlin, a young man, less than ten years his senior, had published a book which had created an immediate sensation and must have been excitedly talked about in student circles in the summer of 1907. This was Albert Schweitzer's *Von Reimarus zu Wrede*, translated into English in 1910 under the title *The Quest of the Historical Jesus*. Its conclusion contrasted sharply with Harnack's major claim—that it was possible to construct a reliable picture of the Jesus of history who could be seen as the reflection, within the concrete actualities of human life, of the character of the eternal God Himself. Such a picture, Schweitzer held, was no more than the attempt of the individual imagination to create a plausible coherence out of the New Testament records. It failed completely to give adequate attention to that strand of the testimony of the Synoptic Gospels to which a rigorous historical criticism must give major prominence, namely, the *eschatological* conviction which completely governed Jesus' words and actions.

Over against Harnack's Son of God mirroring the heart of the Father, Schweitzer set the Son of Man suffering and dying in order to hasten the coming of the Kingdom. 'This dramatic (and it has been said even Wagnerian) picture of Jesus, convinced of the imminence of the kingdom of God on this earth and, during his ministry, of the necessity for him to sacrifice his own life deliberately in order to save his people from the period of woes believed to presage the kingdom, and so to usher it in— this picture has exercised a fascination over many readers.'[3] But it was never accepted as fully authentic by Dodd. Indeed, it has been said by one friendly critic that he fought against Schweitzer throughout his life. Not that he failed to recognize Schweitzer's greatness, or denied that his reconstruction should be given a proper hearing: when later Schweitzer came to England to lecture Dodd acted as his interpreter on various occasions. Nevertheless, as he began to engage in a detailed study of the New Testament, he became more and more convinced that there was an alternative solution to the eschatological problem. To expound what he believed to be Jesus' own eschatological message constituted one of the major aspects of his later teaching and writing.

V

Returning from this formative period in Germany, Dodd settled back into the family life at Wrexham, walking regularly with his father or with his brothers Ernest and Percy, preaching most Sundays in local chapels, taking an active part in a missionary campaign, and working steadily on his dissertation for submission to the Craven Trustees. The red-letter day, however, in the year 1907 was 12 December when, after dinner that evening, he walked down to Magdalen and saw that he had been elected to a senior demyship in that college in the field of ecclesiastical history. Not only would this afford him reasonable financial security for the next four years; it also gave him a place on the list of men of distinguished scholarship from all colleges who in successive years had been given opportunity by Magdalen to pursue some chosen subject of research.

The unusual title 'demyship' derives apparently from the time when the grant was worth half the emoluments paid to a Fellow of the College. On an average, two senior demies were elected each year (the other successful candidate in 1907 became Professor of English at Yale University) and subjects for which grants were most frequently awarded at that time were philosophy, history and medicine. Three years after Dodd's success the only senior demy elected was T. E. Lawrence (who therefore became his contemporary within the four-year span). Those fortunate enough to be elected were in the happy position of being given valuable facilities by the college for further study without being called upon to assume more than a minimum of duties or responsibilities within the society to which they now in a measure belonged.

The next two terms from January to June 1908 must have been almost idyllic. He now had the status of his demyship; he could concentrate on the aspects of the history of the ancient world which appealed to him most, and he was happy to give an elder brother's support to Percy who was following him in the path of Mods and Greats at Jesus. He enjoyed the company of his Univ friends, Grensted and Streatfield, with whom he was regularly walking and sharing meals and he was free to attend special lectures in Oxford such as were given in summer term by William James of Harvard and Willamowitz of Berlin. He was active in local preaching, assisting in boys' clubs and Bible classes and promoting missionary interests, and during one notable week-end he cycled to London to stay with his old friend Hopwood (now a candidate for the Methodist ministry at Richmond College), to see the Academy Exhibition at Burlington House and to spend a morning in the British Museum. In July came the first opportunity to take part in an activity which had become one of his major interests: for two weeks he worked on the 'dig' at Corbridge under the leadership of Professor Craske of All Souls.

But although for two years since his graduation he had been gaining experience through teaching and had been extending his knowledge of other languages and of special departments of ancient history through research, a firm commitment had soon to be made to preparation for his life's work. It had once been suggested to him by no less a person than Dr. Bartlet that he should go out, at least for a period, to teach in a college in Hankow. Had he continued his research in Graeco-Roman history an Oxford Fellowship might well have been offered to him. But the call to the ordained ministry became ever more insistent. A brief diary entry for 2 June, 1908, records the first step towards preparing himself for this vocation. 'In afternoon called on the Souters and afterwards interviewed Dr. Fairbairn about entering at Mansfield.' On 14 June he sent in his application and on 18 June appeared before the Board and was elected an exhibitioner of the college. On 10 October he dined at Mansfield for the first time as a member of the college with which over the next twenty-two years he was to be constantly and intimately associated.

Notes

1. These two quotations are taken from the Preface and the first Chapter of the English edition of *What is Christianity?*
2. W. Pauck, *Harnack and Troeltsch*, pp. 17f.
3. *The Pelican Guide to Modern Theology*, III, ed. R. Davidson and A. R. C. Leaney, p. 256.

6

Training for the Ministry

I

DODD'S FINAL COMMITMENT TO PREPARATION FOR THE MINISTRY OF THE Congregational Church came about as the result of a long process of thought and prayer. When finally he presented himself for ordination, one of the questions to which he made public reply was, What are your reasons for believing that you are divinely called to the work of the Christian Ministry? This was his answer:

I believe that God has called me to the ministry *first* because since first the idea of it took definite shape in my mind, during my second year at Oxford, the times when I felt myself nearest to God have been the times when I felt most constrained to seek this form of service and because, in spite of my shrinking from it, the desire to enter upon it has grown with growing experience;

secondly, because of the way that I have been led and the influences under which, without my seeking, I have been brought; in which I cannot but trace the divine Providence;

thirdly, because of the satisfaction I have already found in the work, particularly during a year as student pastor in the village of Benson;

fourthly, because the congregation meeting in this place, being a true Church of Christ, guided as I believe by His Spirit, has ratified the inward call by inviting me to be its pastor.

My call to the ministry was not a single experience but a growing conviction, making way against many doubts and much hesitation, that this is the field within which God means me to face the double task that awaits every man: that of working out his own salvation and of serving his generation according to the will of God.

In this statement there is no hint of a crisis of conversion or of a dramatic decision between two major alternatives. In his home the ministry had been held in highest esteem: at Oxford the study of divinity and preparation for ordination were still accorded an honoured place within the life of the university. Both in Wales and in Oxford he had associated himself with evangelistic movements and had attended campaigns led by evangelists such as Gipsy Smith and Torrey and Alexander. But in his own religious development he seems to have avoided any extreme emphases, whether towards an excessive stress on emotional experience or towards an insistence upon a particular theory of biblical interpretation. He was eager that the Gospel should be proclaimed and that its implications should be worked out in service to the neighbour. But he believed that this must be done within the context of a constant search for knowledge of the truth and a disciplined application of the intellect to interpret data in accordance with recognised methods of valid historical enquiry.

The question of the particular church in which his ministry was to be exercised presented no problem. In Wrexham the Congregational church to which his family belonged commanded his own complete allegiance: this was maintained through his regular association with Mansfield College and George Street Congregational Church in Oxford: and in spite of the dominant Anglicanism within his own undergraduate college and his intimate friendships with fellow students who were Anglicans, he seems never to have wavered in his loyalty to the principles of independency and rational dissent. At his ordination he was asked, Why do you prefer to exercise your ministry in a Congregational Church? And to this he replied, 'I am persuaded that the independent or congregational church-order, at its best, conserves most fully the spirit of the primitive Church and the liberty of the Gospel: and that it gives the fullest opportunity for the exercise of a spiritual ministry, unfettered by superfluous forms whether of Church government, of ritual or of Dogma.' For order and form Dodd had a concern which bordered on reverence: but these, he believed, must never become inflexible or 'superfluous'. Nothing human must be allowed to impede the free movement of the divine Spirit.

II

The theological course at Mansfield on which he now embarked had obvious links with his earlier specialisations in Oxford but set them in a new context and gave them a new direction. Under Dr. Souter, his splendid equipment as translator of the texts of ancient Greece could be applied to the problems of New Testament text and exegesis. Under Dr. Bartlet, his knowledge of the history of the Graeco-Roman world could be related to the investigation of the progress of early Christianity. The entirely new departure—and it was to prove of immense significance for his future work—was the study of Hebrew and of the Old Testament. This brought him increasingly into contact with Dr. Buchanan Gray, who later supplemented his Hebrew with instruction in Aramaic and Syriac and inspired him to begin the exploration of the rich inheritance of Semitic culture which later on would supply him with a powerful counterbalance to the Greek. Few institutions can have been so well equipped at that time to preserve a fruitful balance between the two cultural foundations of our western civilisation than Mansfield with its two eminent teachers, Souter and Gray.

Souter was a genial, friendly figure, an exact scholar, a typical representative of Browning's Grammarian. When lecturing, for example, on the Epistle to the Colossians he was known to reach verse 13 of chapter 1 by the end of term. (His pupil, though devoted to his teacher, would never have emulated him in this respect; he was always careful to maintain the *form* of any exercise in which he might happen to be engaged.) Buchanan Gray was stocky of build but an intellectual giant. His absolute sincerity, his utter repudiation of the pretentious and the vague, his patience in unravelling the meaning of a difficult text, were all reflected in the later career of the young student whom he first introduced to the glories and the complexities of Old Testament scholarship.

III

The year 1909 brought new interests outside Dodd's course of study at Mansfield. On 1 March he left Oxford to travel, with breaks at Lucerne and Como, to Rome. There he spent more than a month studying at the British School, the Lateran Museum and the Vatican Library. He inspected ancient sites, attended Pontifical High Mass at St. Peter's celebrated by his fellow countryman Cardinal Merry del Val, kept the balance by visiting the Presbyterian church and hearing the minister lecturing on the 'Primacy of Peter', and took some part in meetings of the Italian Student Christian Federations where the great missionary leader, John R. Mott, was speaking. From Rome he went on to stay a few days in Naples, 'swotting inscriptions', making excursions to Pompeii and

Pozzuoli, and incidentally celebrating his twenty-fifth birthday in the neighbourhood of amphitheatre and catacomb. Finally he began his homeward journey on 12 April, travelling via Ravenna, Parma and Brescia (in each of which there were inscriptions to see) and reaching Oxford in time for examinations at the beginning of Trinity term.

The new term was significant for him in at least two ways. First, it began a close association with one who was to become an intimate friend and counsellor in the coming years. In April, Dr. Fairbairn, who had some months earlier announced his intention of resigning the principalship of Mansfield on account of failing health, left Oxford and was succeeded by Dr. W. B. Selbie, who had been exercising a powerful preaching ministry in Emmanuel Church, Cambridge. His emphasis in the teaching of doctrine was less on metaphysical issues, more on the ethical and psychological problems involved in seeking to relate the Christian faith to the life of the twentieth century. He had come originally from Manchester Grammar School to Brasenose College at a time when Dissenters were a rarity in Oxford and, after a distinguished academic career, both in the university and at Mansfield College, had been appointed to a pastoral charge where his gifts as a preacher were quickly recognised. When he returned to his old college as Principal, although he proved himself entirely capable as administrator and scholar, it was through his preaching that his greatest influence was exercised in Oxford life. His practice was to preach on every other Sunday during term and large numbers outside his own denomination were to be found regularly in the congregation. His successor in the principalship has written, 'The pulpit was his throne. No reprinting of his sermons . . . would explain his power. This lay in his directness, his simplicity, his passionate concern. . . . He was preacher, pastor and very humble man of God.'[1] This was the man under whom Dodd was to complete his training for the ministry and then, after a short absence from Oxford, was to join as colleague for some fifteen years. He often turned to Selbie for advice and it was Selbie who, after encouraging him to go away from Oxford for a while into a pastoral charge, brought him back to the position in Mansfield where his gifts and training could find rich fulfilment in preparing others for the ministry.

The second important event in Trinity Term 1909 was his 'call' from the congregation in the village of Benson to be their student minister. Situated about ten miles out from Oxford in the Henley direction, it was within cycling distance, and when he stayed overnight he could explore a new area of the countryside on foot. He enjoyed the hospitality of families belonging to the church and gained further experience in the task, which he had already begun in Wrexham, of communicating the

Christian Gospel to people with no background of academic training and to children who gathered for instruction in the Sunday School. Though devoted to research and to exact scholarship he never lost the concern to bring the Bible into the range of the appreciation and understanding of ordinary folk and to do all in his power to encourage and assist lay people who were Sunday School teachers or Bible Class leaders to do their work intelligently and effectively. Benson Free Church gained a secure and honoured place in his affections.

IV

In ordinary student life at Mansfield he was entirely at home. Nathaniel Micklem was slightly junior to him, but what he has written about the Mansfield J.C.R. in 1911 would have applied equally to the period of Dodd's residence:[2]

> The J.C.R. at Mansfield was a singularly gay and free companionship. Our theology by all modern standards was imperfect; we were rejoicing in our relatively recent deliverance from subjection to old Calvinist dogma and were less interested in dogmatic theology than in the discovery of how little one might believe without ceasing to be Christian. Our theology, no doubt, was lamentable, but perhaps our religion was not all too bad. To that generation the great appeal was made by the Foreign Missionary cause with John Mott telling us that at the moment Japan was open to receive the Gospel, that if we entered into our opportunity Japan might lead the Orient to Christ, but that the door would not be open long.

Inspired by this challenge many students offered themselves to take part in missionary campaigns in various parts of the country, upwards of eighty being organised during the early years of this century. In the autumn of 1909 Dodd acted as manager of the Croydon and district campaign and in the report subsequently issued it was claimed that it had been one of the most successful ever held. Here in a local situation the power of the missionary concern to draw together old and young of varying church traditions and allegiances to serve the one cause was demonstrated on a limited scale in the way that it would be on a world-wide platform in the great Edinburgh Conference of the following year.

The early spring of 1911 found him in Italy again. Nearly six weeks were spent visiting museums and libraries in Rome and the provincial cities, gathering information which could later be written up for learned journals. In June he completed his course of training at Mansfield and in December his tenure of the senior demyship came to an end. The question was obviously, What next? A teaching post? A pastoral charge? He had preached in many chapels in England and Scotland and was becoming well known in the denomination. At the same time he had already gained a place in the world of classical scholarship by his research in numismatics and inscriptions. The next step could be crucial for his whole career.

The diary for 21 January, 1912, carries the significant entry 'Preached at Brook Street Congregational Church, Warwick, morning and evening. In afternoon visited Sunday School and heard Countess of Warwick at P.S.A. [Pleasant Sunday Afternoon]. Wretched weather: cold raw fog all day.' Evidently the depressing weather did not prevent him from commending himself to the people of Warwick for 6 February reads, 'Dined at Univ and then heard Bishop Gore lecture on "The Reconstruction of Belief". Received call from Warwick.' He consulted Selbie who is reputed to have said, 'Go to Warwick and gain some pastoral experience. Then in due course we'll have you back here at Mansfield.' So the call was accepted, digs were booked at 23 West St. and in April he was ordained and welcomed to the pastorate of Brook St. Church.

By a coincidence, on the day before the call came he met James Moffatt at Mansfield for the first time. Alexander Souter had left the college in the summer of 1911. To succeed him the Council had invited a Scot, whose scholarly fame was in the ascendant, to come South.[3] Maybe Selbie saw already that Moffatt's call to a chair in Scotland was not likely to be long delayed and that then their own man would be ready to fill the gap. Be that as it may, this in fact happened, for Moffatt assumed the Chair of Early Church History in Glasgow in 1915. But one result of his stay in Oxford was that he became acquainted with Mansfield's own rising star and in course of time this was to lead to important consequences.

Notes

1. N. Micklem, *The Box and the Puppets*, p. 42.
2. *The Box and the Puppets*, pp. 45f.
3. While still a parish minister at Broughty Ferry Moffatt had written a massive *Introduction to the Literature of the New Testament*. This was published in 1910, the year before he came to Mansfield.

PART 3

A Search for Fuller Reality

7

The Warwick Pastorate

I

WARWICK PROVED TO BE AN ALMOST IDEAL SETTING FOR DODD'S ONLY experience of extended pastoral ministry. It was within easy reach of Oxford by train and yet far enough away to enable him to make a real break for a period with his many academic associations. It is a historic town whose castle and parish church of St. Nicholas are famous. The fine tower of the church can be seen from miles around and the ancient buildings in the centre of town are a delight to the antiquarian. With his archaeological and architectural interests Dodd must have found such an environment particularly congenial.

Not that Brook Street Congregational Church possessed any beauty of form. Originally built in 1758, it was enlarged forty years later and extended still further to gain its present spaciousness in 1826. It was obviously designed primarily for a preaching ministry. A central pulpit commanded rows of pews in the arena and a semi-circular gallery above. The Calvinist tradition in Congregationalism gloried in the preaching of the Word of God and, besides the regular Sunday services, meetings were often held in the week for instruction and discussion. It was not until 1871 that an organ was installed (costing £70!). The facts that a new organ was built in 1882 and that before the end of the century the church hall was enlarged and class-rooms added indicate that Congregationalism in Warwick was a flourishing cause in spite of what must have seemed the dominance of the parish church.

Yet from 1900 onwards there had been a succession of pastors, each occupying the charge for a relatively short time, and the congregation must have been anxious to secure a more settled ministry. A young man of twenty-eight could be expected to remain with them for a reasonable period and this would indeed have been the case had not the call to return to Mansfield come so soon. There is no doubt that the new minister quickly established himself in Warwick, gained warm attachments to many families in the Brook Street congregation and found real fulfilment in his pastoral charge. It was in no sense a case of putting in time before returning to academic work.

Though he had his independent lodgings his bachelor status meant that he was constantly invited to tea or supper with church families. One family in particular almost adopted him—the Coltarts—and the association was strengthened by the fact that the unmarried son, William Coltart, was church secretary. He was a manufacturing chemist, a mathematician of some distinction who had taken a London degree. Although his background of academic interests had been so different from Dodd's, the two became fast friends and walked together regularly on Saturday afternoons. For walking was a habit which could on no account be abandoned. On his day off on Monday Dodd explored the countryside around Warwick; during the week he walked to make his rounds of visiting; and over the week-ends, besides the Saturday afternoon with his friend, he would fit in whenever possible a walk as part of his Sunday schedule. To walk seemed almost as sacred an obligation as to pray.

II

He took up residence in Warwick in April 1912. The days immediately before the move he had spent on holiday with his father on the North Wales coast and the strength of the bond between them was revealed in signal fashion when the father spoke to commend his son at the recognition meeting prior to the ordination service. This took place on 18 April, a red-letter day for himself, for his family, and for those who had been his pastors during the long period of preparation.

His father spoke of his son's own deliberate choice and of how he would never seek to 'run the show' but rather to share with the congregation the best that he had to give. The Mayor of Wrexham declared that of all the testimonials he had ever given none had been sent with so great pleasure and confidence for the future as that which had been requested for the present ordinand. Dr. Selbie gave the solemn charge to the candidate at the ordination service; Mr. Huffadine, the minister from Pen-y-bryn, the charge to the congregation. And the central figure in the ceremony bore witness to the way in which he had received his call to the ministry.

When asked, in the questions put to the candidate, to give a brief outline of the principal doctrines which he intended to teach, he replied in generally orthodox terms, though with his own distinctive stamp upon the language he employed. In his final declaration he affirmed, 'I intend to teach that love to God is shown by service to man and faith in Christ by following His steps; and that all faithful followers of Christ form the one Holy Church of God throughout the world, to which is committed the message of the Gospel for the salvation of every creature.' And then in characteristic fashion he concluded, 'These doctrines it is my present intention by God's help to teach while I look always for fresh enlightenment, being very confident that the Lord hath more truth and light yet to break forth out of his Holy Word.' With patent sincerity he dedicated himself to the double office of pastor and teacher within the congregation worshipping at Brook Street Chapel in Warwick.

Not unnaturally he felt a special responsibility for the young people. Within a few months he had initiated a preparation class for those desiring instruction in the principles of church membership. William Coltart's nephew, who in his boyhood used to spend holidays in Warwick, has written:

I can't remember the time when we did not attend Sunday morning service at Brook Street with our older relatives. Consequently my memories of 'Mr. Dodd' are childlike and vivid. We used to be entranced with his simple and delightful Children's Sermons delivered during the earlier part of the Service, when the Sunday School was in attendance in the first 4 or 5 pews. They departed after the collection but we three sat with our family (somewhat grandly I fear!) and remained for the full service. Consequently we listened to Harold Dodd's quite wonderful sermons and it is a tribute to him that they were really intelligible and gripping to a small boy like myself of 8 (in 1914). I must have acquired much of my biblical knowledge from those sermons at that very receptive age. More often than not Dodd was at our home for midday dinner after the Service and thereafter used to go for a good walk with Uncle Bill until tea time. I believe the two had great respect for the other's intelligence and this forged the bond of their friendship.

I remember Dodd as a small, spare figure of a man. Always spruce and immaculate in his dress and appearance. He had a good sense of humour and a ready laugh. A great and natural appearance of vitality always, and an easy and unconscious concentration in conversation on any subject under discussion. A wonderfully alert and logical brain.

It is not surprising that he quickly commended himself to the people of Warwick as he went in and out of their homes, often a guest at meals, playing croquet one afternoon, taking part in a reading of *The Tempest* one evening, encouraging Sunday School teachers and youth leaders through weekday activities, and giving of his best in the pulpit on Sunday.

III

For more than two years he carried on his work in a small well-ordered county town where divisions socially and denominationally were accepted without serious question and where, within the chiefly middle-class Free Church section of the community, he was highly respected for his character and scholarship. Old friends came to stay with him. There was the occasional visit to Oxford with a chance to work in the Bodleian Library. From time to time he was away at the week-end preaching in Worcester or Leicester or even farther afield. August brought a four weeks' vacation in some seaside resort, and at Easter time in 1914 he was enjoying a long Cotswold walk with his brother Percy, covering more than eighty miles in five days.

His lot was cast in what seemed to be a relatively untroubled part of a relatively peaceful world. He seems never to have involved himself in political activities or civic affairs. He was content to concentrate on his studies but to apply them now, through preaching, to the needs of his own people. He was proving in his daily experience the truth of Luther's words, 'Nobody can understand Virgil who has not been a shepherd or farmer for five years—nobody can understand the Scriptures who has not looked after a congregation for a hundred years. We're beggars, that's the truth.'

It is strange that in his diary he makes no reference to the world-shaking events of early August 1914. On the 3rd and 4th he was enjoying long walks with his father around Warwick. On the 5th he was travelling to Aberdeen, and on the 6th enjoying the beach and 'pictures' there. The only suggestion of anything unusual is an entry in the diary for 7 August. 'In morning went to Intercession at E. St. Nicholas.' Life for the time being could take its normal course. There was as yet no thought that the Europe which he had known in Berlin and Italy, as well as in Great Britain, could never be the same again.

Looking back to those days, Dr. Nathaniel Micklem, when asked about pacifism, exclaimed, 'We were all pacifist in 1914. Nonconformists had never thought of engaging in war. There was no tradition of army service amongst nonconformist families and no Free Church chaplains in the armed forces.' It was regarded as tragic that no way of resolving the conflict had been found, but at first there was no sense that the total community would ultimately be involved. The real testing time arrived when it became clear that the voluntary system was failing to produce enough recruits. By 1916 Dodd was active in the National Council against Conscription.

But although his sympathies were entirely on the side of those who were opposed to war as a method of settling human conflicts, he never became a crusading pacifist. He was a member of the Fellowship of Reconciliation and attended a peace conference in Cambridge in December 1914. He could find no categorical command about war and peace in the Bible which could be regarded as applicable to all men at all times. Nor could he find any unequivocal course of action enjoined upon the individual Christian. So he recognised that, while there must be the constant search for 'the mind of Christ' on this matter, there could never be a final definition.

In a carefully worded address to the Congregational Union Autumn Assembly in 1929 on 'The Teaching of Jesus on Christianity and War' he began by saying that it would be useless to search in the Gospels for such explicit teaching of our Lord about war as would set the question at rest for His followers. A study of the Gospels would not directly solve our concrete problems. Yet, he concluded, 'it would be something gained if we could agree that war is in its nature a thing abhorrent to the spirit of the Gospel and lacking any sanction in the teaching of our Lord, even though we might still differ as to how far any individual, at any given moment, is free to dissociate himself from a war which his country may have undertaken.' It could not have been without significance for him that the brother with whom he shared the five days of idyllic walking through the Cotswolds in March 1914 was in July 1915 writing to him from a musketry camp in Yorkshire, lamenting the fact that he had had no holiday since then. Percy served as an officer and, although he survived the war, his health was damaged to such an extent that he died at a comparatively early age.[1]

IV

Dodd made few innovations in church worship except that he introduced services on Christmas morning and on Good Friday. He was happy with his people and they had confidence in him. There was no reason to think that he would move to another pastorate. However, in May 1915 the General Assembly of the United Free Church of Scotland met in Edinburgh and one of their decisions was to affect indirectly his whole future career. The Chair of Church History in the Glasgow College was vacant and Dr. James Moffatt was nominated to fill it. His gifts were so outstanding that his own Church was only waiting for a suitable vacancy to recall him from Oxford and now it had come. Moffatt would leave Mansfield. Who would take his place?

In the minds of the College Council there was virtually no hesitation. Dodd was their own man. He had in every way commended himself during his residence in the college and his academic record was such that he had no obvious rival. The Council met on 18 June and resolved unanimously to offer him the post of Yates Lecturer in the New Testament, in the first instance for three years: thereafter, if all went well, he would become Yates Professor.[2] In the letter of invitation the Principal made clear how delighted his colleagues would be if he would join their ranks.

It might perhaps have been expected that the young minister would jump at the opportunity to return to Oxford and to all the familiar associations at Mansfield. But the decision was not easily made. He had committed himself to a preaching and pastoral ministry and had found immense satisfaction and fulfilment in the charge at Warwick. People with few educational qualifications had responded to his teaching and welcomed him into their homes. Was he to leave this kind of ministry for the far more specialised study of texts and fine points of scholarship which, as he knew well, could easily become remote from the needs of ordinary life?

Probably his sense of loyalty to his Church was the major factor in his final decision. He knew that there were very few outside the Church of England who could represent the highest standards of Oxford scholarship within Oxford itself. His Church needed him in this position at this juncture. There would still be many opportunities for preaching around the country and for pastoral work amongst candidates for the ministry. From Colwyn Bay, therefore, to which familiar spot he had gone to think things over, came a letter to the Brook Street deacons written on 26 June informing them of his decision to accept the Mansfield invitation. 'It will cause me much regret to sever myself from Brook St. Church but I have come to feel that this invitation to Mansfield is a call to the service of the Church at large which I cannot refuse.' And he concluded, 'No minister, I think, could have had happier relations with his deacons than I have had.' As it later turned out, the severance was not final, for at the end of 1917 Mansfield had temporarily to close and he returned to his old charge from

January 1918 until April 1919 when the college opened again. But the die was cast. From now onwards Dodd and the New Testament would be indissolubly bound together. His specialisations hitherto had been in ancient inscriptions and early church history. All his resources would now be assembled and brought to bear on the history and interpretation of the New Testament Scriptures.

The congregation at Warwick felt the loss keenly but were in no way surprised. Their pastor seemed admirably qualified to serve in the training of future ministers and they were proud that he had been called to succeed so eminent a scholar as Dr. Moffatt. Their approval was matched by that of a wide circle of friends who wrote to congratulate Dodd on this early distinction. His former teacher and valued friend Professor Souter wrote, 'You are in fact the one man in the denomination for the post, though you may not be aware of the fact. I remember your saying to me that you would be ready to take up academic work once you had had five years' pastoral experience. Well you have had four (actually a little over three) and you have left your mark deep on Warwick. I have read every word of every sermon you have sent here and have felt their effectiveness very deeply.'

Frank Lemwood, who had known Mansfield so intimately in the first decade of the century, was enthusiastic. 'God be with you in it all—it's the key to the position for the near future—I mean for twenty years on. Make them know the N.T., not about it and teach them how to make it live in the Churches. Go on to victory in the name of the Lord. "In the year of the great war C.H.D. was appointed to teach N.T. at Mansfield"— Who knoweth but that thou wert called to the Kingdom for such a time as this.' Less exuberantly, but with deep feeling, R. I. Hopwood, who had gone with him from Wrexham to Oxford in 1902 and who remained a close friend ever afterwards, wrote from a Methodist manse in Harrogate,

No such good news has reached us since we have been here. We both congratulate you very heartily. My wife seems even more pleased about it than I am, if that were possible. (Curiously enough, we both came to the conclusion from the preamble of your letter that you were about to announce your engagement!)

No call could be clearer on the human side. Scotch [sic] professors are excellent in their way, so are some other erudite Englishmen, but for the purposes of Congregationalism in England and Wales I have felt they needed men at Mansfield (and elsewhere) with a different kind of 'touch'. You have just that blend of scholarship with the Welsh 'timbre' which will be so effective from my point of view—prejudiced no doubt.

It was a perceptive judgment. The Welsh 'timbre', the Oxford scholarly discipline, the Warwick pastoral experience (in his letter to Hopwood Dodd had confessed that he would have preferred to remain in ordinary ministerial work), had given him a combination of qualities which together constituted a firm foundation for all his future work. He would now be free to build upon this foundation a structure of New Testament scholarship as fine as any that this century has produced. In September 1915 he said good-bye to his friends in Warwick and took up his residence in the tower of Mansfield College.

V

He could hardly have returned to Oxford at a more difficult time. The full impact of the war was now being felt, especially amongst the age-group of those who would normally have been entering university. The supply of men for the ministry was declining and it soon became evident that the college might have to close for a period. In some ways, of course, this was an advantage to the new member of staff for it gave him more time to prepare his lecture-courses than would have been possible with a full college. So far he had given no special attention to Aramaic; now under the ready guidance of Dr. Buchanan Gray he was able to gain proficiency in this language.

He regularly introduced his classes to the study of the New Testament by leading them through a rigorous critical and linguistic analysis of Mark's Gospel. Textual and historical problems must be given proper attention before more comprehensive courses such as 'The Holy Spirit in the New Testament' could be offered. In addition to the lectures (which were open to members of the university), he took his full share in college tutorial responsibilities but, as his diaries show, he in no way confined himself to teaching and research. He was constantly entertaining Oxford colleagues and friends and visitors from outside: a solitary meal must have been a rare occurrence. In addition he was frequently on the move, travelling at week-ends to preach, often in churches far distant from Oxford, attending committees in London, taking part in conferences and retreats, visiting the family at Wrexham or his old friends at Warwick: his small and sprightly figure must have become one of the most familiar sights on the platforms of Oxford railway station. He sang at soldiers' clubs, he went into camp with boys in the summer, he took over an allotment and dug for victory, but whatever the day might bring, somehow the walk (or occasionally the cycle ride) would be fitted in.

There were societies and study groups, too, in Oxford which welcomed him as a member. Perhaps the most notable of these was Professor Sanday's seminar on New Testament Studies. Though Professor S. R. Driver had brought fame to the university by his outstanding work on the Old Testament and though patristic studies flourished within the Oxford classical tradition, it was the New Testament which was the focus of interest in theological research. Whatever its deficiencies compared with other European centres of learning, Oxford could at least claim proficiency in the study of the language and literature of Greece, and, with this equipment, its New Testament scholars could tackle the problems of textual criticism and documentary analysis with full confidence. Dodd, sharing their academic background, could readily play his part within the general enterprise and could enter into friendly co-operation with such men as B. H. Streeter, N. P. Williams and A. E. J. Rawlinson who were soon to make major contributions to New Testament studies.

However, it was not until Michaelmas Term 1919 that anything approaching normal life could return to Oxford. Then large numbers of men who had done war service were admitted to undergraduate colleges and the theological colleges looked forward to an increasing supply of candidates for the ministry. For Dodd the long years of disciplined study were about to find their fulfilment in lectures which captivated his audiences and in books which brought illumination and encouragement to countless readers. Yet two events took place around this time, one of which proved to be significant for his whole future career and the other of which affected him deeply in his own personal life.

VI

On 5 February, 1919, when, as his diary records, there was a heavy snowfall most of the day, he received a deputation from Cheshunt College, Cambridge, offering him the Presidency. Cheshunt, for some reason, had never attained the same status in Cambridge as Mansfield had gained in Oxford. It had a strong missionary tradition, but its academic achievements had not been noteworthy: in this respect it was somewhat overshadowed by Westminster College where Presbyterian learning had won high respect in the university. Now, however, with war ended and the presidency vacant, it seemed possible to make a fresh start. The College Council was determined to secure, if possible, a man who could build up the college, intellectually and spiritually, win confidence and respect in academic circles in Cambridge and act as a worthy representative of Congregationalism in East Anglia.

Already Emmanuel Church was noted for its preaching and social concern and the incumbent at the time was a Mansfield man, H. C. Carter, who had succeeded Selbie when he went to be principal of his old college. Carter knew of the promise and rising fame of the young New Testament professor and strongly supported the proposal to offer him the presidency. So, in company with two other members of Council, he waited on Dodd on the snowy February day and tried to urge the claims of Cheshunt, even at the expense of those of his own former college.

Obviously there was much in the proposal that was attractive. There were famous New Testament scholars in Cambridge. Cheshunt was at a critical stage in its history and as president Dodd would have the opportunity of leading it into a new era. He could work out his own ideas and, in co-operation with Carter, could perhaps make Congregationalism a vital force in Cambridge. Yet, if he became busy here and there, what would happen to his specialised study of the New Testament? And would it be fair to Mansfield? He had been on its staff only three and a half years and almost half of that time he had been carrying pastoral responsibilities at Warwick while the college had been virtually closed. It was of particular concern to him that the college had continued to pay him a full salary during the time he was away. Could he honourably leave them so soon?

Doubtless he sought advice from his Oxford friends who, one can imagine, were unanimous in trying to keep him. Even from Cambridge a wise letter put a strong case for waiting a while before assuming a post with such varied responsibilities. He did not decide quickly but within a month his mind was made up and to the great disappointment of the Cheshunt Council their invitation was declined.

VII

The nature of the crisis in his personal life is less clearly defined. It was undoubtedly related to the possibility of marriage and to the resolving of inner psychological conflicts of which he had become acutely aware. In many respects his life hitherto had been wonderfully sheltered. He had grown up in a home where he was the eldest son, cared for by a devoted mother, encouraged in all his scholastic efforts by an approving father. He had never lacked for male friends, both among his own Oxford contemporaries and among the teachers who fostered his developing academic achievements. He impressed all by his vivacity and at the same time by his modesty and became an ever welcome guest in homes first at Oxford, then at Warwick. It was in no way unnatural that older women should delight to entertain the young bachelor pastor to meals. He could find 'home' away from home, whether with the Coltarts in Warwick, the Souters in Aberdeen, or the Bartlets in Oxford. It was in so many ways a pleasant manner of life, an extension of boyhood's exemption from domestic responsibilities in order the better to concentrate on educational and vocational demands.

But could such a state of affairs continue indefinitely? When Dodd returned to college life at Mansfield in 1915 he had passed his thirtieth year. Many of his friends were finding fulfilment in marriage. Did he lack some quality which would enable him to gain a woman's affection and a family of his own? He had been like a second father to his younger brothers and had related himself easily to children in his pastoral charges. Was this all that he could hope to experience in this particular sphere of human relationships? Except for the continuity in the Brook Street Church at Warwick, almost every week-end was spent in a different place with incessant travelling and adjustments to the *ménages* in which he was 'put up'. And there was no real home to return to in Oxford.

A dramatic entry in the diary of 6 December, 1918, reveals the depths of his own feeling. Normally only the weather, the walk and bare details of engagements are recorded. But in capital letters, such as he used for recording inscriptions, this day is introduced with the words INCIPIT VITA NOVA. He had gone to London and called for Lesley Griffiths, walked with her round Hampstead Heath and then taken her to tea. Before Christmas she had visited Warwick and they had become engaged and in the early months of 1919 they were together in Wrexham, in Oxford and in Lesley's home in Bromley. They shared common interests in the Free Church Fellowship and the Student Christian Movement, and it seemed that at last he could look forward to a more settled form of life. But on a day in March of 'wretched weather, cold and raw with sleet and snow continuously' the engagement was broken off.

This experience left a deep scar and some months later he was seeking the help of Dr. J. A. Hadfield, one of the earliest practitioners in England of the new methods of psycho-analysis. Over a period of more than four years he paid periodic visits to Dr. Hadfield and, although the nature of his treatment is not known, it is abundantly clear that at this stage of his life he became aware of the profound importance of what was then called the New Psychology, not only on account of its interpretation of the place of religion in human life but also of the possibilities which it offered for resolving in a positive way his own emotional problems. He never attempted to become an expert in the study of psychological theories but he gained sufficient knowledge of the new insights which psychological

investigations had made available to use them effectively in his interpretation of the writings of the New Testament, in his grappling with the
question of authority and later on in his consideration of the constraints
which were hindering the cause of reunion amongst the churches.

VIII

In his student days before the War of 1914–18 he, like many others,
became aware of the deep impression made by the first attempt in modern
times to examine religious experience analytically and 'scientifically'. The
famous Gifford Lectures of William James were published in 1902
under the title *The Varieties of Religious Experience*. Subsequently the writings
of R. R. Marrett of Exeter College anticipated in some measure the more
celebrated work of Rudolf Otto, whose *The Idea of the Holy* was published
in Germany in 1917 and translated into English in 1923. The full
impact of Freud's psycho-analytic theories, which had been delayed by
the war, came increasingly to be felt in British intellectual circles in the
early 1920s.

In Oxford Dodd was in close touch with men who were trying to
acquaint themselves with the New Psychology and to work out its
implications for the interpretation of religious experience. Cyril Emmet,
the chaplain of his old college was one such. B. H. Streeter, a specialist
like himself in the field of New Testament criticism and exegesis, was
another. Still more important was the welcome given to the new emphases
on psychological factors in religious experience by his own principal,
W. B. Selbie, and by the chaplain, E. R. Micklem. And, although he
did not return to Oxford until 1925, L. W. Grensted, who had been an
intimate friend since 1903, was in process of building up an assessment
of the relationship between psychology and theology which he was to
give as the Bampton Lectures in 1930.

While these matters were being discussed academically in Oxford, there
were those in other places who were beginning to work out the implications of the New Psychology in the consulting room and in actual
pastoral ministry. A leading representative of the former was Dr. J. A.
Hadfield; of the latter the Rev. W. Fearon Halliday. Dodd consulted
both with his own problems: he arranged for both to visit Oxford and
address meetings where the result of their own therapeutic work could
become more widely known. While both men were Christians, it would
probably be true to say that whereas Hadfield exercised the greater
influence on Dodd in helping him to come to terms with his own deep-

seated personal inhibitions and complexes, it was Halliday who helped him to use psychological insights in interpreting the Bible and in applying the Gospel message to the pastoral needs of men and women to-day.

The opportunity to consult Hadfield came about in a fortunate way. Hadfield was an Oxford man who first read theology and then, recognising the importance of the psychological insights of William McDougall, who was teaching in the university at the time, decided to qualify as a medical doctor. After completing his course at Edinburgh, he served in the First World War and thereby gained first-hand experience of the paralysing effects of nervous ailments. He was still working at the War Hospital in Oxford when Dodd first consulted him, though soon afterwards he set up practice in Harley Street, and this meant that subsequent visits involved journeys to London.

The two men had much already in common. They were both Free Church men; both were academically trained in theology; both were deeply concerned about problems of morality. In 1920 Hadfield delivered the Dale Lectures at Mansfield and these were subsequently published in 1923 under the title *Psychology and Morals*. The book was phenomenally successful, running into no less than sixteen editions between then and 1964. Its chief value, perhaps, lay in its balanced presentation of the relationship between individual and society, between emotion and will, between morality and religion. Its insights had been foreshadowed in an essay contributed by the author to a symposium on *The Spirit* edited by B. H. Streeter and Dodd drew upon this essay (as well as upon William James's *Varieties*) in his attempt to bring home to the modern mind the meaning of Paul's proclamation of justification by faith.

Hadfield's influence on Dodd through personal friendship and clinical therapy was reinforced by Fearon Halliday. From being minister of St. Augustine's Presbyterian Church in New Barnet, Halliday moved to the Selly Oak Colleges in Birmingham as professor with special responsibilities for pastoral problems. Dr. Micklem, who knew him well, vividly recalls the nature of his influence.[3]

He had the most remarkable gifts, intellectual, psychic, spiritual. He had studied philosophy and been gold medallist at Trinity College, Dublin; he had read through Kant's *Critique of Pure Reason*, as he told me, thirteen times. He was pastor and evangelist first and last. He had a quite uncanny power of reading a man's face and divining the secrets of his heart; moreover he had that curious sympathy which made all those who met him in railway train, on bus or in hotel respond to his immediate and affectionate probing, or of their own initiative open up their troubles to him. . . . He learnt much from the new psychology, but it is to be thought that he achieved more by his curious psychic insight into the hearts of men than by his technical knowledge of psychology.

His two major books, *Reconciliation and Reality* (1919) and *Psychology and Religious Experience* (1929), are by no means outdated. Through them the living theological stream, whose fountain-head was John Oman in Cambridge, flowed out into pastoral work just as, through the writings of Halliday's successor at Barnet, Herbert H. Farmer, it brought refreshment and inspiration to the preacher. Though, as his own copy of *Reconciliation and Reality* reveals, Dodd was not uncritical of certain minor details of Halliday's teaching, in general he welcomed it for the light it cast both on the New Testament and on modern personal problems.

The importance of Dodd's encounters with exponents of the New Psychology for his future ministry can hardly be over-emphasised.[4] He was not now an unscathed man who wanted simply to devote himself to critical and linguistic studies of ancient literature in, as nearly as possible, an objective and impersonal way. Nor was he a man who would ever be content to explicate the meaning of an ancient text without any concern for how it could become meaningful and applicable in the modern age. Not that he ever obtruded references to his own individual experience or became simply hortatory in trying to press home the challenge of what some individual had experienced in the past; but the example of such a man as Halliday kept the pastoral concern ever before his mind and enabled him to show that the psychological needs to which the Gospel originally brought illumination and healing were still present in human nature today and therefore still open to the therapeutic message and methods originally employed. 'I believe,' Halliday wrote, 'that the message which is vital for the present is in essence the same message which was vital for the past, but that its efficacy waits upon our willingness to set ourselves with humility, sincerity and determination to the task of re-interpretation and re-application.' Few men at the time set themselves more willingly and more efficiently to the task than did Dodd himself, and the first-fruits of his efforts, so far as a wider public was concerned, appeared when his book *The Meaning of Paul for To-day* was published in 1920.

This new departure did not come about easily. His friend Nathaniel Micklem, a man younger than himself, had already won considerable literary success; now he gained the support of a publisher to launch a new series of books under the title *The Christian Revolution*. In a general foreword the editor spoke of humanity standing at the parting of the ways—for life or death. 'How shall man be made at one with man, class with class, nation with nation, and all men with God?' This could only come to pass through a revolutionary Christianity involving a complete change in the standard of values by which men live. A company of friends was sending out this series therefore in the hope of furthering fellowship and true religion. In the main the books dealt with ethical and practical issues in the light of the teaching and example of Jesus but two were of a somewhat different character. Fearon Halliday produced a striking re-interpretation of the doctrine of the Atonement with particular reference to the New Psychology; Dodd contributed the one straightforward piece of biblical exegesis—a new application of Paul's theology to the issues of today.

Micklem had prevailed upon Dodd to write, but then, as he recalled many years later, he had almost to stand over him and drag out the manuscript page by page. At the time Dodd seems to have had no special urge to write books, though he had begun to contribute articles and reviews to journals. Fortunately others recognised his flair, and in due course opportunities arose for him to work on the learned volumes which were to constitute his major contributions to biblical scholarship. His first efforts, however, were confined to what could be called in the best sense the 'popularisation' of the results of New Testament scholarship. The book on Paul was followed by an introduction to the New Testament specially designed for Sunday School teachers (*The Gospel in the New Testament*). It was not until 1928 that the big book appeared which gave Dodd a place in the forefront of biblical scholars.

Notes

1. On differing attitudes to pacifism in the Dodd family Mr. E. E. Dodd has kindly supplied the following note:

> There can be no doubt that C.H. was a pacifist—though I think he preferred the word 'pacificist'. He was prepared to go to prison rather than fight; when I asked at what stage he would have disobeyed he said (I hope my memory is right this time)—'when a rifle was put in my hands'. But I cannot be sure whether his resistance would have been on general grounds or because he was an ordained minister; I think it was not yet settled that the exemption of clergy should extend to nonconformist ministers. He took an active part, at that time and, I believe, throughout his life, in the work of the Fellowship of Reconciliation.
>
> As to other members of the family. Early in the First War A.H. joined the R.A.M.C. but whether he would have consented to join a fighting unit I doubt; and he remained very much of a pacifist. P.W. on the other hand

was in the War and his death resulted in this way. At the age of ten he contracted rheumatic fever, which left him with Valvular Disease of the Heart. But he refused, when he grew up, to treat himself as an invalid and (as a lecturer at Leeds) played hockey and joined the Officers' Training Corps. In August 1914 his unit was in camp and remained on service. After a year or two of home service my brother, already a captain, exerted pressure, I believe, to be sent abroad. After a week in France he went down with what was then known as P.U.O. and this, added to Rheumatic Fever and V.D.H. kept him in hospital in France and England for the rest of the War. He returned to work at Leeds, then at Oxford and survived (to the amazement, I believe, of doctors) until 1931; but he was, in fact, a war casualty. For myself I was a 'conscientious objector' within limits: I was allowed, though not a Quaker, to serve in the Friends' Ambulance Unit—in two hospital ships and a hospital train. From all this you may infer that we were brought up in a pacifist family. This is partly true: my father was rather grieved that I could not bring myself to accept any kind of military service, but very angry when the usual unkind remarks (I was not living at home at the time) reached him.

On the general question of attitudes within the Free Churches to the First World War I am indebted to Dr. Norman Goodall for the following note:

I think you under-estimate the response of the Free Churches generally to the wholly unexpected outbreak of war. You are right, of course, about the traditional non-military interests of the churches and the strength of a continuing element of pacificism. But (and this was often used by pacifists as ground for bitter denunciation of the churches) the shock of the invasion of Belgium with its high-lighting as *the* great moral issue of the day resulted in an 'overnight' conversion of the vast majority of Free Churchmen to the necessity to fight. Long before Conscription the youth of the Free Churches flocked voluntarily to Kitchener's Army. Large numbers of our (Congregational) central city churches were denuded, within a few months of 1914, of their 'young men's classes' (often with memberships running into one or two hundred). Notable Pacifist voices such as Leyton Richards, H. C. Carter, and Nathaniel Micklem, were, of course of immense significance—and later became still more so—but they spoke to and for a very small minority. In this respect I think Dodd was to some extent shielded within an élite, and this—combined with his absorption in learning—contributed to the absence of a more heart-rending awareness of the world tragedy amidst which he was living.

2. Mansfield College retained the title 'Professor' as employed officially in the colleges of the Congregational Church. But it was not a university title and Dodd preferred to be known as tutor until he was elected to the Chair in the University of Manchester.

3. *The Box and the Puppets*, p. 63.
4. The distinguished historian G. M. Young affirmed that 'the arrival of the new psychology had much of the excitement that attended the arrival of the new learning at the Renaissance.'
   Quoted by P. Roberts, *The Psychology of Tragic Drama*, p. 1.

8

Back to Oxford

I

DODD'S FIRST BOOK WAS LINKED WITH THE HOPE OF A CHRISTIAN revolution. The shock of the First World War was still being felt. The optimistic outlook expressed through such catchwords as 'free enterprise' and 'scientific progress' had been severely shaken. What could now be justly regarded as the hope of the future? A return to the *status quo*? A new alliance to preserve peace amongst the nations? Dodd was convinced that the true way forward could be found only by recapturing the vision of Paul and re-interpreting it for the new age. It was not exactly revolution. Rather it was rediscovery of a message and a philosophy of life with a view to reapplying them to the interests and problems of the post-war world.

In point of fact, however, he seldom refers to the political and social issues of his time. All of these are, in his view, subordinate to the *religious* problem. If man's deepest need is for a religion that can command his allegiance and motivate his actions, both as an individual and within society, can the Christian way of life be so presented that it can be seen to be the one hope of mankind? He believed that this was possible and that it could be done immediately by examining the contrast between true religion and false religion as seen in the records of the revolution which took place in the life of the apostle Paul.

The short opening chapter is of great significance because of its revelation of the *form* which Dodd found the most appropriate to describe God's activity in the world. It is, he suggested, the form of a *drama*. The Gospels themselves are dramatic in form but they do not represent the whole drama of redemption. The dénouement, the resolution of tragic conflict, is to be found in the later writings of the New Testament and above all in the dramatic story of Paul's own career. From another point of view, however, the drama is still unfinished. The total history of mankind cannot yet be written. Only by an act of faith can the Christian dare to proclaim that the determinative stages of the drama have been realised within human history and that this pattern provides the clue to the meaning of the whole. If the dramatic conflict which culminated in the Cross had stood alone, it must necessarily have been categorised as tragedy—a tragedy of the kind with which Dodd had become entirely familiar through his studies in the literature of Greece. But Paul's career was a further act in the drama, an act which revealed the Cross and its sequel, the Resurrection, as a revolutionary force in human life. In and through his heroic life and martyr's death, the drama was played out, a drama which would constantly be re-enacted in the subsequent history of the Church.

But how does Dodd interpret the plot of the drama? What are the conflicting forces in the tragic encounter? At least at the time when his first book was written he presented the rival protagonists as the Gospel over against a religious system, the liberating message of the Kingdom challenging an imprisoning dispensation of Law. 'On the one hand the Way of the Nazarene, with His startling assertions and denials: on the other hand all that the piety of the time prized as the essentials of a revealed religion.'[1] The Prophet stands over against the established order, the Herald of freedom over against the totalitarianism of Pharisaism. And although he recognised that certain leading Jewish scholars of his time were giving a more favourable account of the Pharisees than had hitherto been commonly accepted, he still argued that if Saul of Tarsus was a true representative of Pharisaism then it was legitimate to posit a first-century system which Jesus challenged and opposed and which Paul in turn repudiated and rejected.

II

In focusing attention in this way on a dramatic conflict, Dodd was evidently giving voice to some of his own deepest convictions. He stood firmly in the Free Church tradition. He had memories of the Boer War and its association with a form of imperialism to which he and his friends were utterly opposed. He had seen the devastating effects of nationalist rivalries in the war just ended. And because he believed that the most powerful force in human life was *religion*, he concluded that evil political systems could only be shaken if the religious outlook which motivated them could be changed. Pharisaism was a particular manifestation of that 'narrowness, formalism, bondage to tradition, proneness to national and class prejudice' which can be found in every age. 'We shall not fight it to-day, in ourselves or in the Church, with the precise weapons which Paul used; but if we can read his essential thought out of its obsolete forms into the living language of to-day we shall at least know how to deal with that undying Pharisee whom most of us carry beneath our hats.'[2]

In the book he made no attempt to introduce neologisms or to depart from the generally accepted religious vocabulary of his time. The only notable exception, so far as I am aware, is the regular use of the term 'The Divine Commonwealth' to refer to the Church, the Christian fellowship, and to God's ultimate design for the world of mankind. The Church is the Divine Commonwealth already in existence in history: when, in Paul's words, the sons of God are finally manifested in glory, then the Divine Commonwealth will be fully established. In the choice of the term 'commonwealth' there are obvious echoes of Cromwell and the sixteenth century but for Dodd there were still earlier associations with the common life of the city state in Greece in contrast to the *imperium* of Rome. Not hierarchy but common life was his ideal, and this he tried to express through the phrase 'the divine commonwealth', viewed as the ultimate goal of history but already realised proleptically in the life of the Christian community here and now.

What then is the nature of the life of the individual within this commonwealth? *Freedom within a web of personal relationships*: this, I think, is the natural corollary of Dodd's emphasis on emancipation and reconciliation as the focal points of Paul's theology. 'The Law' throughout the book is a menacing and tyrannical presence. 'The Liberty of the sons of God' is the glorious alternative. And yet, like Paul, he can never allow himself to belittle the majesty of the moral law of God. But this moral law, the 'righteousness' of God, is conceived in dynamic and personal terms and so can never be finally encoded in any legal system. To be set free from the Law and to live under the constraint of the love of Christ is the ideal for humanity which Dodd found expressed in Paul's writings and which he sought to make vivid and meaningful to his own contemporaries.

To do this he drew upon his own extensive knowledge of ancient history to show how easily a concentration upon metaphysical speculations or mystical flights of fancy could deflect men from facing the challenge of moral realities. Possibly he underestimated the influence of the natural environment and of ritual forms on human conduct, though he always attached great importance to the Eucharist in promoting true fellowship within the Divine Commonwealth. His deepest interest, first and last, was human *history*—the history of man's struggles and achievements, his encounters and relationships, his failures and his aspirations. And amongst the fresh developments of his own time, none seemed more valuable for the interpretation of man's endeavours and frustrations than the New Psychology with its insights into hidden repressions and the interplay of will and imagination. In particular, the conflict within the self, so vividly portrayed in the seventh chapter of the Epistle to the Romans, gains new meaning in the light of the case histories which modern psychologists have recorded.

In the course of his exposition of the meaning of Paul for today Dodd drew upon the writings of the two men to whom he had turned for help with his own problems—J. A. Hadfield and Fearon Halliday. The latter's re-interpretation of the Christian doctrine of Atonement he evidently found entirely congenial and he was able to strengthen and support it from New Testament sources by a careful examination of metaphors used in the Epistle to the Romans. Already he was re-interpreting the Greek words translated as 'justice' or 'righteousness', 'wrath' (the inevitable Nemesis of sin in a moral universe), 'propitiation', in a way which he was to develop with far more attention to lexicographical detail in his later works.

Paul was his first love. It would be hard, even fifty years later, to find a better introduction to the mind of the apostle than is contained in *The Meaning of Paul for To-day*. He entered deeply into Paul's experience; he gained an intimate knowledge of his writings in their original language; he set them within their historic context by providing revealing references to the thought and customs of the Hellenistic world; he made constant reference to the way in which Paul's teaching could bring release and new power to those struggling to live the good life today. His book quickly went through its first edition, and his competence as an interpreter of Paul became widely recognised. In retrospect it is not surprising that his friend Dr. Moffatt soon decided to entrust him with the task of writing the volume in the new Moffatt *Commentary* which many would consider the most important of the whole series—*The Commentary on the Epistle to the Romans*.

III

Dodd wrote the preface to his book in July 1920. An earlier announcement had promised publication in the summer of 1919 and it seems probable that most of the material was ready by then. Meanwhile, however, the crisis within his own personal life had occupied much of the winter of 1919–20 and he would have been insensitive to a degree had he not felt the contrast between what he regarded as a failure in his own experience and the exultant vision of emancipation and moral victory to which he had given theoretical expression. Indeed, in his book he refers to the observation made by Mr. H. G. Wells that the 'self behind the frontage' is in all of us something greater than the self of the shop-window which all the world can see. In his own case the outward self was gaining increasing recognition and acclaim. Yet the inadequacies of the inner self caused him an ever deepening anxiety.

The first recourse was to psycho-analysis—not to regular intensive sessions but to intermittent visits to Dr. Hadfield and periodic consultations with Fearon Halliday. The latter, it seems, was convinced that major therapy would be achieved only when a true partnership in love had been attained. Dodd was not a confirmed bachelor. He longed for a wife, a companion to share his interests, a settled home of his own. He may have exaggerated (though he was always careful in his use of words) when he wrote of the 'misery, failure, disappointment' of which he continued to be conscious after the broken engagement of 1920 but it is certain that it brought about deep heart-searchings, both of a psychological and theological kind.

If ever he had prayed for guidance it was in connection with the engagement in 1919. Yet it had seemed to end in disaster. What had gone wrong?

I know quite well now [he wrote nearly five years later] that guidance *ad hoc* is a doubtful matter apart from guidance of the whole life. Therefore I would not, as I did before, eliminate practically everything but the one thing and demand guidance on that one thing. It was a humiliating experience for me to pray as earnestly as I did for guidance and then to blunder. I almost arraigned God for letting me down. Reluctantly I came to see and admit that since I was the sort of person that I was, God could not deal with me otherwise. Only through misery, failure, disappointment could he bring me to His mind. . . . I presented God with an alternative: am I to continue in my present position or am I to seek love and marriage in *this* way?—and 'this way' was largely the outcome of my fantastic valuation of myself. The Lord said to me in effect: Yes: seek in this way and you shall find yourself out: and so through great suffering I did. Well, if I have got to go through further suffering to learn some further lesson—*fiat voluntas*. I no longer say, as I have often said 'I can't risk going through all that again.' If God wants me to go through it, I'll try by His power to face it.

This was written on November 25, 1924. Two months previously he had gone to London for a board meeting of the London Missionary Society and afterwards had gone out to Harpenden to have supper with Phyllis Terry. Again in mid-October attendance at an ordination service at St. Alban's gave him the opportunity to have tea at Harpenden. And on 29 November he was to have tea there once more. Where was it all leading? Had the real resolution come at last? His earlier experience had left behind a traumatic effect. Dare he venture again? He was determined to be ruthlessly honest with himself in assessing his own inadequacy and failure *then* in order that he might walk more circumspectly but with greater confidence *now*.

IV

The introduction to Phyllis Terry had come about through the initiative of Fearon Halliday. During the time of Halliday's ministry in New Barnet a war-widow with her young son came to live in the area, and, although she was an Anglican, she made Halliday's acquaintance and gained through his pastoral concern the consolation and renewal of life which she needed in a period of deep distress. This was Phyllis Terry, whose maiden name was Stockings. She came from a large family of the upper-middle class prominent in the business world of East Anglia. In spite of variations in the family fortunes she had grown up in a gay and carefree atmosphere. She was sensitive, artistic and highly imaginative, though without the formal education which life in a university would have brought.

She married John Terry before the outbreak of the First World War and, with her husband, soon left for Australia where he represented the family firm. But he could not resist the call to the colours and she returned to England where her son John was born in 1917. The death of her husband on active service was a shattering blow and, although she could count on the fullest support of her family, she was determined to make a life of her own, a life which for the time being was bound to be largely devoted to the welfare of her infant son. A sister, Mrs. Elliot, to whom she was closely attached, had suffered a similar loss; her husband had died at an early age and she had been left with a young daughter to care for. The fact that this daughter was to be educated at St. George's School in Harpenden seems to have influenced Phyllis Terry's decision to move to a flat in that area.

But Fearon Halliday kept in touch with her and his deep concern and

affection for Dodd led him to conceive the possibility of their two lives
being brought together. The six years which separated them in age would
be no barrier to a fruitful partnership and although their domestic,
cultural and ecclesiastical backgrounds were very different, their common
interests were sufficiently strong to transcend these differences if each
should find in the other the object of real love.

The months from November 1924 to April 1925 were as difficult for
Dodd as any in his life. He was fully involved in college work; he was
under constant demand for papers to societies and articles for journals;
he was much sought after as a preacher; there were many friends with
whom he tried to keep in touch. Yet urgent personal questions were
constantly in his mind. Was it right to pursue his friendship with
Phyllis Terry? When could he declare his love? Was he really prepared
for the change of life and the many new responsibilities that marriage
would bring? He consulted Hadfield; he wrote down after the manner of
the *Confessions* of St. Augustine his hopes, his fears, his failings. Sometimes
the self-examination seems over scrupulous but much was at stake, not
only for him but also for the one who herself had already passed through
deep tribulation and suffering. They were months of travail, the record
of which he preserved to the end of his life.

In his scrutiny of his own failings he refers especially to his bitter
resentment of criticism, his sensitivity to any kind of slight and the way
this inhibited him from taking any courses of action which might lead to
his making a fool of himself. He was aware, too, of a 'desperate slackness
and inability to direct and control my work', and of lack of strength 'to
face my unanswered correspondence and go right ahead with it'. He
craved a sense of order in his whole life. 'I do propose by God's help once
again to make a determined effort to order my life, using in particular
such means towards it as a definite hour for rising, a method of dealing
with correspondence, a careful record of engagements and fixed times of
prayer.' (In the light of his difficulties with correspondence, it is astonishing that he was able to keep engagements as well as he did. It was at
about this time that his youngest brother wrote to him to ask him to
preside at his wedding. Receiving no reply he sent a prepaid telegram but
still there was no reply! Probably the matter had to be resolved by a personal
visit.) He admits that he was 'run down' and it is likely that physical
and mental exhaustion were more powerful factors in his dissatisfaction
with 'unaccomplished tasks' than he knew. Yet with the memory of 1919
and the hope of 1925 there is no wonder that he travailed in spirit lest
the relationship with Phyllis Terry should prove abortive as before.

'I pray that in all my thoughts of P.M.T. I may be realistic, frank,
honest, wholesome; unsentimental though by no means unemotional;

recognizing and seeking the true values concerned; open-eyed to the truth and to the limits of my knowledge of the truth; enterprising and courageous in facing the full issues; and truly and sincerely ready for the divine leading.'

He is realistic about his earlier failure. He had never allowed sufficient time for a true friendship to develop. He had 'soared at once into romance' and tried to maintain this on a 'lofty intellectual and spiritual' level. Now he determines to be more realistic and more concerned with the full range of relationships which marriage involves—physical, emotional, cultural and spiritual. He will not ask God for special treatment—a sudden revelation, an unmistakable sign. Rather within a developing friendship he will seek conviction that each will find fulfilment through commitment to and relationship with the other.

V

The extracts which I have just quoted reveal the depths of his concern about his own pattern of life at that period and the exalted character of his hopes for the married state. A further extract gives a glimpse into his practice of prayer and the way in which he sought to subdue all his personal preferences to the will of God.

In setting my heart on marriage I hope of course for happiness. But I want to set down clearly that I do not seek marriage for the sake of increased pleasure or comfort or even the early solution of my psychological problems. I seek fuller reality, a greater intensity and depth of living, an enrichment of the stuff of life for joy and pain alike. I have lived and am living a life largely sheltered from reality, in which I am little more than a spectator of the world of human experience (as Hadfield has reminded me). At rare points the reality of things has touched me but in large measure my troubles are mere phantasms and my pleasures artificial. Sometimes when I have thought of marriage I have shrunk in distaste from the difficulties and anxieties and sorrows to which the married man is exposed. But really I am half-sick of shadows: I want the real thing. Marriage means a plunge into reality— a laying of myself open to the common trials of mankind—an invitation to the changes and chances of life to carry me with them. I am desiring marriage with one to whom life has been tragic and who has accepted the tragedy and been 'initiated'. I am utterly unworthy of her unless I am ready to accept life on terms which include the tragic element in it. There will be the difficulties that poverty entails, the anxiety inseparable from the coming of children (if such be the will of God) and the ever-present possibility of all sorts of terrible blows from which the bachelor is immune, just because he is alone, and which I don't particularly want to think of. These things, however, are the common human lot, in which I wish to share. After all, in my solitary and sheltered life, real happiness is a comparatively rare visitant. An intangible depression over nothing is frequent. These are mere vapours. The deepest happiness lies, I feel sure, in getting effectively outside myself and 'letting myself in' for what life brings. If Phyllis is willing I want to enter with her on all this, confident that facing life together we shall find the deep and rich 'blessedness' which can never come to the shirker of contact with reality

In the presence of God, therefore, and in reliance on divine grace and guidance, I register my purpose, subject to the leading of His providence, to seek Phyllis for my wife, earnestly desiring that He would make me fit and ready for marriage and more worthy of her; asking also that He would guide me to the best moment and manner of approaching her, keeping me alike from ill-advised rashness and from cowardly hesitation. Above all I pray that in the whole matter I may be steadfastly subject to His will and open to His guidance and that whatever comes of it, attainment or failure, I may receive what He desires to give for the fulfilling of my destiny and the perfecting of my life. May our Father grant to us both so to act that we may experience His mercy and power in our lives through that which has come upon us and serve Him the better.

Things moved faster than he dared to hope. In January 1925 Phyllis visited Oxford for the first time; at the end of February they were engaged; in June they were married. Just before the engagement was announced Dodd wrote:

We have become firm friends, delighting in one another's company and rapidly increasing in knowledge of one another. Our friendship has a very deep basis in religious experience. She has found her way through to a religious position in which we find common ground and can help one another; and in the Sacrament we both find our strength. Our friendship further carries within it a real community of interests—in books, in nature (walking and gardening), in art.

Then having referred to her 'gracious motherliness' and 'delightful home' he went on:

Looking deeper, I see in her a character formed in suffering, with a serenity that comes not of inexperience but of experience lived through. She has faced her trouble and acknowledged its worth in the divine purpose for her. A certain strength, courage, independence of character is shown by her taking her own line (which is also my line) in religion and politics against her family: and yet this has evidently not made a break with her family with whom she is clearly on affectionate terms.

He was conscious of the 'social gulf' between them and of his own 'poverty' but this never in fact caused any difficulty between him and his wife's relations. They accepted him gladly and rejoiced in his idiosyncrasies, even though Mrs. Stockings, herself a fine handsome woman, exclaimed after his departure on the first occasion that his fiancée brought him to see her mother, 'He seems a very nice man but we've never had a *little* man in the family before. I suppose it will be all right.'

It was, indeed, very much all right. Two sensitive people, each of whom had known disappointment and suffering, came together within an alliance which brought healing to their own lives and enrichment to countless others. The marriage was, in all senses, a turning-point for Dodd. It brought him the intimate companionship for which he had craved; the sense of having someone constantly beside him on whom he could implicitly rely; the home in which his own base of operations was sedulously guarded; the release from the details of domestic organisation from which an impecunious bachelor cannot escape; and the pleasure, in this case immediately, of close relationship with a growing child. For him, without question, new life had now really begun.

When the news of the engagement was made public, Dodd's friends were delighted. Fearon Halliday, who had first brought them together, ended his letter with a flourish: 'Hurrah for Presbygationalists!' Nathaniel Micklem, who had met Phyllis at Selly Oak, wrote, 'I am all hallelujah within. It is really quite ridiculous for an outsider like me to be so flustered and pleased but I cannot help it. And how admirable, most admirable, for Mansfield; she will be the most ideal addition to the spiritual resources of the College.' And, to give one more example, his friend from schooldays, R. I. Hopwood, writing from a Methodist manse, said:

I do rejoice with you greatly—all the more because of the past. But it was worth waiting half a lifetime—and more if need be—to be sure you have found the right one. It seems to me from the account you give that you have realized the ideal as it is given to few mortals to realize it. I have had some experience of ministers and other folk now but I have never known one with so lofty an ideal of marriage and a life so consistent with it in every detail as your own. The reward will extend to wider circles than you can think of now.[3]

Notes

1. *The Meaning of Paul for Today*, p. 13.
2. Op. cit., p. 53.
3. Dodd was always popular as a performer at the Mansfield College smoking concerts. At the same time the students did not hesitate to 'take him off' in the sketch which normally formed part of the proceedings.

   In December 1924 the sketch proved to be strangely, though entirely innocently, prophetic. Some months before the concert took place, an exciting event happened in New Testament circles—a Dutch professor had discovered what came to be known as the Leyden Magical Papyrus and Dodd reported this to his class with enthusiasm. Now, in the programme, a set had been designed which obviously represented Dodd's study, and a young professor, Harold Nikon (played by J. S. Whale), appeared as the central figure in the drama. His consuming passion was to search for ancient manuscripts and this reached fever pitch when he learned that a certain widow, Mrs. Weed, had inherited from her husband the priceless 'Mansfield Magical Papyrus'. How could he possibly acquire it? Other methods having failed, the only way left was to marry the widow and this Harold Nikon proceeded to do before an imposing policeman arrived and arrested him for fraud. Within three months Dodd had announced his engagement—to a widow!

   This became perhaps the most celebrated association of Dodd with a 'smoker'. But for the close-of-year dinner it has long been remembered that on one occasion a visiting American pastor, having been asked to give the speech of the evening, closed by evoking Vernon Bartlet and Dodd in heaven, with Bartlet admonishing the Church Fathers for their errors and with Dodd telling the Apostles 'what they really meant'.

9

Fulfilment in Marriage

I

DODD'S DESIRE FOR A 'FULLER REALITY', 'A GREATER INTENSITY AND depth of living', through sharing in the common trials of mankind was soon realised after the honeymoon in North Devon was ended. Arrangements had to be made for the conclusion of the tenancy of the flat at Harpenden and for the transfer of the furniture. House-hunting in Oxford constituted a real problem and was only finally resolved by the purchase in 1927 of 3 Bevington Road, a house conveniently situated in North Oxford near the main entrance to the University Parks. Moreover he had to concern himself immediately with the interests and needs of a growing boy—his education and his recreations during holidays. There were social calls for the newly-married couple—a practice still observed in Oxford at that time—and the engagement of domestic help. Poor man! He had now to deal with such crises as arose when the maid went off on Phyllis's bicycle and succeeded in wrecking it: it was a new experience to sit in judgment and dismiss the offender.

Then there was the allotment to care for, a task also associated with a bicycle incident, for in 1923 he had himself been involved in an accident which might have had serious consequences. While he was riding out to do his afternoon's stint, carrying various implements, his coat became entangled with the front wheel. Thrown over the handlebars, he escaped with a broken jaw. He never learned to drive a car and in the early days of married life the bicycle was the chief means by which he introduced Phyllis to the countryside with which he was himself so familiar.

Naturally it was the first pregnancy which brought the major new responsibility, and from the middle of 1926 this was the parents' chief concern. But the situation became unexpectedly complicated when a letter arrived just before Christmas, opening out the prospect of a move from Oxford to the U.S.A. With the housing question still unsettled and with a child due to arrive within three months, it was hardly the time that they would have chosen to consider the possibility of such a change.

The letter was from the Dean of the Divinity School of Yale University. Their distinguished New Testament professor, Benjamin W. Bacon, would be retiring at the end of the academic year 1927–8. They were already considering possible men to succeed him in the Chair. Knowing something of Dodd through his books and his work at Mansfield they would like to make his closer acquaintance. Could he arrange to travel to America during the coming year and give a course of lectures in the Divinity School?

Evidently family responsibilities did not prevent him from responding favourably to this advance, for during the coming months a programme was worked out by which he would spend nearly a month in North America in the Fall. Meanwhile on 2 March the contract was signed for the purchase of 3 Bevington Road; on 3 March Rachel Dodd was born; in June her father was appointed Grinfield Lecturer on the Septuagint in the university. His commentary on Ephesians, Colossians and Philemon for the *Abingdon Bible Commentary* was finished in August and work was in progress on a major book on the authority of the Bible, a book which was ready in manuscript form early in the following year.

In the midst of all this he took off from Southampton in the *Carinthia* on 21 September and was soon involved in a busy schedule of lectures in Yale Divinity School, in Hartford Theological Seminary, and in Oberlin College. In each place his theme was 'Development in the thought of Paul' and the impact both of his lectures and of his personal friendliness was such that, before the end of his stay in New Haven, it was made clear to him that it was the strong and unanimous desire of the Faculty that he should join them and that the issue of a formal invitation would follow in due course.

II

The attractiveness of such an offer can easily be imagined. Harvard and Yale stood pre-eminent amongst American universities and Professor Bacon, who had taught at Yale for thirty years, stood pre-eminent amongst American New Testament scholars. Moffatt had recently come to New York to the Union Theological Seminary, and this meant that an old friend of Dodd's would be close at hand. Unhappily the prospect of his being appointed to a university Chair in England was remote there being only one professorship of divinity that was open to non-Anglicans. In Yale there would be classes of nearly two hundred students of divinity each year and Congregationalism held the lead amongst the denominations represented. The Faculty included notable scholars such as Clarence Shedd, Robert Calhoun and Kenneth Latourette, and was a particularly harmonious group at that time. There was no doubt at all about the warmth of the desire that Dodd, now coming to the fullness of his powers, should throw in his lot with them. This was made abundantly clear when the formal invitation, written by the newly appointed Dean, Luther Weigle (who by a coincidence was to play so large a part later in the new American translation of the Bible, the Revised Standard Version, just as Dodd played later in the New English Bible), was delivered in Oxford at the beginning of December.

Meanwhile there had been time for plenty of consultation. Two of his friends had moved to North America quite recently, Leonard Hodgson from being Dean of Divinity at Magdalen to become Professor at General Theological Seminary in New York, and Nathaniel Micklem from teaching at the Selly Oak Colleges in Birmingham to become Professor at Queen's University in Kingston, Ontario. Dodd corresponded with the former about the financial considerations involved, while on the way from Oberlin to Montreal to embark on his return sailing he was able to discuss the matter fully with the latter. What the feelings of Phyllis were, faced with the possibility of moving again less than three years after marriage, with a baby less than a year old, can only be imagined. To say that the decision was an important one would be a platitude: probably in regard to Dodd's career it was the most important that he ever made. But his reply to the invitation was firm and definite. The Dodds would remain in Oxford.

A letter written to Leonard Hodgson sets out clearly the considerations which weighed with him in making his decision. It is characteristic of the man that *loyalty* occupies the central place—loyalty to Mansfield and to the Church which had nurtured him. But would he remain indefinitely at Mansfield? Would he be a candidate for the principalship when, as must happen before very long, Dr. Selbie would retire? These were questions which must have been in the minds of many Mansfield men, even though the fear of losing their outstanding scholar to America had been removed.

III

After the excitement and uncertainties of 1927, there came two years in which routine matters of home and college took pride of place. 3 Bevington Road became a centre of hospitality for friends and relations, while every stage in Rachel's development was recorded with fascination by her father. His health gave cause for concern—he was only just over 100 lbs in weight—and in September 1928 he underwent a successful operation for appendicitis. A month earlier he and Phyllis had experienced the sadness of a stillborn baby girl and a month later came news of the critical illness of Dodd's father in Wrexham. When he visited him on 29 October he found him barely conscious and two days later he died. Superlatives are easily written but it is hard to think that anyone in the history of Welsh education over the past century exercised a wider influence for good than did the headmaster for thirty-five years of the Victoria School in Wrexham, or that a more sustained relationship of affection, trust and mutual respect between father and son could be found during that period than that which existed between Charles Dodd and his son Harold. They walked together literally thousands of miles and seem never to have tired of one another's company. Words which Dodd used of Jesus, 'greeting God as Father and Friend in everything and at every point', came very near to being true of his own relationship with his earthly father.

It was a pleasure to him that his old friend from undergraduate days, L. W. Grensted, was now back in Oxford, and they saw a good deal of one another. Another link with the past was forged when his former pupil, the brilliant young historian, J. S. Whale, was appointed in June 1928 to succeed Vernon Bartlet on his retirement. Besides his regular teaching at Mansfield, Dodd was being called upon to take an increasing part in university responsibilities, such as examining in the Honour School of Theology and serving as a member of the Board of the Faculty of Theology. In 1927 he was appointed university lecturer in New Testament Studies and in the same year began his course on the Septuagint as Grinfield Lecturer. He was probably more aware of new developments in German theological scholarship than anyone else in Oxford and in Michaelmas Term 1928 offered a course of lectures on 'Form-criticism', the discipline so closely associated with the name of Rudolf Bultmann. He acted as host to Professor Frick of Marburg when he came to give the Dale Lectures early in 1930, and about this time brought to the attention of an Oxford audience the significance of the theological revolution initiated by Karl Barth.

But so far as his writing was concerned the great event was the publication in 1928 of his first 'big' book. *The Authority of the Bible* won immediate acclaim as a fresh and constructive treatment of a highly important though difficult subject, and early in 1930 his standing in the world of biblical scholarship was marked by the conferring of an honorary doctorate, the first of many he was to receive. Aberdeen led the way and in due course was followed by Oxford, Cambridge, London, Manchester, Glasgow and Wales in Great Britain; by Harvard, Oslo, and Strasbourg overseas. The Aberdeen award brought congratulatory messages from far and near but one expressed in a special way the feelings of those on the home base. Romilly Micklem had been a constant companion throughout the twenties, had explored with him the implications of the New Psychology and, with his wife (Dodd had been the best man at the wedding and had caused considerable anxiety about the production of the ring), had given warm hospitality to Phyllis during her early visits to Oxford. He wrote:[1]

Please accept my very genuine and delighted congratulations on the honour you are receiving from a very famous University. It is so good for once in a way to see the fitting, proper and right thing done; and I am glad that the first University to honour you with a doctorate is one whose doctorate it is an honour to possess!

Shall I confess to one childish regret? (a regret which is really quite swallowed up in pleasure). No longer shall I be able to boast that our most distinguished scholar was simply and sufficiently designated as *artium magister*. A plague on the psychologists! No doubt they would explain this easily: here was a distinction which the least learned member of the community was able to share with the most learned! Well, well, let them prate and show our motives for the miserable things they are. Nothing can hide the truth that the news I read in *The Times* this morning gives me unfeigned delight.

IV

Marriage in 1925 brought the critical turning point in his personal life: 1930 brought a similar crisis in his academic career. By general consent he was the key figure at Mansfield. Selbie, the Principal, was drawing towards the end of his reign. Dodd, now Vice-Principal, was the chief link between the college and the university. He had become well known throughout the denomination and was held in the highest esteem and affection by the students. On any question of conduct or belief he was the man that they most naturally sought to consult. In many ways he seemed to be the obvious man to succeed Selbie. Yet would this mean the forcing of a square peg into a round hole? He was not exactly noted for administrative ability and in fact his interests did not lie that way. Did this imply, however, that he was never to hold a position of major responsibility where he would be free to organise his own research and to give new leadership in biblical studies?

Perhaps some had already thought of him as successor to the most distinguished Free Churchman then occupying a university Chair in England. If so, their hopes seemed possible of fulfilment earlier than expected for Professor A. S. Peake of Manchester did not live to retirement age but died in August 1929. The Vice-Chancellor of the university at the time was Walter Moberly, who had been three years senior to Dodd in reading Greats at Oxford and had then begun to teach philosophy. His father had written one of the most original and profound books in the history of Anglican theology and the son shared his father's deep concern for the things of the Spirit. The appointment of Peake's successor was a matter of more than ordinary interest to him and it is likely that he was one of those most eager to attract Dodd to Manchester.

It was from Moberly that Dodd received the first intimation that Manchester wanted him. A letter came informing him that the selection committee wished to make him their sole nomination to the Senate and Council. It was made clear that whereas Peake had taught both Old and New Testament they wished that his successor should be primarily a New Testament man. He would be leader of the Faculty and the bridge between it and the Senate. The amount of actual teaching and administrative work would be small, leaving him considerable freedom for study and writing. Finally Moberly indicated how delighted he would be at the prospect of working with him and told him that in a conversation with Peake not long before his death the latter had affirmed that it was his hope that Dodd would succeed him in his Chair. After learning that he was at least willing to consider the invitation, Moberly spent an evening with the Dodds in Oxford and in April entertained them at his home in Manchester when they went to explore the situation. On 17 April Dodd wrote to accept the offer and the end of his long and intimate association with Oxford and Mansfield was now in sight.

V

Peake's career, before he became first incumbent of the Rylands Chair of Biblical Criticism and Exegesis at Manchester University, had been strangely similar to that of his successor. Born in 1865, he gained a scholarship to Oxford and became the first Free Churchman (he was a Primitive Methodist) to be appointed to a research Fellowship in the university. This he held at Merton College and at the same time taught Hebrew and Old Testament at Mansfield. Though he might have remained on its teaching staff, he decided to accept an appointment to the college of his own denomination in Manchester, and his election to the Rylands Chair in 1904 brought him the distinction of being the first Nonconformist to become a Professor of Divinity in an English university.

Until that time all Chairs of Theology—at Oxford, Cambridge, Durham and King's College, London—had been restricted to members of the Church of England and no modern university had attempted to establish a Faculty of Theology: indeed, in certain instances the statutes of the university prohibited the teaching of religion in any shape or form. But Manchester broke through the barrier by establishing a Faculty in which, in the first instance, instruction was to be given in the Bible and in Comparative Religion, the teaching of Doctrine and Ecclesiastical History being left to the theological colleges.

The endowment of the new Chair was provided by John Rylands, a wealthy Manchester merchant, and after his death his widow determined to create, as his memorial, a great library in which theology was to be given pride of place. Peake not only made his Chair famous: he also devoted time unsparingly to the administration of the library and, by his advice on purchases, made it the key centre for theological research in the north of England. Large numbers of continental books were bought and when the time came for Dodd to consider the move to Manchester he could be assured of ample resources in the Rylands Library for any piece of research on which he might happen to be engaged. It is probably true to say that when Peake died in 1929 no biblical scholar in Britain was held in higher repute and no single Chair carried fuller responsibility for leadership in every department of biblical studies.

But it was no easy matter to leave Oxford where Dodd had comparatively recently gained increasing recognition so far as the university was concerned and where his family was happily settled in an attractive part of the city. Moreover, an addition to the family was expected in June just before the move would have to be made. (A son, Mark, was born on 17 June.) Most painful of all was the prospect of leaving Mansfield, a college which had become part of his very life since he came to Oxford as a freshman in 1902 and to which he felt a deep loyalty. He naturally consulted Vernon Bartlet, who had been almost a second father to him since they first met. Bartlet had only recently retired after devoting his whole life to the service of the college and when Dodd came to see him he did his best to persuade him to remain in Oxford—only to be conscience-stricken afterwards that he had added to the strain of his friend's decision-making. His final letter was characteristic of the man:

> I am satisfied that you have done the right thing on the data before you, and now for the first time made available to me also by your loyal consideration for my concern. I am particularly reassured on the crucial point of gains and losses by Grensted's judgment, since he knows both situations and you in relation to both.[2] Happily our ultimate standard is the same, to wit, the interests of the Kingdom of God, as the *summum bonum* for the Christian man. I will add one element to those you refer to in this connexion, viz that as 'a son of the Kingdom' in its catholicity, as regards denominational divisions, I rejoice greatly that the co-ordinating influence should at Manchester fall to one who has the Congregationalist's catholicity without loss of loyalty to the communion which has made catholicity native to him.

Other reactions from old Mansfield men were expressed with less sense of *gravitas* than that displayed by Dodd's venerable colleague. 'Poor dear old Mansfield'; 'to the best of my knowledge there simply is *no one* to take your place there'; 'you would be astonished how my thought of Mansfield is like that of Hamlet without the prince of Denmark.' And these were echoed from within the university where Anglicans of all types had come to recognise how valuable a contribution to biblical scholarship was being made by their Congregationalist friend. F. W. Green, who stood firmly within the Anglo-Catholic tradition, wrote to send his warmest congratulations and then added, 'Really it is like being made a Bishop, it is so exalted. But there are few who will not deeply regret your departure from here. For us at Merton it is a great satisfaction to know that you will so worthily fill the place of our former and beloved fellow, A. S. Peake.'

So to Manchester, ominously described in a letter from the editor of the *Christian World* as a 'ghastly city to live in' but redeemed by the professorship which 'makes it worth while enduring the unrelenting rain there; and to be able to read the *Manchester Guardian* over breakfast is a joy to be coveted!' A house had to be found, farewells made, John Terry's future schooling provided for, and all the while the coming of the new baby complicated domestic arrangements. Dodd began the term alone, staying at Lancashire College, but soon after the middle of October the family was re-united, taking up residence at 2 Kingston Avenue, Didsbury, which was to be their home for the next five years.

Notes

1. Nathaniel Micklem's brother.
2. Grensted had studied theology in Manchester and become warden of Egerton Hall, the Anglican Theological College in that city, before returning to University College, Oxford, as chaplain.

PART 4

A Leading New Testament Scholar

10

The Rylands Chair at Manchester

I

THE MOVE TO MANCHESTER BROUGHT ABOUT A RADICAL CHANGE IN Dodd's whole pattern of life. In Oxford he had been at the heart of a closely-knit and supportive community. He had known, often intimately, generations of Mansfield men, had tutored them individually, had worshipped with them, walked with them, eaten and drunk with them. Besides his fellow-tutors, certain dons in the university had been close friends, and the Dodds were acquainted with many families in North Oxford. Their house was in easy walking distance of the college (near enough for him on one occasion to excuse himself at the beginning of a lecture in order to walk home again with his faithful dog in order to collect the right notes, the class sitting patiently to await his return), and the Bodleian Library was not much farther away. Home and college and resources for study were integrated into a convenient and harmonious whole.

Now, however, his home was in the suburbs, some miles distant from the university and the centre of the city where the Rylands Library was situated. His office was in the university area, but there were few opportunities for meeting other members of the teaching staff except at lunch or in committees. The denominational colleges were scattered around a wide area and, although he might visit each on some special occasion, he no longer had any direct association with collegiate life. The almost inevitable effect of the new conditions was to divide his life sharply between study at home and public lectures in the university or to special audiences. He became almost withdrawn from the kind of easy social intercourse which had characterised his life in Oxford. But whatever the loss may have been for himself and others in direct personal relationships, the results in his output, both in books and in outstanding series of lectures, were impressive to a degree.

By universal consent, as a lecturer he touched the heights. A fellow-professor in the field of New Testament studies expressed it vividly when he remarked that a lecture by Dodd was comparable to a ballet performance. He came into the room with a dancing, bird-like movement, took his place on the rostrum and then, in speech and gesture, even in the writing on the blackboard, played out a drama in which the whole man became intensely involved. Always the lecture was carefully planned to finish at the appointed time (it was said that the dog who in Oxford days accompanied him and slept at the foot of the desk while the lecture was in progress knew exactly when the time had come for the proceedings to end) and its general *form* became familiar to all his students. Two who owed much to him in Manchester days have written:[1]

At a rapid pace [he] would proceed first to expound the linguistic data of a passage—with a wholly unjustified assumption that his hearers would follow his quotations in Greek, Hebrew, Latin, Syriac, German, French (he condescended to his audience sufficiently to write the Syriac on the blackboard); next the relevant passages from the Bible would be brought to illumine the text under notice; then would follow a précis of different lines of exegesis, where he regarded these as well-founded and important, with his assessment of them. Five or ten minutes before the end, the spectacles would be removed, the note book closed; we, gasping a little from this rapid immersion in the deeper water of scholarship would be given a brief, lucid and penetrating exposition of the theological import of the passage, related to contemporary philosophical ideas, or social changes, or ethical issues. In these last few minutes of each lecture we saw the relevance of all the preceding linguistic and exegetical study to the understanding of what God was saying to men to-day through the witness of the Bible. We realized that we were sitting at the feet of a man who was not only a first-class scholar, but who owned a deep—and deeply simple—allegiance to God through Jesus Christ.

These are the recollections of two who were students at the time in the Congregational College in Manchester (Lancashire Independent College). Others might have questioned the appropriateness of what might be regarded as *doctrinal* teaching coming at the end of a lecture within a university setting. In Manchester, Jewish and Unitarian interests had been strongly represented and the teaching of Christian doctrine had been given no place in specifically university courses. Yet no objection seems to have been raised to the new Professor's excursions into the 'theological import' of biblical texts. No one could be unaware of his insistence on high standards of exact scholarship in the study of the Bible. Indeed, in his first year he failed almost the whole New Testament class in a terminal examination. But he made no attempt to conceal his own faith or his conviction that the Bible was the medium through which divine words could still be spoken into contemporary life. And his lectures not only illuminated the past but also challenged men and women to relate the past to the problems of the modern world.

Besides giving regular lectures in the university he served as extra-mural lecturer to more popular audiences and periodically treated some specialised theme through a lecture which was subsequently printed in the *Bulletin* of the John Rylands Library. Two, given in 1932 and subsequently printed under the title *The Mind of Paul: A Psychological Approach*, not only made a profound impression upon their hearers but also made a signal contribution to the development of Pauline studies. They focused attention upon the apostle's self-revelations as they appear in the Second Epistle to the Corinthians, and suggested that they provide evidence of a kind of 'second conversion'. Even after he had yielded his first allegiance to Christ Paul had still retained 'a touchiness about his dignity' and a certain authoritarianism in relation to his fellow-Christians. The result was inner anxiety and outward friction. 'So long as he chafed against unavoidable disabilities and reverses which wounded his prestige, he was losing the spiritual liberty and power which come from the abandonment of personal claims. But when he accepted his limitations, he was liberated afresh.' In the light of Dodd's own records of self-analysis, it is hard not to feel that in this description of Paul's experience he was revealing some comparable movement in his own. Other printed lectures on the Johannine writings were in the nature of experimental forays into fields which he was to explore in far greater detail at a later date.

From study desk to lecture platform he went to and fro and this constituted the dominant pattern of the Manchester years. He took little part in university administration and made no substantial changes in the workings of the Theological Faculty. He tried, after a period, to secure the university's sanction for a departmental library and premises and for the appointment of an additional lecturer in the Philosophy of Religion—this, if possible, to be an Anglican. But, as he himself wrote long after-wards, his time was too brief to do much towards developing theology generally in the university. He regarded it mainly as the period during which the foundations were laid for his subsequent contributions to New Testament studies. His relations with his colleagues and particularly with the two Vice-Chancellors under whom he served—Sir Walter Moberly and Sir John Stopford—were altogether happy, and the Dodds often accompanied the Stopfords to Sunday morning worship at the Grosvenor Square Presbyterian Church. Stories are still told of the Vice-Chancellor coming to the rescue of the Professor when the latter was fulfilling some preaching engagement and found that he had left his sermon notes at home.

II

It was in his home that the writing and research went steadily forward. He was a devoted father and carefully reserved times when he could be with the children and tell them stories. Back in the Wrexham home he had done this for his younger brothers and his children's addresses in morning worship had become famous. Ultimately a book was published, There and Back Again, containing a selection of the stories told to Rachel and Mark, a map by his stepson John, and a series of illustrations drawn by his wife. Though concentration on his own work in progress seemed sometimes to inhibit him from easy intercourse outside a limited circle, he could always establish a happy relationship with children and entertain them with stories or with recitations of ballads which he remembered from boyhood days.

From the beginning, however, the home in Manchester was organised by Phyllis in such a way as to give the maximum of privacy and undisturbedness to her husband for the pursuance of his work. A neighbour who became a close friend called on them in early days. 'My impression,' she wrote later, 'was that Phyllis was cushioning Harold from the outside world. His study was sacrosanct, and in spite of later intimacy I never saw inside it. Complete silence was the rule even outside the door and the nursery quarters were as far removed from it as possible.' Yet, paradoxically, although he may have been cushioned from the outside world and took little interest in either the social round or in public affairs, he was in no way remote from the struggles and deepest needs of ordinary individuals. He was entirely ready to spend time in counselling a maid who was in trouble about a love-affair. Moreover, the books which came from his isolated study spoke in an extraordinary way to the hearts and minds of those who had received no special theological training. Many years of preaching and pastoral work had not been in vain.

This was perhaps above all true of the *Commentary on the Epistle to the Romans* which was published in 1932. As far back as 1919 he had composed a paraphrase designed to present 'in a plain way the continuous sequence of the argument while suggesting the free epistolary form of the original' and this had been published in the *Student Movement*. Subsequently he lectured regularly on the Epistle and thereby identified himself more and more closely with the Apostle's thought. At length the opportunity came to express his detailed interpretation of the text as translated by his friend Dr. Moffatt. It was a happy combination, for only in a few instances did he question the translator's accuracy or judgment. Still happier was the combination of careful scholarship and its application to Christian living which was contained in the commentary itself. For thousands of readers the Epistle to the Romans took on new meaning and relevance as they used the interpretation which had assumed its final form in the Manchester study.

Dodd had the knack of taking his readers immediately into his confidence. They felt that he was sharing their difficulties and wrestling with their perplexities. With never a trace of arrogance he wrote with supreme confidence, on occasion differing from Moffatt and even daring to express sharp criticisms of Paul's own pronouncements at a number of points. He can call one of Paul's arguments 'obscure and feeble'; his treatment of Scripture in one important chapter 'artificial'; his exposition 'unenlightening'; his illustration of a particular Christian thesis is said to have 'gone hopelessly astray' and his apologetic in one instance to appear 'little better than solemn trifling'. These strictures, however, do not seem in the least to diminish the splendour of Paul's thought as revealed in the Epistle. A few shaky arguments and unhappy illustrations could be exposed and allowed for and still the tremendous proclamation of the Epistle as a whole would in no way lose its power.

The balance of the *Commentary* is remarkable. There are no long-drawn-out discussions of detailed points of exegesis but the key words and ideas of the Letter are given ample treatment. Every attempt is made to give the document its proper setting in the past but constantly the reader is helped to see its relation to the present. The theological significance of what God has done in Christ is celebrated with glowing conviction but what it all implies for man's responsibility in daily living is never forgotten. When Dodd speaks of Paul as a first-rate thinker as well as a man of the deepest religious insight, he perhaps unconsciously reveals his own ideal of the double-sidedness which ought to characterise everyone who undertakes to expound such 'a comprehensive and reasoned statement of the fundamentals of Christianity' as is to be found in the Epistle to the Romans.

C.H.D.—8

III

Reading again the *Commentary*, to which I have often turned since it first appeared, I have been struck by the author's recurring reference to two collections of writings—one ancient and one modern. He finds the illuminative background of the Epistle in the *prophetic* literature of the Old Testament: he finds the illuminative connection with human experience today in the literature of modern *psychology*.

As Dodd devoted himself to the study of the Gospels he became increasingly convinced that if there was one category which could be applied without hesitation to Jesus in His earthly career it was that of *prophet*. This conviction he expanded in a fresh and original way in his essay published in *Mysterium Christi* in 1930. There he claimed that in the external aspects of His ministry, in the purport of His teaching and in some at least of His personal traits, Jesus stood essentially in the succession of the prophets and was regarded as a prophet by the populace at large.

When it came to Paul the same could hardly be said, for he was a Pharisee of the Pharisees, disciplined from his youth in the schools of Rabbinic learning. Yet Dodd was convinced that after his conversion Paul, like his Master, found his chief inspiration and pattern of ministry in the prophets of the Old Testament rather than in the Law-givers.[2]

> Paul divined . . . that legalistic Judaism was after all a one-sided development of the religion of the Old Testament. In the prophets, in the Psalms, and even embedded in the Pentateuch itself, there is a conception of God in His relation to men which goes far beyond the merely legal conceptions of orthodox Judaism in Paul's time and is in the most real sense the 'direct antecedent of Christianity'. Paul's citation of Old Testament passages often strikes us as arbitrary, and his interpretation of them as fanciful, but at bottom what he is doing is to appeal to the prophetic strain in biblical religion against the legal strain which prevailed in the Judaism of his own time. Jesus Himself had insisted on the continuity of His own work with that of the prophets and had deliberately set the prophetic conception of religion over against the Pharisaic, and in this Paul followed Him.

The implications of this general thesis for the interpretation of particular words and passages are far-reaching. The dominant words of the Epistle—righteousness, faith, justification, salvation, wrath—he sets within the context of prophetic utterances rather than within the common usage as found in Hellenistic literature. The contrast between Spirit and

Law is shown to have had its foreshadowing in prophetic religion. The divine control of history is seen through the eyes of the prophets rather than through those of the guardians of a legal system. All this gives the *Commentary* a dynamic quality, and the reader can scarcely fail to sense the possibility of becoming involved within a movement of history stretching far back to the prophets of Israel and still stretching forward to the Day of the Lord when God's secret purpose, revealed in Christ, will find its ultimate fulfilment.

IV

This is the wide sweep of the process of history. But within it individual men and women struggle with suffering and sin, frustration and guilt. How can they be liberated into courage and confidence and hope? Paul has his answers in the Epistle but the language and the illustrations and the movement of his thought are not easy for the ordinary reader to apprehend. Dodd himself had passed through struggles of a personal kind and had found help towards understanding them and resolving them through the insights of modern psychology. He did not hesitate therefore to appeal to those insights to elucidate Paul's descriptions of conflict within the human psyche—above all in the great chapter, Romans 7. So far as I can judge, he regarded this chapter as the very heart of the Epistle, seeing that it corresponded so obviously to crises in his own experience. Besides quoting twice from Dr. Hadfield's book *Psychology and Morals*, he remarks that three of its important chapters admirably illustrate Romans 7.

There have of course been developments in psychological theory since 1932, but Dodd's familiarity then with the language of the New Psychology—instincts, sentiments, complexes, repressions—enabled him to write in terms which brought Paul's analysis of human nature and human experience right into the midst of the twentieth century. He demonstrated clearly that the Epistle was no remote compendium of doctrine but that at many points it was rather the *cri de coeur* of a man who had known moral failure and despair and then had found release and moral victory through a new-found faith. This had been set forth in outline in *The Meaning of Paul for To-day*. In the *Commentary* it is given detailed exposition as passage after passage reveals some profound psychological insight.[3] Like Paul, Dodd had known the agonising search for 'the condition of inward harmony when all elements of the personality are organized about a single centre and division and conflict are at an end'. (Comment on Romans 8: 6.)

It is still today a great commentary. The author is marvellously frank and down to earth in his judgments. There are engaging touches of wit: 'If we ask why the cut was made so clumsily at 14: 23, there is perhaps no answer but the illimitable stupidity of editors'; when commenting on the allegory of the olive and its branches in Chapter 11, 'A truly remarkable horticultural experiment! Paul had the limitations of a town-bred man.'

But besides wit, there is wisdom; there is sympathetic understanding of human struggles; there is, one feels, a magnificent imaginative leap into the mind of Paul himself. And beyond all these the *Commentary* throbs with its celebration of the 'everlasting mercy' revealed in the redemptive love of God in Christ. There is no belittling of divine judgment or of the Wrath ('the Nemesis of sin'). But the whole emphasis is on God's initiative, His intervention in grace, His purpose to bring all mankind to share the likeness of Christ. Dodd exults in Paul's words at the end of Chapter 8 that nothing 'in all creation will be able to part us from God's love in Christ Jesus our Lord' and comments curtly, 'There is no arguing with such a certainty. Either you simply don't believe it or you recognize it as the word of God.'

V

At the conclusion of his commentary on the great eighth chapter of the Epistle Dodd pauses to look back on the 'high argument' which had begun at Chapter 1: 17.

We have here a co-ordinated presentation of Christianity in a rich variety of aspects. The chain of argument is continuous even though it may drag at times, and have a weak link or two. The difficulty that we find in following it is largely due to the extensive *background* in Paul's own mind, which we have to divine, often from mere hints. But we know that the *background* is there and that, even if sometimes the relation of ideas is obscure to us, *it would become clear if we knew the background.* How far the Romans followed the argument is a question to which one would like to know the answer. They shared the general *background* of Paul's thought, more or less, but they no more than we had that personal knowledge of him which would be necessary for a full understanding. No doubt to them, as to us, the epistle became really thrilling when argument passed into prophecy, and with its 'I am certain' challenged, not logical discussion but spiritual assent. [My italics.]

'*If we knew the background!*' If we could dig down to the very *foundations*. If we could discover 'the *substructure* of New Testament theology' (the sub-title of a later book, *According to the Scriptures*). If we could uncover the *form* behind the forms. This was the problem which had intrigued and fascinated Dodd for many years, perhaps ever since he sat in Harnack's class-room in Berlin and heard him trying to penetrate to the very *essence* of Christianity. In so many ways his own training had been along these lines. Studying original documents, deciphering inscriptions, estimating the significance of coins, taking part in archaeological expeditions, observing geological strata—in all these ways he attempted to press back to the very origins of phenomena. If only we knew the *background*!

As I have thought of his constant efforts in these various directions, one puzzle has remained unsolved. Why did he never visit Palestine and why did he put off visiting Greece until his eightieth year? Is there any more obvious way of obtaining *background* knowledge than by living for a period in the environment where events took place? Countries change in the course of the centuries but so much in Israel and Greece has remained unchanged. Arnold Toynbee, who became a student of the world of Hellenism soon after Dodd, went off for a period and lived rough amongst the Greek peasantry, absorbing the sights and sounds of rural Greece which, at least at the end of the nineteenth century, were little different from what they had been two thousand years before. But Dodd never adopted this method. His concern, after the initial study of sites and inscriptions, came to be with *language*, with translation, with style, with the semantic background lying behind overt expressions in written form. Continental scholars were tending to lay increasing emphasis on the *oral* background of the writings of the New Testament. He recognised the importance of this quest but still believed that it was possible to make new discoveries by excavating, as it were, the literature itself.

VI

The first-fruits of this side of his activities were presented to a wider public when *The Bible and the Greeks* was published in 1935. Much of the material had been used in his lectures on the Septuagint, delivered in Oxford between 1927 and 1931, and it is probable that the origins of the book may be found in discussions with his former teacher George Buchanan Gray whom he celebrates in the dedication as master, colleague and friend. The studies, he says, were undertaken 'from a desire to find firm footing in certain parts of that wide field which is commonly referred to as "the background of early Christianity" '. In effect, the first part of the book is a detailed examination of the influence of Hellenistic Judaism on the vocabulary of early Christianity, while the second part investigates its influence upon the theological tractates contained in the Hermetic literature.

The result was a volume which captured the attention of scholars in the two fields of New Testament studies and the literature of the Hellenistic age. It was recognised as a highly original piece of research and as an example of sound critical judgment. By its fresh examination of the terms 'sin', 'righteousness' and 'propitiation', it has influenced the development of atonement theology in this century, and by its interpretation of the Hermetic writings it has thrown light on the background of the Johannine literature in the New Testament. On both sides of the Atlantic it won immediate acclaim and there have been few attempts to criticise or question its conclusions.

On a more popular level the invitation to give the Shaffer Lectures at Yale during the spring of 1935 afforded him the opportunity to present the results of his extensive studies in New Testament eschatology. Ever since he began serious study of the Gospels he had been aware of the central importance of the eschatological background for any would-be interpreter of the story of Jesus. What do we know about the future expectations of those among whom Jesus grew up? What do we know about His own view of the ongoing purpose of God and the end towards which it is directed? How far can the eschatological pronouncements attributed to Jesus be regarded as His own authentic utterances? Some had virtually dismissed them as no more than the imaginative constructions of early Christians; others, notably Schweitzer, had seen them as the vital clue to the nature of Jesus's own ministry, the evidence of His belief that the Kingdom's manifestation on earth was imminent and that His own death would usher it in. Dodd found himself unable to accept either of these positions. For years he sought for *solid ground* on which to build an alternative interpretation of the eschatology of the Gospels.

If there was one element of the Gospel writers' testimony that virtually all critics acknowledged as authentic, it was the claim that Jesus spoke in *parables*. But were the parables, as recorded, His own creations or had processes of adaptation and re-interpretation been applied to them before ever they appeared in written form? Seeing that the parables were pre-eminently concerned with the Kingdom of God, an answer to the questions concerning the parables would do much towards solving the deeper questions concerning the nature of the Kingdom and its manifestation in the world. Dodd therefore set to work to study each parable within the context of the whole gospel story, always with one question in mind: what was the

original *intention* of Jesus as He unfolded this or that parable in its
historical setting? Could the layers of post-resurrection adaptation and
interpretation be peeled away so that the parable as originally spoken
could be seen in its sharp simplicity? Could the dramatic impact of the
parable in its original setting be reconstructed and re-experienced? At
least it was worth trying. And the book *The Parables of the Kingdom* was the
result.

This book will always be associated with the phrase 'realised eschatology',
an expression which the author admitted was not very felicitous but to
which it was not easy to find an alternative. 'Proleptic' and 'inaugurated'
were suggested by others, but 'realised' has held its ground as best
expressing the author's own convictions about Jesus and the Kingdom.
In contrast both to the 'eternal now' of Hellenism and to the 'final then'
of Hebraism, Dodd advocated an intermediate position in which the
'now' had an eschatological reference, the 'then' an immediate realisation.
Put in simple terms this means that while God's rule must ultimately be
established in the whole universe, in the present era, which we call
history, that rule has been realised once, in dramatic immediacy, in the
personal career of Jesus of Nazareth:[4]

> The absolute, the 'wholly other', has entered into time and space.
> And so the Kingdom of God has come and the Son of Man has come,
> so also judgment and blessedness have come into human experience. The
> ancient images of the heavenly feast, of Doomsday, of the Son of Man
> at the right hand of power, are not only symbols of supra-sensible,
> supra-historical realities; they have also their corresponding actuality
> within history. Thus both the facts of the life of Jesus and the events
> which He foretells within the historical order, are 'eschatological'
> events, for they fall within the coming of the Kingdom of God.

The Parables of the Kingdom gave a brilliant and original re-appraisal of the
nature of a parable and the method of its interpretation. To regard a
parable simply as 'an earthly story with a heavenly meaning' or as a
fabulous coating to sweeten a moral pill were seen to be woefully
inadequate views. To employ abstruse allegorical methods of interpretation
could lead to mystification and even falsification. To relate the parable to
its original setting, and then in turn to illuminate the setting by the help
of the parable—this was the double task confronting anyone who wished
to interpret the Gospel parables rightly. And Dodd, by a masterly
analysis of the situation and a detailed criticism of individual parables,
suggested new lines of interpretation which brought conviction and
illumination to a very wide circle of readers. Naturally they were far

from universally accepted. The notion of 'realised eschatology', in particular, many found hard to swallow. But that a real breakthrough had been made few were disposed to deny. Not often were British books praised by German critics, but Dodd must specially have prized a generous tribute by Joachim Jeremias of Göttingen: 'In this extraordinarily important book the attempt has actually been made for the first time with success to relate the parables to their situation in the life of Jesus, and thereby to open a new epoch in the interpretation of the parables.'[5]

VII

The journey to America to deliver the Shaffer Lectures proved full of interest. Dodd sailed from Liverpool at the end of March and as always on his travels made easy contacts with his fellow-passengers. This time on the *Scythia* he had a long conversation with an economist from London University on the impossibility of combining a planned economy with civil liberty and another with a Lancashire solicitor on the history of copyhold estates, conversations of which he kept careful notes. The ship touched at Boston and he saw the landmarks to the south: 'the coast is grim and unattractive—high banks of earth rather than cliffs, with drab coloured grass and a few mangy trees. I don't wonder the Pilgrim Fathers felt their hearts sink!' Finally they put in at New York on 9 April 'in a cold drizzle', but soon his spirits were revived by a letter from home and the hospitality of Reinhold and Ursula Niebuhr at Union Theological Seminary.

After delivering the Shaffer Lectures in Easter week he went on to Boston and gave the annual Ingersoll Lecture on the 'Immortality of Man' at Harvard. In Cambridge, Massachusetts, he met friends, old and new, but specially welcomed the chance to discuss common interests with experts in his own field—Thomson, Professor of Arabic, on the influence of Hellenism on Muslim mysticism, and Arthur Darby Nock, Professor of the History of Religions, on the Hermetic literature. The latter had caustic comments to make on the 'pathetic' character of the Oxford theological faculty. Even Streeter had suffered from being too much with his inferiors and not exposed to the 'cold wind' of criticism from his peers. Clearly Dodd had by now been fully accepted by his 'peers' in the study of the history of the ancient world. He had in fact attained recognition as a leading authority on Hellenism and Christianity, and this was notably demonstrated in the following year when, at a great international assembly in Cambridge, Massachusetts, to celebrate the Harvard Tercentenary, he was invited to lecture on that subject within a series which included on its panel of lecturers such notables as Jung, Jaeger, Rostovtseff and Norden.

By the middle of May he was back in Manchester, but not for long: the end of the academic year was to mark the end of his tenure of office in the university. As he wrote in a letter thirty-five years later, he remained immensely glad that he had spent the five years in the Rylands Chair, and they had certainly been fruitful for him. But a call to Cambridge was one that he could not resist. When his friend T. W. Manson, who was to be his successor, consulted him about the Manchester offer he described his own work there as not burdensome and allowing a great deal of independence. He had missed his tutorial work and had not enjoyed the climate. He had been involved in a certain amount of administration ('which in these modern "business" universities is done with a most unbusinesslike expenditure of time') and had been called upon to represent the faculty on committees of various kinds ('the scientists have it too much their own way anyhow!'). He had lectured a great deal, to his regular classes, to colleges of education, and to extra-mural courses, and had obviously increased his skill in this particular method of communication. He had no regrets at having gone to Manchester. Nevertheless it was with few regrets that he left to take up what was to be the most satisfying and fulfilling post of his whole career.

Notes

1. From a letter written jointly by the Rev. Eileen K. Orchard and the Rev. Ronald K. Orchard.
2. *The Epistle of Paul to the Romans*, p. 74.
3. I have counted at least fifteen places where reference is made to the insights or the vocabulary or the value of 'modern psychology'.
4. *The Parables of the Kingdom* (Fontana Books), p. 81.
5. Quoted by S. C. Neill, in *The Interpretation of the New Testament*, p. 256.

The Authority of the Bible

I

DODD SPENT THE FIRST EIGHTEEN YEARS OF HIS LIFE IN AN ENVIRONMENT where the authority of the Bible was regarded as absolute. Questions about dates or apparent discrepancies might occasionally be raised but that the Bible was the final authority on faith and conduct was the firm conviction of those who worshipped Sunday by Sunday in the Pen-y-bryn Chapel. The minister's task was to expound the Scriptures and to give clear guidance to his congregation on what they should believe and how they should act.

Such an attitude to authority was by no means exceptional in the last decades of the nineteenth century. A literary critic has recently written:[1]

> In the Victorian Age there was a widespread and willing submission to the rule of the Expert; the Voice of Authority was accepted in religion, in politics, in literature, in family life. . . . It was not the acceptance of any single body of doctrine that distinguished the Victorian but his insistent attitude of acceptance, his persistent belief in (but rare examination of) the credentials of Authority, his innate desire to affirm and conform rather than to reject or question.

So in church life generally it was through the Bible that the voice of authority was heard and accepted.

Yet in university circles in particular the *nature* of this authority was beginning to be seriously debated—by Anglicans such as Driver and Sanday; by Free Churchmen such as Peake; in Scotland by the likes of Robertson Smith and George Adam Smith. It was not that they denied the authority of the Bible but that they rejected such terms as 'inerrancy' and 'infallibility' to define that authority. The Bible, like other forms of literature, must be subjected to historical and literary criticism, and in the light of the results of this process of careful analysis the whole notion of authority must be reconsidered. Must the Church be regarded as the authoritative interpreter of Scripture? Or could the individual be trusted to recognise a unique disclosure of authority whenever he came with serious intention to the reading of the Bible? These questions, which gained only limited attention in England before the First World War, caused increasing distress and even division in the Churches after the war and it is doubtful whether any issue in religious circles was more hotly debated than that of the authority of the Bible.

At the time there existed in the University of London a distinguished group of scholars, representing various denominations, who were united in their general attitude to biblical criticism. They believed that the rejection of formerly accepted views of the nature of biblical authority presented the Churches with a new opportunity to work out a constructive theology, based upon religious *experience* in the widest sense. Two leading members of the theological faculty were W. R. Matthews, Dean of King's College, and H. Wheeler Robinson, Principal of Regent's Park College. These men welcomed the opportunity, offered by a publisher, to edit a Library of Constructive Theology—a series of volumes whose authors would be commissioned to think out afresh, in the light of modern knowledge, 'the foundation affirmations of our common Christianity'. The emphasis would be on *experience*, and two of the earliest volumes to appear were entitled *The Christian Experience of Forgiveness* by the distinguished Scottish theologian, H. R. Mackintosh, and *The Christian Experience of the Holy Spirit* by Wheeler Robinson himself.

In the early 1920s Robinson and Dodd lectured together in various conferences at a time when moves were already afoot for Regent's Park College to establish itself in Oxford. This took place in 1927, but prior to this Robinson, who had once been a student at Mansfield College, evidently formed a highly favourable opinion of its New Testament professor. Almost certainly it was his commendation which caused the latter to be entrusted with what was in many ways the key issue of the whole series—*The Authority of the Bible*. Hitherto Dodd's writings had been mainly devoted to problems of New Testament interpretation. Now his task would be nothing less than that of defining the role of the Bible in the total life of the Church, assuming that it could no longer be appealed to as an infallible source-book for guidance on beliefs to be held and laws to be obeyed. It was a challenge to him not only for the sake of a wider public but also for his own sake. His life's vocation was to study this one book—its language, its history, its background, its interpretation.

How could he justify the spending of his time and talents on one book unless it could be shown to have a significance and an authority beyond any that could be accorded to other sacred writings or to other forms of literature?

II

The editors had described the post-war crisis as essentially 'a questioning of authority if not a revolt against it'. They were convinced that the number of people content to rest their religion simply on the authority of the Bible or of the Church was steadily diminishing, and with this judgment Dodd found himself in general agreement. Twenty years of close attachment to a college where freedom of criticism was encouraged, and where the idea of development in history was fully accepted, had resulted in a very definite change in his whole conception of the nature and function of authority. 'I assume,' he writes in his own Preface, 'that the function of authority is to secure assent to truth; that for us the measure of any authority which the Bible may possess must be in its direct religious value, open to discovery in experience; and that this value in turn will be related to the experience out of which the Scriptures came.' On the basis of such an assumption he could proceed to study 'the specific religious value of the Bible in its various aspects, laying emphasis everywhere less upon the word than upon the life behind the word, and upon that life as part of an historical context whose meaning is determined by "the fact of Christ" '.

The life behind the word, the life as part of a wider history, that wider history finding its meaning in and through the things concerning Christ— these were his leading concerns as he approached his task, and they remained central, I think, within all his later work. He loved words, he was fascinated by words, but he was always conscious that behind words there was the speaker or writer of words and that he in turn played a part in the total history of mankind. No word could be interpreted in isolation but only within its historical context, and that could only gain final meaning within the context of universal history. But where could any clue be found to the meaning of universal history? It was because he believed that there was such a clue and that that clue was 'the fact of Christ' and that the Bible in all its parts converged upon that 'fact of Christ' that he was still able to speak of the authority of the Bible, an authority contained not in words as such but in the life behind the words and above all the life of Him who is rightly called the Word of God.

III

It is clear from the Preface that he planned the book with great care. He wanted to leave no doubt in his readers' minds about the kind of authority by which he felt constrained in his own experience. These are so important for his whole philosophy of life that they deserve to be recalled in some detail.

1. *The Authority of Individual Inspiration*

It was not for nothing that Dodd had grown up in a land of great preaching, amongst a people who possessed so many affinities with the ancient Hebrews. They knew the rigours of a mountainous terrain and infertile soil. Amongst them eloquent men, like the prophets of old, proclaimed the word of the Lord with music in their voices and poetry in their spoken words. On occasion a man would speak with surpassing power. He seemed to be divinely inspired and his message had an authority beyond that of ordinary speech. And when Dodd came to Oxford the experience of the Welsh chapel was confirmed by preaching at Mansfield, of a different kind indeed, but still by men who through their inspired utterances exercised a comparable authority.

That which he had experienced in some measure through listening to countless sermons was given a secure historical and theological foundation in the early years of his own disciplined study of the Bible. It was a period when almost suddenly the splendour of the prophets of the Old Testament had gained fresh recognition. Instead of being regarded as remote and mysterious foretellers of future events or as chosen instruments of divine judgment, they had come to be seen as men living at the very heart of human affairs, relating themselves to the dramatic movements of world history, men of vision and imagination and poetic genius, men whose message could be applied to the struggles of nations today just as much as to the power conflicts of Assyria and Egypt and Israel two and a half millennia ago. The brilliant writings of George Adam Smith and A. B. Davidson in Scotland, of John Skinner in Cambridge, of Dodd's own teacher, G. B. Gray, in Oxford—all had contributed to an entirely new appreciation of the inspired genius of the men who proclaimed, 'Thus saith the Lord.'

Not only, however, was it a time when the relation of each prophet to his own historical situation had gained fresh recognition. It was also a time when the place of prophecy in the whole development of the religions of mankind was being interpreted in a new way. Advances in the disciplines of social anthropology and of the psychology of religion shed new light on the phenomena of 'numinous' experiences and ecstatic utterances. Rudolf Otto's book *The Idea of the Holy* had created a deep impression in theological circles, while the theories of Freud were becoming increasingly known. Dodd seized the opportunity to apply this new knowledge to the Old Testament and in particular to the records of the major prophets. He traced the progress of religious experiences, from its early manifestation as an overwhelming sense of the presence of an object both awe-inspiring and fascinating, to its altogether higher expression as a tense yet wondering consciousness of standing in the presence of the living God and listening to words of judgment and grace—an experience supremely illustrated in the story of the vision of Isaiah in the temple at Jerusalem.

In the first section of his book, he drew together in a remarkably comprehensive way the researches of historians of religion, psychologists, and Old Testament experts, and combined them with his own studies of the works of poets and moral philosophers to produce a fresh and convincing interpretation of authority as manifested in the spoken and written words of 'inspired' men. He rejected any facile notions of automatism or irrational ecstasy and concentrated rather upon vision (which is not clairvoyance) and imagination (which is not fantasy) and poetic form and ethical insight. It is the individual who has 'the capacity to explore independently the regions of the spirit and to convince others of the reality of that which one has discovered' whose words 'without being infallible carry creative power'.[2] Such were the prophets of the Old Testament and we still honour them as men of authority.

2. The Authority of Corporate Experience

Besides listening to men of greater or less talent proclaiming the word of God, Dodd had for many years been a devoted member of a worshipping community within which he had enjoyed experiences of enlargement of vision, stirrings of conscience and intimations of grace. In his own home, as in the homes of many other families he had known in Wrexham, in Oxford and in Warwick, life had been suffused by 'religion'. This had never been confined to church services, though in the sanctuary intensifications of common experience could often be enjoyed. The Old Testament and the Gospels showed in unmistakable fashion that 'religion', far from being something abnormal and sporadic, could be the very atmosphere within which a community could live and move and have its being.

This being already his own conviction, he proceeded to survey the literature of the Old Testament (with some reference also to the Gospels) which dealt with the ongoing life of the Hebrew people in its social, economic and cultic manifestations. Many of the organisational details could obviously be paralleled in the records of other peoples, but was there some distinctive quality, some pervading ethos within the common life of Israel, which set it apart from that of other communities and thereby gave it an *authority* which they did not possess?

Clearly he believed that such was the case, and yet it is hard not to feel that the second section of his book carries less conviction than the first. He was well aware of the dangers within the Jewish community of a narrow particularism, an excessive legalism, a despairing apocalypticism or a deadly formalism in worship. He could paint a vivid picture of the simple piety nurtured by the Psalter and of the high ethical ideals set forth in such books as Deuteronomy and Job. Over against the dangers already mentioned could be set the fine universalism of the Book of Ruth and the heroic faith of the Book of Daniel. But illuminating as his survey of the literature was, it somehow failed to communicate the sense of *authority* which it was his chief purpose to convey. That a study of the corporate experience of the Hebrews through the millennium before Christ can lead to the enlarging and enriching of the area of experience within which truth reveals itself (his own terms) may be granted: but that it confirms or restores in any marked degree a sense of the Bible's authority is surely open to question.

3. *The Authority of the Incarnation*

The Bible was vividly associated in Dodd's memory with the piety of the Wrexham home and the preaching of the Wrexham chapel. But once he had begun to study Greek, he found that he could enter into the world of the New Testament through its original language. For something like ten years Greek literature was his meat and drink almost day and night. Though there is no record that, like Arnold Toynbee, he dreamed in Greek, the language and the philosophy, the art and the history of that ancient civilisation filled his thoughts and stirred his imagination. To relate the Greek New Testament and subsequently the Septuagint to the wider Hellenistic world within which they took their origin became perhaps the dominant ambition of his scholarly research.

It is not surprising, then, that as he approached his third main theme it was the significance of Hellenism within the development of God's purpose that fascinated him. Why was the Old Testament incomplete? Why was the authority of prophetic inspiration only partial in its realisation? Why was Jesus' ministry exercised in Galilee, the section of Palestine most open to Greek influence, and why were the earliest Christian scriptures circulated in the Greek language rather than in Hebrew or Aramaic? Did the New Testament possess at least some of its authority because of its relation to Greek culture?

Though he did not formulate his questions in precisely this way, they seem to be implied in the method of his exposition. In the first two sections of his book he had shown that Christianity is 'of the Jews', and claims as part of its own authority the authority of the prophets who spoke to men in the name of the Lord. But he went on from there to emphasise the specifically Hellenistic elements in the 'new spiritual movement' to whose distinctiveness the writers of the New Testament bear witness. 'The New Testament largely speaks the language and answers the questions of that cosmopolitan civilization which is in so many ways the forerunner of our own' (p. 198). In other words it speaks with authority because it is no longer confined within a strictly Jewish tradition and specifically Jewish thought-forms. By its Hellenistic ambience it is now able to speak to the whole world.

With characteristic felicity he proceeded to spell out in detail the leading features of the Hellenistic context into which Christianity came. There are noble titles, 'Lord', 'Saviour', 'Logos', which mirror the spiritual longings of that world. There are sacramental observances which answer to a widespread need of the Gentile world expressed through the Mysteries. There is an ethic which corrects but also fulfils the finer aspirations of Stoicism. There is a total philosophy of life which has many affinities with Platonism, even though the claim that the Son of God had lived as true man and died upon a cross would have found no place within a consistent Platonic system. Dodd was profoundly convinced that the Christ-events did not happen within a Jewish ghetto or even in a remote corner of the Roman empire. They were such as could be related both to the Hellenistic world of the first century and to the long tradition of Hellenistic ideas and language-forms which had preceded it.

It is perhaps strange that he did not attempt to deal with the question of whether the very notion of *Incarnation* is more Hellenistic than Jewish. He was content to see Jesus as the looked-for Messiah of Jewish anticipation, destined to deliver and redeem His people. If He was indeed the One who was to come, then His authority within the context of Jewish history was assured. But would this necessarily be the case in Hellenistic circles, where no such expectation of a Messiah was entertained? By stressing the authority of *Incarnation* Dodd may have suggested more than he immediately demonstrated. Future studies of the Johannine writings would one day serve to amplify this section of his thesis.

But to speak of the authority of the *Incarnation* at least implies that the Christ of the Gospels is more than one amongst other outstanding figures in the religious history of mankind. As he writes, 'His authority over the Christian soul can never be simply that of a prophet, however great, who speaks to us through a written record' (p. 231). He then turns aside, as it were, and takes his readers into his confidence.

What do you mean by saying that this or that is 'un-Christian'? You do not mean that Christian people do not do it, for they do many 'un-Christian' things, and even do them without being conscience-stricken. You do not mean that it is explicitly condemned in the Gospels, for many of our ethical problems do not appear there. Do you not mean that in some sense Christ is One who stands in the midst of the world to-day, representing an ethical standard in advance of common ideals and practice? From this to the lofty 'Christ-mysticism' of Paul, which some Christians, though they have never been a majority, today as always share, there are many imperceptible gradations of Christian experience. For them all an appeal to a Christ contemporary because eternal is natural and indeed unavoidable, over and above any reference to the New Testament records. At the risk of raising philosophical problems which we are not in a position to solve, may we not say in general terms that for Christians, even for Christians who would hesitate to assent to any traditional creed, Christ is in some way identical with 'that of God in us', the inner Light, the indwelling Spirit, whatever it is that we live by at our best? His authority, therefore, is the one and only authority we have declared to be absolute, the authority of truth, the authority of God. There can be no discussion of it (pp. 231f).

I have quoted this passage at length because it so vividly illustrates the Greek strand in Dodd's whole approach to the subject of authority. Incarnation, Immanence, God in us, the absoluteness of goodness and truth, contemporary because eternal—all these are concepts inherited from the world of Hellenism with which he had become intimately familiar. At times he must have been tempted to make it his sole habitation, his permanent home. But he could never forget the onward march of *history*, the fact that early Christianity was a *movement* in time. So after rising to the heights of speculation in the above passage, he immediately comes back to earth with the statement: 'It is characteristic of Christianity to find its Christ in history as well as above history.' This naturally leads him on to the development of his final theme, a theme which was to occupy his attention more and more over the next twenty years.

4. The Authority of History

At the beginning of his undergraduate career, the idea of evolution had won its way to general acceptance in educated circles. Many questions were still being asked about the details of the evolutionary process, but that the life of the universe was to be conceived as evolving and therefore as, in certain respects at least, progressing seemed a reasonable deduction

C.H.D.—9

from the known evidence. Every theory of smooth or automatic progress, however, received a staggering blow through the events of 1914–18 and the problem of the *meaning* of the whole historical process became more complex perhaps than ever before.

In face of this situation Dodd boldly appealed to the *particular* history recorded in the Bible and claimed that through this history the meaning of universal history had been disclosed. The implications of such a claim were far-reaching. No pains must be spared to investigate biblical history as carefully as possible. But this did not mean a mere hunting for dates and sequences of events. It meant rather a constant exposure to events as interpreted by men who experienced them. 'It is claimed that in the Bible we have a record of facts thus understood and interpreted, with an interpretation imposed by the facts themselves upon responsive minds' (p. 248). Such a claim is ultimately an act of faith. But faith is only justified when every effort has been made to enter into the minds of those who first interpreted the facts and tried to gather together into a coherent whole the conflicts and cross-currents, the continuities and discontinuities of the historical process as they themselves experienced it.

Dodd himself had made his act of faith. He believed profoundly that through the particular history recorded in the Bible the meaning of all history had been revealed. And at the centre of biblical history there was the witness to the history of Jesus Christ. That history, he believed, could not be viewed in isolation, for all who bore witness to it belonged to the tradition represented by the whole biblical story. Nevertheless, it was upon that limited history of roughly the first century A.D. that he focused his own attention; he then used every available means to record it accurately and authentically through his own writings. He was not unaware of the universal tendency to interpret the past in accordance with one's own predilections and even prejudices. Yet he remained convinced that it was possible to speak of the *authority* of history. History is greater than any individual's interpretation of it. God's purpose in history has been disclosed through the historical career of a particular person and to submit my history to the authority of that history is the ultimate act of faith.

IV

Amongst all his writings *The Authority of the Bible* stands out as the most systematic, the most theological and the most definitive of his own personal convictions. It presented a system of thought in a clear fourfold division; it enunciated a comprehensive doctrine of revelation; it revealed his own approach to the book to the study of which all his powers had been dedicated. When after ten years a new edition was called for he made no change in its general form or character but confined himself in a new preface to a brief commentary on Part IV of the original. He recognised that the question of the meaning of history had received ever increasing attention during the period since his book first appeared and he therefore saw fit to give a fresh summary of his own convictions.

This time he referred explicitly to an 'inner core' of history which is recorded or reflected in the Bible. This 'inner core' is concerned with the conquest of evil and error, and for this reason it is this 'inner core', this 'sacred history', which deserves to be regarded as the clue to the meaning of all history. He fully granted that events in history do not stand alone: they are only known to us through their interpretation by others. Yet he insisted upon the *actuality* of the biblical history. Events actually happened and therefore must be studied by rational and critical methods used in normal historical investigations. This does not prevent us, however, from recognising that these events may be related to an overall divine purpose: it is in fact eminently reasonable to regard them as such. Through his apprehension of the 'sacred history', the Christian finds the necessary key to unlock the meaning of all history.

Once more he returned to the question 'What is the Bible?' when invited to give the 'open lectures' in Cambridge in 1945. This series had already become famous through courses on Christian Doctrine given in 1940 by his friend Dr. J. S. Whale, and on Science and Religion in 1943 by his colleague Professor C. E. Raven. His own course in printed form was entitled *The Bible To-day* and was quickly recognised as a fresh and arresting treatment of a familiar subject. The remark attributed to Queen Victoria: 'We are the people of a Book—and that Book the Bible' was by no means obviously true in the middle of the twentieth century. It was Dodd's task, in the presence of an audience drawn from all faculties, to present a reasoned case for giving a central place still to the Bible in the religious and ethical life of contemporary society.

In its doctrine of revelation and response, of God's 'interventions' in history and of the centrality of the Christ-event, *The Bible To-day* retains the theological scheme developed in *The Authority of the Bible*. There is still the emphasis on the prophetic literature as providing the clue to the understanding of the Old Testament as a whole and to the significance of 'the life of a community conscious of a continuous history'. There are references to the 'excellent principles and methods of Greek scholarship' and to the 'subtle and powerful Greek intellect'. But more urgently than in the earlier book Dodd is concerned with the Bible and history. The

Bible not only reflects the movement of history but it gives meaning to that movement by interpreting it as the outworking of the purpose of the living God. 'The Bible differs from other religious literature in that it stakes everything upon the assumption that God really did reveal Himself in particular, recorded, public events' (p. 145). The events were public: it was given to inspired individuals to interpret them as critically significant for the understanding of the whole historical process.

From one important new source he brought reinforcements to the position adopted in the earlier book. During the 1930s the first six volumes of Arnold Toynbee's *Study of History* had appeared and had evidently made a profound impression on Dodd. The notion of the 'transfiguration' of history he found particularly appealing and proceeded to apply it to the situation in which his hearers found themselves as they approached the conclusion of the Second World War. Just as in times of disastrous upheaval among the nations the prophets and Jesus lifted men's eyes to the judgments and saving mercies of God, so now the Bible could guide us in the same direction and thereby 'transfigure' our own situation. In moving terms he spoke of a great rhythmic pattern in history: the negative, denying false values, judging human pretensions, challenging demonic powers: the positive, when all seems lost, bringing forgiveness of sins and renewal of hope. Such a 'transfiguration' could take place in the situation created by the crisis of war. The biblical interpretation of history, in other words, was no merely antique theory devised by an insignificant people. It was related to all peoples at all times and to none more than to the peoples of Europe at the end of a devastating war. In his own concluding words, 'If we are to "live ourselves into" the history which is God's revelation of Himself to man, we have no need to take a flying leap into a remote and alien past. The Church is heir to that history and makes us free of it. What happens then lies between a man and his Maker' (p. 163). Whatever else the Bible may be it is supremely the medium through which the Word of God has come to mankind and through which the individual has found his way to God.

Notes

1. A. C. Ward, *Twentieth Century English Literature*, 1901–60, pp. 2f.
2. *The Authority of the Bible*, p. 129.

12

The Centrality of the Gospel

I

IN THE PEN-Y-BRYN CHAPEL THE MINISTER'S CENTRAL TASK WAS TO preach the Word of God as contained in Holy Scripture. The time came when Dodd himself assumed the role of preacher and tried to fulfil the task as faithfully as the many pastors to whom he had listened in the chapels of Wales and England. Still further the time came when he accepted a position on the staff of a college designed to train men for the preaching ministry. It was no wonder that his mind turned often to the question, What has been the bearing of all my studies—in languages, in history, in philosophy, in literary criticism—upon the central task to which I was ordained and for which I am now seeking to prepare the men under my charge?

This question gained increasing urgency in the period after the 1914–18 War when many old certainties had either been destroyed or were being strongly challenged. Inhibitions in the social structure and dogmas in the religious context, for the abolition or loosening of which liberals had struggled, had in many cases been removed. But what that was positive and constructive had been put in their place? If the absolute authority of the Bible could no longer be taken for granted and if the Christian inter-pretation of universal history could no longer, at least in its traditional form, be given uncritical assent, what was to be the basis of the preacher's own authority, what was to be the regulating pattern of his message? Was every man to preach simply that which came out of his own individual experience?

Such an appeal to experience, valuable as it might be in a period when traditions and dogmas seemed to be too firmly entrenched, was not with-out its own dangers. It could lead to an excessive individualism and subjectivism. In the first two decades of this century one of the most passionate voices warning against these dangers was that of a preacher within Dodd's own denomination—a man to whom he had often listened in Mansfield College chapel. This was P. T. Forsyth, the Principal of Hackney College, London, who, through his many wide-ranging writings, had returned again and again to the centrality of *the Gospel*. Christ indeed was the central figure in the universe but Christ became known to men only through the Gospel. Not the Church, not the Bible, was the final seat of authority but rather *the Gospel*. Christ Himself came proclaiming a Gospel and it was through a continuing proclamation of the Gospel that the world was to be saved.

> Christ [he wrote], did not come to bring a Bible but to bring a Gospel. The Bible arose afterwards from the Gospel to serve the Gospel. We do not treat the Bible aright, we do not treat it with the respect it asks for itself when we treat it as a theologian, but only when we treat it as an apostle, as a preacher, as the preacher in the perpetual pulpit of the Church. . . . The Bible, the preacher, and the Church are all made by the same thing—the Gospel.

I know of no specific reference to Forsyth in Dodd's writings but he certainly owed a debt to Karl Barth who brought a new direction into theology in the 1920s and he was also well aware of the powerful emphasis upon the primacy of the Word which was appearing in the writings of the New Testament scholar, Rudolf Bultmann. Whatever may have been the influence, it is, I think, clear that whereas in the 1920s Dodd focused his attention upon the importance for the interpretation of the New Testament of the new insights which had been made available through advances in the study of psychology and of general religious experience, in the 1930s he set his sights in another direction—on the Gospel itself, on the preaching of the Gospel in early Christianity, on the question of how the Gospel is to be proclaimed today.

II

In the performance of this task he concentrated on three aspects of the subject.

A The Form of the Gospel
B The Historicity of the Gospel
C The Interpretation of the Gospel

From 1908, when he began his serious study of theology, he had been familiar with the central interest of Oxford New Testament scholars in the *literary* sources of the Gospels—how they had come to be written, what was the nature of their relationship to one another. But after 1920, in Germany in particular, emphasis had increasingly been placed upon the *oral* sources which lay behind the written records. Was it possible to distinguish forms of the *spoken* word which were subsequently woven together into written narratives?

It was an invitation to give a series of special lectures at King's College, London, towards the end of 1935 that gave Dodd the opportunity of making his own signal contribution to the new emphasis upon *form* in the study of the New Testament.[1] In so doing he was able to bring together in a remarkable way his concern for exact biblical scholarship and his sense of the never-ending responsibility of the preacher to declare the Word of God to his own contemporaries. By careful analysis he tried to discover the form of the earliest apostolic *preaching* (though he was quick to point out that it was not 'preaching' in a church context—the usual interpretation of 'preaching' today), and to distinguish it from the *teaching* which was later given to those who had accepted the Christian faith.

Dodd, rather like a musical composer, found a dominant theme, a recurring sequence, to which he delighted to return again and again and around which he created innumerable variations. This theme he found in its earliest and simplest form in 1 Corinthians 15: 1–3. The Gospel (or, using the Greek word denoting the proclamation made by a herald or public announcer, the *Kerygma*) there defined ran as follows:

> Christ died for our sins according to the Scriptures.
> He was buried;
> He rose again the third day according to the Scriptures,
> He was seen by Cephas.

Comparing this formulation with other examples of evangelical proclamation recorded in the New Testament, Dodd came to the conclusion that a regulative pattern of first-century Gospel-preaching could be discerned. Whatever the nature of subsequent exposition or elaboration or refinement might be, the basic theme remained firm and determinative. It could be expressed in these terms:[2]

> The prophecies are fulfilled, and the new
> Age is inaugurated by the coming of Christ.
> He was born of the seed of David.

He died, according to the Scriptures, to
    deliver us out of the present evil age.
He was buried.
He rose on the third day, according to the Scriptures.
He is exalted at the right hand of God, as Son of God
    and Lord of quick and dead.
He will come again as Judge and Saviour of men.

Some ten years later he summarised the *Kerygma* in his commentary on the Johannine Epistles. This time he included a statement—'He did mighty works and gave a new and authoritative teaching on law'—which he evidently regarded as sufficiently attested by the evidence. In addition, he believed, the Gospel early included a reference to the Church as the fellowship of the Spirit and to the forgiveness of sins, and if this was the case the *Kerygma* was already approximating in form to the earliest version of what we have come to call the Apostles' Creed. Perhaps he was tending to make his basic form a little too elaborate. His original dependence on 1 Corinthians 15: 1–3 gave him a simple series which he liked to speak of as the 'substance' or the 'historical core' of the Gospel, its 'central strand of testimony', the 'deposit', the 'crystallization' of essential Christian faith.

The discovery of the remarkable convergence of the New Testament writings towards a single apostolic Gospel gave him a new confidence concerning the book as a whole. In the first quarter of the twentieth century the emphasis had lain upon the *variety* of the several writings and upon the *individuality* of the different authors. Now, however, it could be seen that behind all the variations there was a real coherence arising out of the urge to proclaim the same basic truths about Jesus the Christ. By a rediscovery of the apostolic Gospel, Christendom could move towards that unity which should characterise it as the one Body of Christ.

Secondly, the discovery of the form of the Gospel provided him with a welcome check to his earlier appeal to *experience*. This is brought out strikingly in a comment on 'spiritual' manifestations referred to in the second chapter of the first Epistle of John:[3]

The appeal to the indwelling Spirit easily declines into an appeal to the individual experience of 'inspiration'. If such experience is made the criterion, persons with little grasp of the central truths of the Gospel may mistake their own 'inspirations' (or bright ideas) for the truth of God and so the corporate, historical tradition of Christianity is imperilled. Our writer found that this was actually happening within his sphere of influence. If, on the other hand, we are referred to the Gospel itself, which is a recital of what God did for us in the life, teaching, death and resurrection of Jesus Christ—to the Gospel not as merely heard, believed and remembered, but as livingly apprehended and retained as a power in our lives—then there is an objective standard by which the faith of the Church is kept true to what is distinctive in the Christian revelation. The interior testimony of the Holy Spirit is confirmation of the *datum* in the Gospel.

A *datum*, an objective standard, a historical tradition, a distinctive revelation—through this emphasis Dodd enabled many in all denominations to gain a new sense of their unity with one another through their allegiance to the one Gospel. At the same time he restored the confidence of not a few ministers who had been shaken by biblical criticism as well as by world events and were seeking a message of salvation which they could whole-heartedly proclaim. But although he had brilliantly uncovered a common pattern of testimony, the question still remained whether the testimony pointed to events which actually happened in history, to a career which belonged to the real world of the first century A.D., or whether it was a beautiful story representing no more than the wishful thinking and the fervent imagining of a group of disappointed disciples. This was the second matter to which he felt constrained to give special attention.

For thirty years and more he had been an enthusiastic student of the history of the ancient world. He had pored over texts, he had sifted evidence, he had disciplined himself in the recognised methods of historical research. What now could be said about the Gospel and history? Undoubtedly the Gospel was primarily a *religious* affirmation proclaiming to men the way of salvation. Did that mean that the Christian could be indifferent to questions about whether events recorded in the New Testament actually happened? Above all could he be free to regard the saving events proclaimed in the *Kerygma* as myth rather than history in the generally accepted sense of that term? This problem was never far from Dodd's consciousness, for we find him referring to it in many different contexts. The opportunity to face it squarely and give his own considered judgments came when in 1938 he delivered the Hewett Lectures in America 'History and the Gospel'. This series involved a threefold repetition—at Union Theological Seminary in New York, at the Episcopal Theological School in Cambridge, Massachusetts, and at the Andover-Newton Theological Seminary. This meant that he was presenting his views before some of the most highly qualified biblical scholars in the United States whose outlook on history was not necessarily the same as his own.

III

By this time Dodd recognised that the problem of history and its meaning had moved into the foreground of thought in the whole field of humane studies during the previous decade. To say that Christianity is a historical religion is not an immediately self-explanatory statement. What is history? How can the truth of history be determined? And is there any meaning in history?

In all his treatments of these problems he moved to and fro between pairs of polar antitheses. On the one hand contingent facts of history: on the other hand eternal truths of religion. On the one hand actual events whose location in time and space can be determined with reasonable exactitude: on the other hand the meaning attached to those events by those who witnessed them at the time of their occurrence. On the one hand the whole course of human affairs since history first began to be recorded: on the other hand a series of events which constitute a kind of inner stream and through which the true significance of the whole is disclosed.

In his study of history he rejected entirely the aim of isolating 'bare facts', or of recording private events as a diarist might, simply for his own satisfaction. Neither a chronicle nor a diary can be regarded as authentic history, though each can be of service in the writing of history. History must in some way be related to *public interest* and must in some way convey *meaning* to those for whom it is recorded. 'History in the full sense consists of events which possess not merely a private but a public interest, and a meaning which is related to broad and permanent concerns of human society.'[4] This is a crucial definition in Dodd's understanding of the nature of history. It leads on to his well-known insistence that a historical 'event' is an occurrence *plus* the meaning which the occurrence possessed for the persons involved in it. There is a number of large assumptions to be found here in regard to the interests and permanent concerns of human society, but the main result of adopting such a definition was that he remained dedicated to the task of exploring what actually happened at a particular time and a particular place. He uses such terms as 'crude actuality', 'concrete actuality', 'brute historical event': before the question of meaning could have arisen *something must have happened*. Behind the proclamation of significance there must have been *an event*. He was never content to confine himself to such phrases as the story of Jesus, the picture of Jesus, the drama of Jesus, much as he valued the artist's approach to the Gospel records. He wanted something quite firm as foundation beneath all forms of evangelical witness or artistic expression. He recognised fully that without the witness we should never have known anything about most events: at the same time without the event there could have been no impulse to bear witness. Therefore, to proclaim that an event in space and time did actually happen seemed to him an important part of the true historian's responsibility.

In all this he revealed the nature of his own religious commitment. He dissociates himself from the quest of the mystic, from the flight of the alone to the Alone, from the pure contemplation of forms and abstractions. He is concerned rather with *action* and so with a God who acts. If God really acts in human affairs, that in itself establishes the priority of action, action which inevitably produces some form of *crisis* in the midst of the even flow of merely human occurrences. It was the Bible's constant reference to the acts of the living God and to the crises they produced in human affairs that he found so compelling. *Something* must have happened. The quest for knowledge of what did actually happen was consequently a worthwhile pursuit. The goal could never be finally attained but this did not free the Christian apologist from joining with fellow historians in sifting evidence and struggling with the problem of what in fact Jesus of Nazareth did and suffered during a limited period of time around A.D. 30. He knew that all the New Testament documents had been written by men of faith and that in consequence they could all be called 'religious' documents. Yet he refused to divorce 'historical' writings from 'religious'. The search for what happened must never be abandoned, and the very fact that the Gospel story is so intimately connected with recognisable places in Palestine and with attested events in Roman history means that the Christian emphasis on God's acts in history and the crises they produced is not totally conjectural or without substantive foundation. There was room for a wide variety of opinion about the authenticity of details in the Gospels: it would be a bold man who would assert that the Gospel itself was pure fabrication with no relation whatever to events which actually happened in Palestine in the first half of the first century A.D. Dodd summed up his own convictions on this particular matter in an essay contributed to a composite volume on *The Study of Theology* (1939).[5]

The aim of all theological study of the New Testament is to recover and illuminate the Gospel, in its whole scope, as fact and as meaning . . . For better or worse, Christianity grounds itself upon a revelation *in history* and history consists of events (including the meaning borne by events but necessarily including what actually happened). It remains therefore a question of acute relevance, *what actually happened* [my italics]. Historical criticism must retain its place in the study of theology.

IV

Yet with all his insistence upon the necessity of historical criticism Dodd never lost sight of the higher level which he wanted to reach and where he could speak with the greater authority if he had, as it were, come up the hard way. More than once in his writings he referred to the study of the New Testament as an ascent in stages. At the base there was the critical study of texts, a discipline which had flourished most notably in the mid-nineteenth century but which must still be undertaken today. Historical criticism, involving the study of languages and comparative history, constituted a further stage in which outstanding work had been done at the turn of this century. But at least since the 1930s there had come the growing recognition that the chief task to which all else is preparatory is that of *interpretation*. What did the words of Holy Scripture *mean* to those who first spoke and wrote them, to those who heard or read them, to us who read them today? To interpret the *meaning* of the Gospel for our contemporary world had been his aim from the very beginning of his ministry. Yet when he gave his inaugural lecture at Cambridge in 1935 he committed himself to this particular task with a new intensity. Event and meaning were still held together, but the bias now was to be more towards the latter.

In particular he believed that there was still a great task to be undertaken in seeking a deeper and truer understanding of the Fourth Gospel.[6]

> I am disposed to think that the understanding of this Gospel is not only one of the outstanding tasks of our time, but the crucial test of our success or failure in solving the problem of the New Testament as a whole. The Fourth Gospel may well prove to be the keystone of an arch which at present fails to hold together. If we can understand it, understand how it came to be and what it means, we shall know what early Christianity really was and not until in some measure we comprehend the New Testament as a whole shall we be in a position to solve the Johannine problem.

Again there is a characteristic polarity, this time between the part and the whole. The interpretation of the Fourth Gospel needs an understanding of the New Testament as a whole: the key to that understanding may well be a more adequate interpretation of the meaning of the Fourth Gospel. In point of fact, when *The Interpretation of the Fourth Gospel* finally appeared, it was set in a far wider context than that of the New Testament. In language, symbolism and ideas it was shown to have many similarities with the religions and philosophies of the Hellenistic world of its time: in turn its own affirmations throw light upon the wider religious quests of that period of history. Dodd knew that the task of interpretation can never come to an end. New light shines upon God's Holy Word: new light breaks forth from it. Through the dialectic between the part and the whole, between the Gospel and its environment, he found a constant source of renewal and a constant challenge to fresh endeavour. His definition of the interpreter's task set forth in the Cambridge Inaugural has become famous and deserves to be quoted once more:

> The ideal interpreter would be one who has entered into that strange first-century world, has felt its whole strangeness, has sojourned in it until he has lived himself into it, thinking and feeling as one of those to whom the Gospel first came and who will then return into our world, and give to the truth he has discerned a body out of the stuff of our own thought. If there are other qualifications of which it is less fitting to speak in an academic lecture, I may be allowed to hint at them in a phrase familiar to theologians—*testimonium Spiritus Sancti internum.*
>
> This is an ideal. That any of us, or all of us together, will be able to realize it fully or to give a final interpretation of the New Testament, final even for our own age, is not to be supposed. But here our task lies.

Notes

1. These lectures were, in fact, a résumé of a survey course given to his Manchester students.
2. *The Apostolic Preaching and its Developments*, p. 17.
   The Johannine Epistles, p. xxviii.
3. Op. cit., pp. 63f.
4. *History and the Gospel*, p. 26.
5. Pp. 223, 241.
6. *The Present Task in New Testament Studies*, p. 29.

PART 5

The Fulness of His Powers

13

The Norris-Hulse Professor
of Divinity

I

DODD'S ELECTION TO THE NORRIS-HULSE CHAIR OF DIVINITY IN THE
University of Cambridge was an event of peculiar significance in the
history of English theological scholarship. Since the Restoration, all
divinity professorships in Oxford and Cambridge had been confined to
members of the Church of England. Usually they had been held by
clerics, but occasionally, as in the case of the Norrisian Chair at Cambridge
from 1906–35, by a layman. This was Francis Crawford Burkitt, a man
who possessed an extraordinary range of learning—archaeology, philology,
textual criticism, history of early Christianity, Hebraic and Syriac studies
—and was at the same time editor, musician, and translator. When he
died the Norrisian and the Hulsean professorships (the Hulsean was left
vacant after the death of W. Emery Barnes) were reconstructed and one
new Chair—the Norris-Hulse Chair of Divinity—was established with
the restriction to members of the Church of England removed. There was
a strong hope in Cambridge that the first incumbent would be a Free
Churchman and that his particular expertise would be in the field of New
Testament Studies.

Naturally the electors' chief concern was to find the man most likely to
be a worthy successor to Burkitt in the areas of scholarship which he had
adorned. It was obvious that Dodd had attained a position of eminence
amongst biblical scholars in England and Wales, and he was a greatly
respected Dissenter. So for the first time a non-Anglican was accorded full
status as a divinity professor within an ancient university, the only continuing restriction being that he was not permitted to exercise the

privilege accorded to his Anglican colleagues of preaching university sermons in Great St. Mary's Church.[1]

The election to the Chair did not automatically carry with it an official Fellowship at a particular college and the fact that Dodd had never previously held a teaching post in Cambridge meant that for a short time he was, as it were, without a settled home in the university. But his participation in the British-German theological conferences organised by Dr. Adolf Deissmann and Bishop George Bell had brought him into a friendly relationship with two Cambridge scholars, Edwyn Hoskyns and J. M. Creed, and it was the latter who suggested to Mr. Gardner-Smith that Jesus College, of which he was then the Dean, might elect the new Professor into a Fellowship. Happily the college agreed and he was thus admitted to full membership of a society with a long and honoured tradition. There was a further link in that the house the Dodds had chosen to rent was Jesus College property. 3 Park Terrace, an early nineteenth-century building whose windows had a fine view over Parker's Piece, remained their home throughout their period of residence in Cambridge.

II

Jesus College, Cambridge, occupies a very different kind of location in the university from that of University College, Oxford, in which Dodd's undergraduate days had been spent. The latter is on the busy High Street at the very centre of university life. Jesus College stands in splendid isolation, in a park of its own, not far indeed from the centre of Cambridge but with none of its buildings fronting on a town street. In date of foundation (1496) it is tenth amongst the colleges, but in parts of its structure it is the oldest of all, its founder having given it the buildings of the Benedictine nunnery of St. Radegund which had been established in the twelfth century before the university even existed. The full title of this ancient foundation is therefore 'The College of the Blessed Virgin Mary, St. John the Evangelist, and the Glorious Virgin St. Radegund, commonly called Jesus College'. It was a happy association for Dodd in that no task occupied him more intensively during his stay in Cambridge than the study of the writings of the Evangelist St. John.

There were two personal links with the college which must have added to Dodd's pleasure at the time of his election. One of his most famous predecessors in the study of early Christianity and the Hellenistic world had been F. J. Foakes-Jackson, for many years Dean of Jesus and subsequently Professor at Union Theological Seminary in New York. He was a great character, still vividly remembered in Cambridge, whose works Dodd had admired and whose acquaintance he made on one of his American visits. In the small portrait gallery of the college, striking pictures of 'Foakie' and Dodd are today given places of honour in close proximity to one another.

The other link, not so much in scholarship as in concern for the finest traditions of Congregationalism, was with Bernard Manning who was then senior tutor of the college. Manning came to Jesus as an undergraduate in 1912, was tutored by Foakes-Jackson, was elected Fellow in 1919 and served the college with complete devotion until his death in 1941. Son of a Congregational minister, he remained an 'Orthodox Dissenter' to the end, though few can have had a deeper appreciation of other forms of worship or have had closer friendships with members of other denominations. Dodd, like him, often attended services in the college chapel and doubtless felt something of the atmosphere so sensitively described in the memoir of Manning written by his friend Frederick Brittain:

In this beautiful cruciform chapel the nuns had sung their office from Norman times until the Tudors were settled on the throne. Here Cranmer, as undergraduate and Fellow, had for 25 years enjoyed the peace that was denied him from the day he left the College. Here, in the seventeenth century, a Master of the College, Richard Sterne, had been arrested by Cromwell during service time and committed to the Tower for his High Church practices. Here, in the eighteenth century, Richard Sterne's great-grandson Lawrence had attended service and meditated on his debts; and here, sixty years later, Samuel Taylor Coleridge had acted as Chapel Clerk to eke out his Rustat Scholarship.

From the time of his election as Fellow in 1936 to the end of his residence in Cambridge in 1951, Dodd went in and out of the college, attending chapel and sometimes preaching, dining often but normally excusing himself before 9 p.m. in order to reach home for the radio news, serving in quiet ways on college committees and speaking, when called upon, to undergraduate societies. He was always ready to listen to those who had different spheres of interest from his own and quickly gained the respect and affection of his colleagues, who, on his retirement from his Chair in 1949, elected him an Honorary Fellow. His link with Jesus College was extended within his own family when his son Mark was admitted as an undergraduate and proceeded to attain distinction as an oarsman. Had it not been for a wrist injury he would probably have gained his blue. As it was, his father rejoiced in his rise to the ranks of a celebrity—a status which he never dreamed of possessing himself! There can be little doubt that Jesus College, Cambridge, gave Dodd that sense of belonging to a closely-knit community which he had always valued, which he had missed in Manchester, and which helped to make his Cambridge days probably the happiest period of his life.

III

With home and college affiliation settled, Dodd was in a position to plan his professional work. This proved to be in four main sections.

1. *His Regular Lectures*
From beginning to end these always drew large audiences.

His lectures were lucid, structured carefully, comprehensive, and, above all, often penetrating in their newness and, sometimes, lightened by a quick wit. Precise, and master of the right word to an almost uncanny degree, he could also pour forth a torrent of controlled data with an eloquent rapidity that brought into the drabness of the lecture room a vital freshness. It was then, perhaps, that the Celtic strain which had mingled with the English in his veins broke forth—in his peculiar sparkle and almost fiery enthusiasm. For students inadequately prepared his lectures could be baffling, but to those who were prepared they were excitingly illuminating.[2]

He gave regular courses on 'The Holy Spirit in the New Testament' and 'The Fourth Gospel'. They were so well prepared, and delivered with such zest and conviction, that the attention of his audiences never flagged. So long as he was speaking, nothing else mattered. As one of his hearers commented, the effect of his treatment of the New Testament was to inspire in you the assurance that its truth was coherent with the ultimate meaning of the universe. His last lecture before his retirement made the briefest reference to the impending event in its final paragraph and then concluded with the simple words *'Deo gratias'*.

2. *His Own Research*
In his inaugural lecture he gave a clear indication of the direction in which he intended this to go: it would be concerned with the problem of the place of the Fourth Gospel in early Christianity. Not until 1953 and 1963

did the two splendid volumes on the Gospel appear in print, but they were the fruit of a long period of disciplined study and reflection which covered the whole period of his Cambridge professorship.

3. His Supervision of Advanced Students

This proved to be one of the most significant parts of his work, though the coming of the Second World War reduced the number of graduates from overseas who would have been eager, under normal circumstances, to submit themselves to his guidance. Some of the outstanding teachers of the New Testament in the world today acknowledge their indebtedness to him for his lively interest in their subject of research and for the stimulus which he brought to their endeavours. Though at first he might seem somewhat reserved and even shy, as soon as he recognised that the student was on to something really worthwhile his excitement would kindle and he would give every possible assistance out of his own resources, often by detailed correspondence.

Probably no scholar alive today can speak with greater authority on this aspect of Dodd's activity than Professor W. D. Davies of Duke University, North Carolina. In the Preface to his own magisterial work on *Paul and Rabbinic Judaism* he acknowledges an indebtedness, which cannot adequately be expressed, to his supervisors at Cambridge, Professor Dodd and Dr. David Daube. Both gave unstintingly of their time and learning in suggestions and criticisms; a kind of triumvirate was formed, each helping the others, whose aim it was to create a new atmosphere in Jewish-Christian studies and to reveal the immense importance of the Rabbinic background for New Testament interpretation. Ultimately Professors Daube and Davies became joint editors of the magnificent *Festschrift* which celebrated Dodd's seventieth birthday. In this book scholars from England, Scotland and Wales; from Norway and Sweden; from Germany and Switzerland; from France and America, joined in paying tribute to the man whose major contributions to learning had been in two well-defined fields—the background of the New Testament and its eschatology. As the editors affirmed in a graceful introduction, it had been the combination of exact and disciplined scholarship with imaginative insight and clarity of thought which had given him his pre-eminent position amongst interpreters of Holy Scripture.[3]

4. His Seminar

This, it has been affirmed, was his most distinctive contribution to the academic life of Cambridge. It was not an entirely new venture—Professor Burkitt had for many years presided over a seminar for New Testament studies—but under Dodd's leadership there came reconstruction and a new stimulus. What proved to be so distinctive about the seminar was the enthusiasm with which busy senior members of the university set aside every Wednesday afternoon in term to work together on complex problems of New Testament background, literary structure and interpretation. Regular members included Stanley Cook, the Regius Professor of Hebrew; F. S. Marsh, the Lady Margaret's Professor of Divinity; C. F. D. Moule, who was to succeed Marsh in the same Chair; Wilfred Knox, the distinguished author of books on Hellenistic Christianity; R. Newton Flew, the Principal of Wesley House; and Noel Davey, who collaborated closely with Edwyn Hoskyns in his fresh approach to the study of the Gospels. It would not, however, be unfair to say that the most remarkable of all the features of the seminar was the devoted participation in its labours of two of the outstanding Jewish scholars of the time. These were Herbert Loewe, Reader in Rabbinics in the university and David Daube, who in 1938 became a Fellow of Gonville and Caius College and was later to become Regius Professor of Civil Law in the University of Oxford. The intimate association in the work of the seminar between Dodd and Daube proved to be a major influence upon both men in the development of their own subsequent contributions to biblical theology.

The members of the seminar met for roughly two hours each week, sitting around a large table in the somewhat austere surroundings of the Lightfoot Library of the Divinity School. Dodd sat at the head of the table and directed the proceedings firmly but unobtrusively—some indeed wished that he had talked more himself and discouraged some of the more loquacious members of the group. There was an overall exercise for the term and at each session one of the participants opened with a short paper. If any one aim could be singled out as the most prominent, it was that of penetrating behind the words and phrases used, for example, in the Gospel of Mark, to discover possible background parallels or influences in Rabbinic, Aramaic, or Hellenistic sources. Among those present there were experts in each of these fields and they could be relied upon to produce evidence, either at once or through research between meetings. David Daube was indefatigable at examining Old Testament and Rabbinic sources, communicating the results of his investigations in a succession of letters to the leader.

Jew and Gentile, old and young, joined together in the common task. When one day Wilfred Knox argued that the reference to Parthians, Medes, etc. in Acts 2 could not possibly be original, Herbert Loewe almost painfully enquired, 'May we not then accept Acts as historical?', a remark which led another member of the seminar to comment, 'Things have come to a pretty pass when a Jew has to ask permission of a Canon of the Anglican Church to accept the evidence of the New Testament!' An older member, Mrs. J. W. Adam, read a paper on alabaster flasks in reference to the Gospel incident and concluded that they were not in fact made of alabaster and were possibly like a modern milk bottle with a parchment top! A younger member of great promise, Alasdair Charles Macpherson, soon to lose his life on active service in the war, contributed a highly original paper on liturgical influences which could be detected in the later chapters of the Fourth Gospel while another, J. A. T. Robinson, usually quiet and taciturn, periodically interjected some sharp and critical comment, revealing the quality of his developing powers.

In the earliest days of the seminar, attention was focused on the tradition behind the Gospels. Later, the members proceeded to a close study of the Passion narrative. In this way themes were explored which Dodd was to investigate with the utmost thoroughness in his works on the Fourth Gospel. When he came to write down his own conclusions he knew that they had been exposed to the most thorough examination by a team which included experts on Hebrew and Syriac, on classical languages and ancient history, on the doctrine and worship of the various cults in the Hellenistic world, and on early Christian texts. At times a member of the seminar might appear to be slumbering, but if discussion touched on his own specialism, he immediately sprang to the alert to prevent his colleagues from falling into error.

Dodd, in a quite remarkable way, retained the confidence of the very varied members of his seminar and sustained their interest over a period of some thirteen years. Visiting professors or graduate students from abroad attended sessions while in Cambridge and derived immense stimulus from the experience. The general atmosphere of the weekly assembly has been vividly depicted by W. D. Davies, to whom I have already referred. Having commented on the way Dodd directed his students to the work of German, French and American scholars, he continues:[4]

This openness to outside scholarship was typical of his whole attitude, which was best experienced in his seminar. In this those qualities we have noted, a dignified human sensitivity, expressed in a fine courtesy and easy wit, enabled him to draw out the best in those present. In his seminar, above all, one felt his complete freedom from any dogmatism despite, nay, more probably because of, his massive knowledge, and his unself-conscious openness to all possible positions . . . For this reason, probably, he never formed a school. His students never felt that he expected them to follow his positions and certainly not to follow him. The unexpressed assumption was that we were all together engaged in a high task but each free to pursue it in his own way. It was his freedom within his conscientious dedication that constituted his authority over us and made his seminar so remarkable.

IV

It was three years after the Dodd family took up residence in Cambridge that war came. Dodd was now fifty-five years of age and therefore exempt from any kind of national service, but the strain of the war years took its toll, both on himself and on his family. In the summer of 1941 his health deteriorated and X-rays revealed a minor incidence of T.B.[5] This meant an extended stay at a hospital at Papworth, some twelve miles out from Cambridge. Transport was exceedingly difficult, but Phyllis bravely struggled out two or three times a week, carrying whatever the family had been able to spare or secure of food to supplement his inadequate hospital diet. Books, too, he needed. He decided to read through the whole series of the *Waverley Novels*, leaving technical New Testament scholarship for the time being in abeyance: he also taught himself to knit and darn.

It was a dark period of the year and a dark period of the war but he accepted his situation without complaint and by Christmas his recovery was almost complete. To a friend he wrote on 27 December:

> My progress has now gone so far that I am allowed to be out of bed for 2 hours daily and to take, during that time, short walks in the grounds. I enjoy this mild perambulation quite absurdly! On Tuesday however I was actually allowed to go into Cambridge and spend a few hours at home: and as my wife and children came out here for the afternoon of Christmas Day we managed something of a family Christmas after all.

Progress was sustained and there was never any recurrence of the T.B. He was subject to attacks of migraine (late in life he remarked to a friend that the passage in Ezekiel concerned with wheels within wheels must have been written during a migraine attack: 'that is just how I feel at 5 a.m. when an attack is coming on'), and he worried from time to time about his food and digestion; but his general health was consistently good. Though his physical frame was so small, he was wiry, and he continued his regular walks: his only serious handicap was the increasing deafness which began to afflict him soon after his retirement.

War brought obvious physical discomforts, for Cambridge was near to important military zones and air-raid warnings were frequent. In addition there were strains of conscience and loyalties which Dodd felt deeply. For at least thirty years he had held pacifist convictions: for roughly the same period he had been a reader of German literature and had counted distinguished German scholars amongst his friends. What attitude could he now take, in private and in public, to the war effort? What could he do to maintain cordial relations with Germans in England who were now under suspicion and often under restraint?

On the pacifist issue his attitude was summed up in a phrase used in conversation with his friend David Daube: 'a pacifist with a bad conscience'. He could not abandon his conviction that war was contrary to the Christian ideal. Yet the menace of Nazism and later of Stalinism—the latter particularly—caused him to question the possibility of avoiding in practical politics recourse to the armed conflict which seemed contrary to the law of Christ.

His most careful and considered statement on pacifism is to be found in a joint document entitled *The Bases of Christian Pacifism*. This consists of three addresses given to the Council of Christian Pacifist Groups meeting in London in September 1938. (The other contributors were Canon C. E. Raven of Cambridge and Professor G. H. C. Macgregor of Glasgow). Characteristically Dodd founded his whole case on the revelation of God in Christ, through which His righteousness had been declared and vindicated. Having analysed the principles of the Kingdom as they appear in the New Testament record, he declared that war contradicts these principles point by point. Seeing that Christians must seek to live as already within the Kingdom, they cannot avoid challenging the standards of the secular world even though they cannot withdraw from it.

From time to time [he went on] the tension becomes peculiarly acute—as one or another manifestation of evil in the world becomes flagrant, or as the Christian conscience becomes especially sensitive on a particular issue. The Christian may then be driven to make a stand, even to the extent of withdrawing from the social order in that particular respect at that particular time.

For the early Church the central issue was idolatry. At the present moment the crucial issue for many of us is that of war. We have seen that war belongs to an order of things which is challenged all along the line by the principles of the Kingdom of God. . . . Consequently it represents a point at which the tension between the world order and the

Kingdom of God is at its maximum. The Christian pacifist I take to be one who is compelled to believe that the tension here reaches breaking point and that the only way in which the obligations of the Kingdom of God can be met is by refusing to take a personal part in war (though what 'taking part' may mean under present conditions scarcely admits of logical definition: in one sense every member of a belligerent community takes part in war, willy-nilly).

We should be clear that in doing so we are not delivering our consciences from the tension of which I have spoken. For the order from which, temporarily and *ad hoc* we withdraw our service, is not in itself an evil thing. The Christian who refuses military service is therefore not doing the ideally right thing. He is denying to his country the support to which it is in justice entitled from all who have shared in its benefits. He is denying to his neighbours the particular service they ask of him. When once war has broken out, there is no way, for the time being, of reconciling the claim of God upon us through the social order with His claim upon us through the Christian order. Both claims we cannot satisfy. Either way we must act with a bad conscience.

Then on what ground do we take our stand? I can give no demonstrable ground, beyond the fact that a man, having contemplated the meaning of Christ for the world and having taken stock of the whole situation, is conscious of an inward compulsion which leads him to say

> Here I stand, so help me God:
> I can no other.

The spirit in which such action is taken may be described by adapting language used by Paul in another connection: if I refuse to fight this is no matter for pride. Necessity is laid upon me. If my action were self chosen I should be winning merit, but if it is involuntary I am only fulfilling a trust. (1 Cor. 9: 16–17.)

Our judgment may be mistaken. God alone knows. At best we may say with Paul 'I know nothing by myself yet am I not hereby justified: but he that judgeth me is the Lord.' (1 Cor. 4: 4.)

I have quoted this passage at length because of the way in which it illustrates Dodd's attitude to the State, to war, and to moral crises in history. He recognised the claims of natural justice: if he enjoyed the benefits of living within a particular society he must be willing to fulfil his obligations to it. Yet still more he recognised the claims of the Kingdom of God, the Kingdom whose dynamic is a charity which cares for every individual even to the extent of complete self-sacrifice. Though these two sets of claims need not necessarily be antithetical there come occasions in history, moral crises, when the claim of the Kingdom must take precedence *for the individual* over the claim of the State. But no individual is infallible. He may mistake the issue. He dare not pass judgment on his brother. He can only take his stand and bear the consequences.

These principles he presented for the consideration of the individual, leaving him to make his own decision. He did not engage in any pacifist crusade nor did he discourage anyone from playing his or her part in the war effort. Phyllis worked incessantly in the centre which provided facilities for R.A.F. personnel in the tea-canteen at the station. John Terry, his stepson, while fully supported by Dodd when he registered as a non-combatant (at the tribunal Dodd spoke on his behalf), received equal support when at a later date he decided to apply for transfer to a bomb-disposal squad. Dodd went to the Bible to gain insight and guidance for his own decisions and he was willing to share his own understanding of the biblical revelation with others. But he was always tolerant and unsolemn and ready to face the implications of new circumstances. Though a teetotaler himself he provided wine for guests, and though opposed to the opening of cinemas on Sunday, so far as his own judgment was concerned, he refused to vote against the proposal in Cambridge because of what he regarded as the bigotry of those who were trying to prevent this innovation. He was firm on the Gospel, flexible on the Law. Never would he allow legalism to take precedence over grace and truth.

V

Family memories of 'life with father' at 3 Park Terrace seem to be almost uniformly happy. There was the stress of the war, clouded by father's absence in the hospital at Papworth and by a period in which the children were taken to Shropshire, Cambridge being a likely target for air raids. But in general family life went forward in the normal routine: the process of education in which Dodd never exerted pressure because of the feeling that he had been too much under constraint in his own boyhood; holidays when neither father nor mother seemed able to pack without a frantic last-minute scramble leaving things behind which neighbours were asked to send on; parties at which father provided the star turn in charades or told ghost stories in dramatic fashion; excellent cooking by Phyllis which her husband fully appreciated; Sunday afternoon teas at which students from many countries were made welcome: it was a warm and united family context within which father's quiet for study was vigilantly guarded and his characteristic foibles long remembered.

Many stories of his absent-mindedness are still current. Absent-mindedness may not in fact be the right word. He was so absorbed in his books and in whatever topic he was currently studying than less important matters, as they seemed, received little attention. This was particularly the case in matters of dress. He was never untidy but he was known to have gone off to lecture wearing one of his own shoes and one of his daughter Rachel's. Gown and academic cap were constantly mislaid. At the ceremonies for Smuts's installation, the cap was finally discovered in a corner at Barclay's Bank. When due to preach a university sermon, Dodd arrived very late at the Vice-Chancellor's luncheon party held beforehand, in much confusion because his gown could nowhere be found. Having then been lent one which almost enveloped him, he was greeted at the Senate House by the Clerk enquiring why he was wearing that strange garment: his own gown had been carefully left there in readiness the day before.

The times of greatest apprehension for the family were those of any special ceremony. Rachel's wedding was one such. Phyllis enquired, 'Are you ready, Harold? Let me look at you.' All was well at the top but as she looked downwards strange colours appeared above his shoes. For the sake of warmth he had put on a pair of football stockings belonging presumably to one of the other male members of the family. And whenever, after the outbreak of war and the consequent construction of a chicken-run in the garden, preparation for attendance at some function had to be made, special guard was mounted to prevent father from going out to feed the chickens at the last moment.

His devotion to the chickens indeed came to be a kind of *cause célèbre*. He sang to them, believing that this improved their laying powers. He went out at all hours to feed them, wearing the oddest garments—a heavy coat over a night-shirt with old fur boots and a derelict hat which was almost always knocked awry by collision with some part of the run. A complicated contraption of chair and ladder gave him access to the hens, and every feed became an adventure in which his accident-proneness had full scope. He possessed no mechanical skills—geology and archaeology were the only disciplines of a scientific kind which he ever pursued with any enthusiasm.

He was in no way unsociable, but had no love for formal parties. On one occasion, encountering Professor Dorothy Emmet at an academic sherry party he remarked, 'I meant to forget to come to this show but somehow I forgot to forget.' He was always eager to learn about unfamiliar aspects of the world or human experience, but small talk or gossip made no appeal to him. There were such fascinating explorations to be made in so many fields of interest: he was an avid reader of newspapers; he listened, whenever possible, to news broadcasts and seemed to gain a particular satisfaction in relaying the more gloomy aspects of current affairs.

In addition he had plenty of recreations. For many years he sustained an interest in gardening, not on any large scale but with a limited attention to rock plants or to an individual species such as delphiniums, which he tended to regard as he would his special pupils. He was delighted when his son Mark developed an interest in ancient monuments and they were able to go together on joint explorations. He enjoyed visits to art galleries and museums and never lost his early interest in coins. He loved an occasional attendance at a performance of ballet and particularly enjoyed Charlie Chaplin films—it has been said that he saw something of himself in the physical mishaps that his hero encountered. But his chief recreations were found indoors, in his own home or when away on holiday: crosswords, novels (for example, Trollope, Hardy, Galsworthy), biographies, thrillers (his favourites were Dorothy Sayers and Michael Innes) and patience. Whether he found in the last-named exercise the same pleasure as did T. S. Eliot—who liked it because 'it's the nearest thing to being dead'— we have no means of knowing.

Notes

1. It was a curious position. It was normal for a Divinity Professor to preach a university sermon from time to time, but equally university sermons could be preached only by Anglicans. In 1941 the contradiction was finally resolved, and it became possible for a non-Anglican to be appointed to preach. However, because of Dodd's illness, the first non-Anglican to enjoy this privilege was W. A. L. Elmslie, the Principal of Westminster College. This was in November 1941. On January 25, 1942, Dodd preached his first university sermon in Cambridge.
2. From a memoir by W. D. Davies in *New Testament Studies*, 20, p. iv.
3. In a personal letter describing Dodd's relationships with those engaged in advanced study of the New Testament, Professor W. D. Davies includes the following reflections:
   (1) If C.H.D. had few research students to guide as such, he was a guide to all students working in the field. He was often accused of neglecting his correspondence, but I have heard many beginning and older scholars say that whenever they approached C.H.D. personally or in writing on any serious point of academic concern he invariably replied—in detail, with encouraging illumination.

(2) C.H.D. always made his limitations (and how very few they were!) clear. If he did not know sources at first-hand, he would not guide. This was typical of his method. Many have remarked on the absence of references to other scholars in his works. This was indicative of his concentration on primary sources.

(3) When in time I reported that I could use German, he asked me how I would proceed. He did not provide me with any outline; this evolved as we proceeded. He never imposed himself on me in any way. He pointed out areas of difficulty and dispute and I began with the first. I would spend 3–4 months working on a theme and then visit C.H.D. with a 'chapter' in my hands. He would read it in my presence. He always sat in a high chair and I in a *very* low one opposite him (a psychological datum: I now realize—I think he would so recognize it, as he did with Paul's stature!). As he proceeded, he would correct infelicities of style and reference and make comments, either in confirmation or criticism. When the latter was needed, as was often the case, he offered it forcibly, but he also *always* noted any strength or virtue in what I had done and expressed agreement with warmth and encouragement.

(4) How can I recapture the spirit of working with him? His devotion to his field; the *purity* and *breadth* of his awareness; his enthusiasm; his essential seriousness, and yet his sensitivity to the difficulties of belief (about these we never talked, but they were always silently recognized). For me he was then and has always remained 'The Master Scholar'. This must not be taken to imply that he was in any way 'The Master' as pompous and important. There was absolutely no trace of any clerical or academic 'consequence' about him. He wore his learning—which was never, never advertised—very lightly, so lightly indeed that one could miss the immense detail behind his judgements. He could deal with serious matters sometimes with an almost jaunty casualness (as when he spoke of a great scholar as a 'Big Gun') which deliberately (?) *hid* his seriousness. It was only years later that I glimpsed the deep and essential conservatism (rooted in his early Wrexham years about which only seldom he talked to me) of his religious faith which explains the dimension of his writing, I think, in the midst of its critical austerity.

4. W. D. Davies in *New Testament Studies*, 20, p. v.
5. An old patch in one lung had suddenly become active.

14

A Monumental Work of
Scholarship

I

ON 30 SEPTEMBER, 1949, DODD'S TENURE OF THE NORRIS-HULSE CHAIR came to an end. Though, as the Dean of his college wrote afterwards, he was then at the height of his powers, university regulations at that time demanded retirement at sixty-five. But he would certainly not be idle. He could now busy himself with preparing for publication the major work on the Fourth Gospel which he had made the centre of his interest throughout his years in Cambridge.

However, within a short time, a new and presumably quite unexpected development gave him an official task which occupied him without a break for the next twenty years. In May 1946 an overture in the General Assembly of the Church of Scotland had requested that steps be taken to prepare a new translation of the Bible in the language of the present day. In 1947 a Joint Committee was appointed with Dr. J. W. Hunkin, Bishop of Truro, as chairman, Dr. G. S. Hendry of the Church of Scotland as secretary, and Dr. C. H. Dodd as vice-chairman. The work of translation was entrusted to four panels dealing respectively with the Old Testament, the New Testament, the Apocrypha and the literary revision of the whole. Finally, in November 1949, Dodd was invited to become general director of the total enterprise, with ex-officio membership of all four panels.

Such an invitation could hardly have been declined. Opinions have differed about the loss to New Testament scholarship which may have been incurred by the preoccupation of its leading British representative with the complicated processes of Bible translation. But few have doubted that he was the man outstandingly equipped for the task and that he carried through the difficult work of oversight and co-ordination with consummate patience and skill. From the beginning of 1950 until the completion of the project in March 1970 Dodd led his colleagues forward, giving personal attention to every part of the enterprise and ensuring that no avoidable delays in any one section would impede the progress of the whole.

This did not mean, however, that the publication of his researches on the Fourth Gospel had to be indefinitely postponed. By the time he reached Cambridge in 1936 he had become convinced that this Gospel constituted the most acute and pressing problem in New Testament studies. He agreed to write a commentary on the Johannine Epistles for the Moffatt Series and this served as a useful exploration of the world of thought common to the Epistles and the Gospel. Finally he found himself in a position to draw together the results of detailed studies in many fields of ancient history and to present them to the public in what is probably his *magnum opus*, *The Interpretation of the Fourth Gospel*.

In this Gospel a man who had gained a position of authority in the early Church had set down his mature reflections on the Word of Life and on the way by which all men could enter into a conscious possession of eternal life. But Dodd knew that the writer's testimony depended utterly upon the reality of the One through whom, it was claimed, true life had become possible for men. 'This has been written in order that you may hold the faith that Jesus is the Christ the Son of God, and that, holding this faith, you may possess life by His name.' Was it possible to obtain, through the medium of this Gospel, an authentic portrait of Jesus as He actually existed 'in the flesh', that is, in His earthly life? Or must we conclude that John's portrait, however striking and appealing, was simply the creation of his own imagination with little foundation in fact?

Dodd was fully aware that since 1850 the Fourth Gospel had been the object of an extraordinary range of critical judgments—some, at one extreme, regarding it as the most authoritative record of Jesus and His teaching (being the inspired memories of a beloved disciple); others, at the opposite extreme, viewing it as no more than 'a hotch-potch of borrowings from popular Hellenism' (Dodd's own words). In between, opinions of the most varied kinds had been advanced—for or against apostolic authorship, for or against dependence on the Synoptic writers; for or against assimilation to the thought-forms of the Hellenistic world— and amidst the clash of these debates the great positive contribution of this Gospel to Christian faith and life was in danger of being muted if not completely lost.

Admittedly Christians with differing intellectual convictions were united in finding in the Gospel a treasured stimulus to meditation and devotion. But was this enough? Could Christians remain altogether un-concerned about whether events recorded in the Gospel had or had not actually happened? Many were inclined to answer these questions affirma-tively, largely because they believed that all available evidence had been assembled, every available tool of criticism had been used, and that no firm conclusions about the reliability of the stories recounted in the Gospel could ever be expected. If information about the Jesus of history was to be found anywhere, it was certainly not to be discovered in the Fourth Gospel!

Dodd, however, was convinced that although the long periods of *literary* criticism had ended in a kind of stalemate so far as this Gospel was con-cerned, the new era of *form* criticism had opened up new possibilities. Without going to extremes, he had applied the methods of form-criticism with positive results to the Synoptic Gospels and the Acts of the Apostles. Could he not use them in the field of Fourth Gospel research, to see whether new light could thus be thrown upon what still remained an unsolved, and by many had come to be viewed as an insoluble, problem?

II

It is hard to think of any piece of New Testament investigation in this century which has been carried out with greater patience and thoroughness than Dodd's labours on the Fourth Gospel. First its language-forms must be scrutinised. It was not simply a matter of putting Greek into English or even of noting the usage of particular words in the Septuagint and Philo. Since the mid-1920s, when he had studied in detail and written a critical review of W. Scott's *Hermetica*, he had recognised the immense importance of the Hermetic literature as a key-example of 'the cross-fertilization of Greek and oriental thought which was characteristic of the Near East in the Hellenistic and Roman periods.'[1] In his book *The Bible and the Greeks*, published in 1935, he revealed his mastery of the difficult problems of texts and dates associated with this literature and in the long second chapter of *The Interpretation of the Fourth Gospel* he gave a classic account of the speech-forms used by the Hermetic philosophers in their dialogues dealing with the nature of ultimate reality.

Besides the Hermetic literature, there were the writings of Philo of Alexandria and of Jewish Rabbis. Dodd examined these, together with characteristic documents from Gnostic and Mandaean sources. Surveying this wide spectrum of written forms, he tried to establish a certain range of commonly accepted religious language which could be paralleled to some extent in the Fourth Gospel. 'The evangelist can be shown to be using the idiom and vocabulary common to thoughtful religious persons in circles where Jewish and Hellenistic influences met. He is concerned with *Gnosis*, the knowledge of God, and with eternal life through participation in the divine *Logos*. Any intelligent reader in the Hellenistic world would respond to that; he would be aware of an affinity of thought and language which can be traced in detail all through the Gospel.'[2]

It was an exhaustive exercise made necessary by the currency of theories concerning the dependence of the Gospel on this or that religious sect of the ancient world. His own conclusion was that the language of Rabbinic Judaism, Philo and the Hermetica bore the closest affinity to that of Johannine Christianity and that help could therefore be gained from these sources in the task of interpreting rightly the leading concepts of the Gospel. No comparable examination of the background literature had hitherto been made, and its value can hardly be exaggerated.[3] The only serious omission was any investigation of the new evidence which had come to light through the discovery of the Dead Sea Scrolls. At the time when Dodd was writing there was still considerable uncertainty about their dating and the scope of their influence. He decided that their contribution was not of sufficient importance to demand special treatment but it is arguable that if his book had been written ten or fifteen years later he would have revised this opinion.

III

Having established, as he believed, a reliable background of *language* he was in a position to interpret the leading *ideas* of the Gospel from points of view both of similarity and dissimilarity. This was a delicate exercise of discrimination, and obviously open to special pleading. Yet there could be no doubt that the key-themes of the Gospel—Life, Light, Truth, Knowledge, Glory, Judgment, Word, Spirit—constantly appeared in the writings of the devotees of Hellenistic mysticism. Dodd gave extensive quotations from the background sources before examining the words in their Johannine context. There are remarkable parallels. But the outstanding *differences* he defines very directly, very sharply, at the conclusion of his chapter on 'Union with God'.[4]

He [the fourth Evangelist] makes use of the strongest expressions for union with God that contemporary religious language provided, in order to assure his readers that he does seriously mean what he says:

that through faith in Christ we may enter into a personal community of life with the eternal God, which has the character of *agape*, which is essentially supernatural and not of this world, and yet plants its feet firmly in this world, not only because real *agape* cannot but express itself in practical conduct, but also because the crucial act of *agape* was actually performed in history, on an April day about A.D. 30, at a supper-table in Jerusalem, in a garden across the Kidron valley, in the headquarters of Pontius Pilate, and on a Roman cross at Golgotha. So concrete, so actual, is the nature of the divine *agape*; yet none the less for that, by entering into the relation of *agape* thus opened up for men, we may dwell in God and He in us.

After the leading ideas, the *argument* and the *structure*. Here, as Dodd well knew, he was treading on very debatable ground. Innumerable attempts had been made to re-arrange the order of the material contained in the Gospel. But with none of these had he been satisfied. He had the utmost respect for a document *as it stands*. While ready to recognise that redactors may have been at work, changing an existing order or inserting new material, he was convinced that they would not have acted in this fashion just for the sake of making arbitrary changes. Until he had tried in every way to detect a sequence which advanced an argument or a transition which held together two parts of a structure, he was unwilling to resort to theories of dislocation or interpolation.

The Proem obviously occupies a position of its own. Thereafter Dodd distinguished two major parts—the Book of Signs and the Book of the Passion. In each of these Books there are clear correlations between actions and discourses and pronouncements. The precise order (action—discourse —pronouncement) is not always preserved, but that this general pattern determines the structure of the Gospel seems a reasonable hypothesis. Put in another way, this implies that the Gospel records a succession of events in Jesus' ministry, each of which is to be viewed as a *Sign* holding deeper meaning than appears on the surface. This meaning is drawn out and expanded in a discourse and is summarised in a pronouncement which bears witness to its universal significance (e.g. 'I am the Bread of Life'). The succession of Signs reaches its climax in the Book of the Passion. Here is *the* Sign, the Sign which is in many respects comparable to its predecessors but which possesses one crucial difference. This is so important that it seems best to describe the similarity and difference in Dodd's own words:

As everywhere, so most emphatically in the story of Christ's arrest, trial and crucifixion, what happens and is observed in the temporal and sensible sphere signifies spiritual reality: the life eternal given to man through the eternal Word. In this sense the Passion of the Lord is the final and all-inclusive *semeion*.

Yet it differs from all other signs. The difference might be expressed in this way. The healing of the blind, the feeding of the multitude, the raising of Lazarus doubtless happened (or so the evangelist was persuaded) but the happening had no lasting 'objective effect' in history. The multitude might 'eat of the loaves and be filled', but there the matter ended unless they 'saw signs'. They were soon hungry again. Not the event but the eternal reality it signifies brings real satisfaction of man's hunger for life. Lazarus is raised to life, but in the course of nature his body will die again; the only lasting effect is that which his bodily resurrection *means*: 'He who lives and believes in me will never die'. With the event of the cross it is not so. Here is something that happened in time, with eternal consequence. Though individual men may miss its significance, nevertheless the thing has happened and history is different: the whole setting of human life in the world is different. It is an 'epoch-making' event; in history, things can never be the same again. But more: in it the two orders of reality, the temporal and the eternal are united; the Word is made flesh. It is an event in both worlds; or rather, in that one world, of spirit and of flesh, which is the true environment of man, though he may fail to be aware of its twofold nature. Thus the cross is a sign, which is also the thing signified. The preliminary signs set forth so amply in the gospel are not only temporal signs of an eternal reality; they are also signs of this Event, in its twofold character as word and as flesh. They are true—spiritually, eternally true—only upon the condition that this Event is true, both temporally (or historically) and spiritually or eternally.[5]

IV

The Interpretation of the Fourth Gospel was a magnificent examination of the cultural background, the leading theological ideas and the detailed literary structure of the Gospel. It was steadily directed towards the task of *interpretation*, of discerning the *theological* significance of this early Christian document. In fact, Dodd had taken a stage further the new approach to Johannine studies made by a man who was his colleague when he first arrived in Cambridge but who died shortly thereafter—Sir

Edwyn Hoskyns. Hoskyns had not lived to finish his commentary, but through the devoted labours of his friend and former pupil, Noel Davey, gaps were filled in and the book was published in 1940.

In a long and careful review, Dodd declared that there had been nothing in English to compare with it since Westcott's classic commentary. The author had made the Gospel speak with a clearer voice to our generation, and with his general theological emphasis Dodd found himself in hearty agreement. Yet on two grounds he was not entirely satisfied. First there was the virtual ignoring of the Hellenistic background; secondly there was the imprecision in the handling of the problem of 'historicity'. It would not, I think, be too rash an over-simplification to say that *The Interpretation of the Fourth Gospel* was designed to repair the first of these defects, *Historical Tradition in the Fourth Gospel* the second.

I do not wish to imply, of course, that the problem of 'historicity' only became acute for Dodd when faced with Hoskyns's 'solution'. For years he had been struggling with the question of the place of 'history' in Christian faith and interpretation. How far was it possible to establish *facts* in history at all? Could fact and interpretation ever be separated? How could they be inter-related? All these questions were brought to a focus in what seemed an unparalleled way when any attempt was made to expound the Fourth Gospel and to estimate its significance for the whole life of Christendom. Was the Evangelist concerned only with symbolic operations, with purely theological significance? Or was he directing his readers back to the events which actually happened in space and time, to a human figure who actually spoke particular words and behaved in a particular way? Dodd simply could not bring himself to by-pass these questions. He was as concerned as any scholar of his time for the *theology* of the New Testament. But how was that theology related to historical probability? He recognised that it was impossible to achieve absolute historical *certainty*. But could an absolute historical scepticism be conjoined with a confident Christian faith?

V

Historical Tradition in the Fourth Gospel must be one of the most detailed and painstaking examinations of the Gospel ever made. And yet it is never pedantic or dull. Constantly fresh light is thrown on the meaning of a word in varying contexts; on the subtle differences between the recording of the same incident by the respective Evangelists; on the Aramaisms or the Old Testament echoes which can be detected in the original language-forms; on the peculiarities of structure which tend to recur—all is done as fairly and objectively as possible, rarely if ever pressing a point yet gradually building up a case which becomes hard to refute.

What then is the essence of Dodd's case? It is, as I understand it, that behind the four written Gospels there existed tenacious oral traditions, traditions which became embodied in forms easy to remember and to transmit. The task of the historian examining and comparing the written documents is to ascertain the general pattern of these forms and the 'information' (a significant word) which they convey. He will be specially interested in similarities between the written Gospels, for he will infer that they have either drawn upon an earlier written source or upon a single oral tradition. At the same time he will be interested in variations which suggest that a particular evangelist has drawn upon a writing or an oral form unknown to or unused by the others.

Dodd was convinced that it was possible to discern behind the Fourth Gospel a strain of tradition which at least had not been used by the Synoptic writers and yet which, for a number of well-argued reasons, could be regarded as originating in the Palestinian milieu at a very early date in Christian history. This meant that the theological interpretation of the Fourth Gospel was not to be regarded as mere Gnostic speculation or even as inspired mystical meditation but as the direct outcome of that which had been said and done by One who lived and suffered and died within the concrete actualities of a this-worldly existence. That there had been inspired interpretation was obvious. But that this was *independent* of a tradition which stretched back to the particular man, Jesus of Nazareth, could in no way be assumed. The weight of the evidence, he believed, was on the other side.

At the end of the exhaustive investigation in which his patience and determination seem never to have faltered (though the book was finally published in 1963, his eightieth year, an early version had constituted the first series of Sarum Lectures[6] given in the University of Oxford in 1954–5), he refers with characteristic modesty to the extent of his achievement. He does not claim to have solved the problem of historicity or to have done more than blaze a promising trail in the continuing quest of the historical Jesus. His chief concern had been to show that 'the strain of tradition recovered from the Fourth Gospel is capable of being compared with other strains, corroborating or supplementing them, correcting them or being corrected by them, and of being in the end, perhaps, integrated into a consistent picture of the facts as they were handed down by the first witnesses'.

Strangely, in this concluding statement Dodd is less clear and precise than is normally the case. How can 'facts' be handed down? How can 'facts' be integrated into a *picture*? It is in his use of the term 'fact', I think, that his whole case remains most open to question.

VI

The reception given to his two great works on the Fourth Gospel was generous to a degree. Fellow scholars from many lands joined in the chorus of praise which saluted the completion of the mammoth tasks which he had undertaken. I suspect that he might have valued most the judgment of Professor Arthur Darby Nock of Harvard, a man internationally recognised as a leading authority on the history of the Hellenistic world. In a short review of *The Interpretation of the Fourth Gospel* he wrote, 'It would not involve any lack of gratitude to the practicality of Bauer's commentary or the suggestiveness of Bultmann's[7] to call it the most important contribution made in this country to the study of the Fourth Gospel.' This tribute was echoed by scholars working more specifically in the field of the New Testament itself.

There were reviews in French, German, Dutch, Spanish, Greek, by men drawn from all the leading Christian denominations. The anonymous reviewer in the *Times Literary Supplement* gathered up a wide range of reactions when he spoke of the 'rich learning', the 'sound judgment', and the 'deep insight' revealed in Dodd's treatment of the Gospel. An American spoke of 'the wisdom of a scholarship which can only be described as genuinely great'. In an altogether appropriate way the two books constituted the crown of a writing career which had extended over more than forty years.

Naturally there were criticisms on particular issues. One acute and very interesting observation was made by Bishop Cassian of the Greek Orthodox Church. 'I must confess,' he wrote, 'that, in interpreting the Fourth Gospel I do the same thing as Professor Dodd: I too insist on its unity, try to follow its line of thought and seek for signposts in its structure which help to trace that line. It is all a question of holding the balance. My listeners will probably say that I sometimes overstate my case. It seems to me that Dodd's book (i.e. *Interpretation*) suffers from the same defect—less than Bultmann's *Commentary* with its exaggerations and arbitrary assertions, but on the same lines: *it leaves an impression of too much orderliness* [my italics]. Such systematic perfection is not found in real life. It seems at times that in Dodd's interpretation, life has flown from the Fourth Gospel.'

The Bishop, I believe, put his finger upon a real danger in Dodd's labours in the field of literary criticism. He had so disciplined himself to find the exact phrase, the balanced sentence, that he tended to expect in ancient writers a striving for perfection of form such as he aspired to himself. He was always on the lookout for *patterns* in literature, and his discovery of patterns has brought stimulus and illumination to countless readers. But too much orderliness can be inhibiting. It is at least possible that patterns which he thought he discerned may not have been as consciously intended as he imagined.

But perhaps the most serious questioning arose about his conclusions concerning the audience to which the Gospel was addressed and the way in which the Evangelist accommodated himself to the thought-forms of his (assumed) non-Christian hearers. Had he not over-emphasised the apologetic character of the Gospel? At times he seemed to allow that the Evangelist had written with the object of deepening Christian believers' understanding of the faith. Yet he was obviously convinced that the Gospel was primarily directed to non-Christians who were familiar with the philosophical and religious imagery of the Hellenistic world. Was this so certain? Mr. Noel Davey wrote, 'Do such contrasts as phenomenal—real, lower—higher, outward—inward, material—spiritual, formulate the interpretation of the Gospel too concretely?[8] Was there not the danger of attributing to the Evangelist the very kind of theoretical dualism which in fact Dodd strove to avoid?

The nature of the audience and the governing framework by which the meaning of the Evangelist's leading words and statements is to be determined—these were the large uncertainties which sympathetic reviewers felt had by no means been removed by Dodd's patience and industry. But whatever perplexities still remained, all agreed that a monumental contribution had been made to Johannine studies. 'Nothing is derived,' Henry Chadwick wrote of *Historical Tradition in the Fourth Gospel*, 'every opinion is fresh.' Another friend from Cambridge days, Stephen Neill, concluded his review of *The Interpretation of the Fourth Gospel* with these words:

Those of us who sat at the feet of Alexander Nairne learned long ago that theology is a department of the worship of the Church. Without adoration, no good theology. Dr. Dodd writes so well and movingly of the Fourth Gospel only because over twenty-five years he has drunk of its spirit, and learned that same attitude of adoring reverence face to face with the mystery of the Word made flesh, which is characteristic of the Fourth Evangelist.

Notes

1. *The Interpretation of the Fourth Gospel*, p. 12.
2. From a broadcast given by Dodd on 'New Testament Scholarship To-day' and printed in the *Listener*, December 19, 1946.
3. H. Odeberg had examined the rabbinical background in his book: *The Fourth Gospel Interpreted in its Relation to Contemporaneous Religious Currents* (1929).
4. *The Interpretation of the Fourth Gospel*, p. 200.
5. *The Interpretation of the Fourth Gospel*, p. 439.
6. By statute the Bampton Lectures can be given only by ordained ministers of the Anglican Communion. Permission was obtained for a surplus of funds within the Bampton endowment to be used for the foundation of a new series—the Sarum Lectures—which could be given by a minister or a layman from any denomination.
7. Dodd did not receive Bultmann's commentary until *Interpretation* was complete. In *Historical Tradition* there are only a few footnote references to Bultmann. The latter's elaborate *source*-criticism of the Gospel receives no consideration in Dodd's writings.
8. *Journal of Theological Studies*, October 1953, p. 244. See also an important article by D. E. Nineham in *Theology*, November 1953.

15

Visits Overseas

To be alone in his study with a Greek Testament was, for Dodd, a foretaste of ultimate bliss. He became oblivious of everything else— even the ringing of the telephone at his elbow. Time and again his wife would ascend two flights of stairs to answer the call, only to see him lift the receiver just as he noticed her approaching. At length she made a rule: if she came so far to do what he should already have done, she must be allowed to complete the process herself!

But although he loved what she once described as 'the atmosphere of undisturbed bookishness', he was in fact often on the move after he retired in 1949. His first journey abroad since 1938, in fact, took place in the Easter vacation before his retirement, when he went to deliver the Olaus Petri lectures in Sweden and to be guest-lecturer at Copenhagen and Aarhus Universities in Denmark. But once he was free from university duties and his wife from some of her family responsibilities, it became possible for them to contemplate an extended visit to the U.S.A., and this occupied most of the first five months of 1950.

I

Dodd had been invited to spend a term as visiting lecturer at Union Theological Seminary in New York. In addition, he gave series of lectures at Columbia, Yale and Princeton and in the spring went south to fulfil a number of engagements in and around Washington. Phyllis kept a lively diary of their experiences which were for her particularly interesting as she had never been in America before. As far as Dodd himself was concerned the schedule of lectures kept him on the stretch and the round of social occasions allowed few opportunities for relaxation in between. At Union Seminary the Dodds were provided with an apartment which, though warm and convenient, was very different from their own home.

Our flat had a very negative air when we arrived and the sitting room was just saved from being a Morticians' Parlour by a most lovely cyclamen sent in by Mrs. Van Dusen (the President's wife). While he (the President) was happily fiddling with the refrigerator, two ladies in blameless white from top to toe suddenly materialised. They swept me into the kitchen again and immediately demonstrated the filling of ice pans, defrosting of the refrigerator etc. I agreed warmly with everything and felt thoroughly cowed. I now can remember nothing of what I was told. The white ladies had barely left before two large gentlemen appeared bearing a radio. They told me how much it would be and before I could speak it was plugged in and blaring at us. I was warned that everything was on D.C. and most dangerous. It seems these ministering officials always hunt in couples.

After this auspicious beginning the Dodds settled in, with Phyllis struggling to establish bearable colours for sofa-cover and lamp-shades, her husband intent on securing a typewriter capable of registering Greek as well as English. From all sides came invitations to take meals with old friends or to attend parties arranged in their honour. Dodd had known Ursula Niebuhr from the time when she became the first woman student to obtain a First Class in the Honour School of Theology at Oxford and he had later offered her a position on his staff at Manchester. Reinhold, her husband, whom he had also met on several occasions, found in Dodd's work on the biblical interpretation of history strong support for his own warnings concerning the way in which moral factors operate within the ongoing experience of human societies. With the leading biblical scholars at Union—F. C. Grant in the New Testament, James Muilenburg in the Old—Dodd felt a particular affinity, and with the Scherers (Paul Scherer, a Lutheran, was Professor of Homiletics) the Dodds forged perhaps the closest friendship of all. It was a peak period in the history of the Seminary—Paul Tillich was at the height of his powers; John Bennett, who had been at Mansfield in the twenties, was becoming a key figure within the ecumenical movement as an interpreter of the social and political implications of the Gospel—and the visiting professor, who by this time enjoyed an international reputation amongst New Testament scholars, brought additional distinction to what was then possibly the most famous theological faculty in the world.

II

The first major event of an academic kind was the delivery of his inaugural lecture, which he entitled 'Thirty Years of New Testament Study'. This kind of survey he did supremely well—revealing himself as obvious master of the whole field, tracing developments with an unerring eye for those which were really significant and fruitful, speaking with a deceptive simplicity and with touches of wit, never forgetting the goal of all New Testament study, which he defined as getting through the book to the life behind the book. The lecture is a model of its kind which can still be read with pleasure and profit twenty-five years after its delivery.

His main concern was to describe and draw out the significance of the reaction in Britain to developments in German New Testament scholarship in the years immediately succeeding the First World War. British scholars had undoubtedly made lasting contributions to the analysis of the *written* documents—their vocabulary, their structure, their origins, their interdependence. But by 1920 the interest of German scholars had swung away from literary analysis to obedience-in-faith, to hearing the Word of God which had been spoken through those who originally proclaimed the Gospel of the risen Lord:

> In Great Britain [Dodd said] the pendulum does not swing with such violence as in Germany; and we took our Karl Barth in water. . . . In place of the older methods of documentary criticism the new school offered a method which they called—rather infelicitously, I have always thought—'*Formgeschichte*'. I well remember, when my lamented friend Martin Dibelius first visited England after the Four Years' War, how we wrestled together with the title of his lectures—*Formgeschichte des Evangeliums*, in the attempt to render the intractable term into English. The attempt met with poor success.

In this reminiscence Dodd revealed himself as having been a pioneer, though a discriminating one, in the study of 'form-criticism' in Britain. In his judgment the new emphasis on forms of speech rather than upon written documents had brought about one consequence of major importance—the recognition of the formative influence of the actual life-situations which existed in the early Church. 'The stories in the Gospels had been told and retold many times within the early Christian communities, and they must have shaped themselves, even without definite intention, to the needs of those communities. . . . The study of the Gospels thus leads to the endeavour to picture to ourselves the communal life of the early Church as realistically as we possibly can.'

Oral tradition and its importance within the life of the Church—this was the theme of the remainder of the lecture. *Kerygma, catechesis,* Old Testament prophecies, liturgical forms were all shown to have been included within the oral tradition as it came to be applied and adapted to the needs of the developing Church. 'We are beginning to discern the lineaments of the living tradition, nurtured on the prophetic faith of Israel, witnessed by the preaching, teaching and worship of the primitive Church, and handed down as a heritage to the Church of succeeding ages.' And with obvious optimism the lecturer concluded that the outcome of this new discernment would be the spotlighting of the crucial event in history ('all lines converge') when God visited and redeemed His people. The quest of the historical Jesus could be pursued with new zest and fresh hope.

III

The delivery of the Bampton Lectures in Columbia University was the other major academic event of Dodd's stay in New York. For this series he chose as his theme 'Gospel and Law' and in the space of four one-hour lectures gave as succinct, as felicitous and as convincing an exposition of the relationship between the theology and ethics of the New Testament as one is likely to find anywhere. Beginning with the way in which those who had committed themselves to Christ were instructed in distinctively Christian patterns of behaviour, he proceeded to uncover what he believed to be the source of this instruction in the teaching of the Gospels. This source, which he finally designated 'The Law of Christ', is neither a set of rules nor a rigid pattern of prohibitions: it is the enactment by Christ Himself of that pattern of self-sacrifice which is the law of our creation within the ultimate purpose of God. To live according to the Law of Christ is to be truly human and at the same time to be a true child of the one Heavenly Father.

No one can ever have had a keener sense of the moral demand of Christianity than Dodd. To profess allegiance to the Christian faith and then to behave without regard either for justice or compassion was to him abhorrent. Yet he was never a legalist. He knew enough psychology to recognise that you cannot make men good by imposing formal laws and prohibitions. The key to his whole approach is to be found in these Bampton Lectures when he declared that the ethical teaching of the Gospels 'is not so much detailed guidance for conduct in this or that

situation, as a disclosure of the absolute standards which alone are
relevant when the Kingdom of God is upon us. These standards, however,
are not defined in general and abstract propositions, but in dramatic
pictures of action in concrete situations; and they are intended to appeal
to the conscience by way of the imagination.'[1] Through the imagination
to the conscience, through dramatic representation to ethical insight: this
Dodd believed was the way of Jesus Himself and it was the way he tried
to follow in presenting the Christian ethic to his own contemporaries.

I have tried to summarise the content of the lectures. The outward
circumstances are best described by quoting from his wife's travel-diary.

> Harold's Bampton Lectures were a great success. The McMillan Theatre
> was well filled and they tell us that there is seldom an audience like
> that even for a secular subject and never for a religious one. He was
> certainly in good form and started off on a fresh line.
> The Vice-President, Dr. Kirk, took the chair the first night; previous
> to the lecture a rather grand dinner party was given in the Faculty Club
> at Columbia—it was hard on Harold. We all went across to the
> Lecture Theatre—a distance of 200 yards—in a cortège of highly
> expensive cars—I remarked it was like a wedding, the Dean of Barnard
> remarked more grimly that it was like a funeral!

On subsequent nights formalities were reduced but even so 'Harold
felt years younger once the lectures were over.' There were speaking
engagements yet to be fulfilled in Massachusetts and Virginia and
Washington but this gave the opportunity to see other parts of the
country in springtime in company with Mark their son who had finished
his national service and came out to join them early in April. While his
father was lecturing at Harvard, he was riding in Kentucky and watching
the Derby: when in mid-May his parents made the journey to Virginia, he
drove the car and enjoyed with them the chance to visit the battlefield at
Gettysburg, to motor along the Skyline Drive and to be transported back
to old colonial days in Williamsburg. Finally they arrived in Washington,
where Dodd was to lecture at the College of Preachers, and from there
they returned to New York for two hectic days of farewell before leaving
for home.

IV

Homecoming was doubly exciting for in February, on a 'dismal Monday'
of snow and icy wind in New York, the afternoon siesta had been

interrupted by a radiogram from their daughter Rachel and Eric Heaton asking permission to announce their engagement. Preparations must be made for the wedding and Mark would soon take up residence as an undergraduate at Jesus College. In contrast to these pleasant prospects, however, there was the question of where the Dodds' own future home should be. They could not remain indefinitely in the college house in Park Terrace, but to obtain alternative accommodation in Cambridge, when the wartime shortage of houses still persisted, would not be easy.

Ultimately the decision was made to return to Oxford to a house owned by Mrs. Elliot, Mrs. Dodd's sister, which she was ready to vacate in order to move to an apartment more suitable for one person. It was a fateful decision and one whose effects, advantageous or otherwise, cannot be estimated by an outsider. Certainly it brought to an end Dodd's happy and easy relations with Jesus College, something which could not at this stage of life be replaced by his own old college at Oxford. Again, for Mrs. Dodd the move meant a severing, not of friendships, but of those frequent contacts with friends which happen when those who share common interests stay for a long period in one locality. On the side of advantage, Dodd was now within easy reach of Mansfield and Mrs. Dodd of her sister: later on, to their delight, Eric and Rachel came to live in Oxford after Eric's appointment as Chaplain of St. John's. But to break away from Cambridge after nearly twenty immensely happy and fulfilling years involved painful adjustments, at least for a while.

Doubtless the situation was redeemed by Dodd's own absorbing interest in the New English Bible and by the constant round of meetings and conferences which were now required. Physically he remained fit and well and so was able to undertake another extensive trip abroad: in the winter of 1956–7 he and his wife travelled by air to Karachi to spend more than two months with their stepson, who was engaged in architectural projects in various parts of Pakistan. Arriving on 13 December, they were not back in London until 28 February. It was the only period of his life through which Dodd kept a detailed diary, and this reveals how enthusiastically he entered into the completely new experiences, both of a social and scenic kind, which the extensive programme of travel arranged for them by John Terry made possible.

John's residence and office were in Rawalpindi. With this as their base the visitors were taken by car to Peshawar (twice), to Mansehra (3,500 feet above sea-level and providing wonderful mountain views), to Lahore, and to the Khyber Pass. Dodd revelled in the views of snow-clad mountains and brilliant sunsets, the beautifully laid-out gardens with Eastern flowers and fruit trees, the temples, mosques and churches, the archaeological remains and the new buildings, some of which his stepson had

designed. His diary recorded his impressions with characteristic attention
to detail and with vivid touches, here and there, painting pictures in
words. I give extracts from the account of the excursion to the Khyber
Pass:

At the entrance to the Pass, the road wound up through bare rocky
hills, barren even of scrub. It kept company more or less with the
railway and the caravan road, which crossed and re-crossed. On the
heights overlooking the road are picket-posts forming a continuous
chain of observation points. For some miles the scenery grew more and
more savage and forbidding. Then we came to a high and fairly broad
valley, much broken with hills between the mountains, dotted with
villages, strongly fortified with mud walls and towers, each of which
houses a family and its dependants.

From the top of the Pass we looked over the mountains of Afghanistan
with the Hindu Kush in the background, sloping down to the Plain of
Cabul. We ran down to Landi Kotal where there is a cantonment. Here
we made contact with Hamid, the political Tassildar, who accompanied
us down to the frontier post at Torkham. Here there is a well-built
guard-house and a pretty rest-house for which John supplied the basic
design (somewhat modified in the process of building) surrounded with
gardens. A chain across the road marks the actual frontier and the other
side an Afghan sentry stands ground.

From Landi Kotal they were taken to a village to lunch with Malik
Samruddin Khan.

A carpet had been spread on the outer courtyard and a table set. Round
it were couches furnished with rugs and cushions and spread with gay
cotton coverlets. We were served by the Malik's son and men-servants:
lamb kebub, lamb grilled on the bone and served with potatoes,
followed by fruit and green tea. After lunch we were conducted by the
Tassildar to Landi Kotal Serai, one of the great traditional markets of
Central Asia (along with Samarkand, Tashkent and Bokhara) through
which, before the Russians came, all the trade of Central Asia was
funnelled into India. It is surrounded by a wall, with gateways furnished
with great wooden gates and guarded by sentries. Along the walls are
shops, mostly frail booths made of wooden posts with reed thatch.
Other booths form alleys and bazaars. In the middle is a large open
space where laden camels and donkeys stood or kneeled. At one corner
is a mosque, its mud walls and minarets whitewashed. We wandered
among the bazaars—food-sellers, cloth-merchants, money-changers

squatting on their counters with battered tin-boxes beside them and piles of coin and notes before them. The whole scene seemed to be all the pictures of the East that one had ever seen come to life, with the immense mountains for background on every side.

But if he found interest in the sights and customs of this unfamiliar land, Dodd was even more fascinated by the extraordinary range of people he met and conversed with during his stay. John's architectural work had brought him into touch with politicians, educators, contractors, military men and those engaged in business. As a result, the Dodds' programme included an almost continuous succession of social events: dinner parties, sherry parties, visits for tea or 'elevenses'—the kind of hospitality that was possible where there was no lack of domestic help and where living quarters, at least for certain classes, were amply planned. Here was a unique opportunity to learn about the results of partition, about attitudes towards the British, about the probable future of mission schools, about the prospects for the whole Christian movement in Pakistan. Dodd kept a careful record of his many conversations, summarised them at the end in a series of 'General Observations' and even compiled an 'Onomasticon' containing more than eighty names with titles and exact dates when meetings had taken place. Of these eighty, roughly half were Pakistanis.

At a Christmas party in Rawalpindi he was able to renew his enthusiasm for charades. But a more noteworthy and unexpected involvement in drama took place when, soon after landing at Karachi, John told him that he was in process of producing a radio performance of *The Importance of Being Earnest* and would like Dodd to play the part of Canon Chasuble, and Mrs. Dodd the part of Miss Prism. To this they readily agreed, shared in the necessary rehearsals, and finally put on a performance which was apparently a complete success. Dodd returned to his labours with the New English Bible stimulated and refreshed and retaining the happiest memories of his visit to the East.[2]

V

Life continued relatively smoothly in Oxford for the next four years. Then came a devastating blow. Phyllis, his wife, sustained a stroke which left her partially paralysed and for a period unable to speak. For more than thirty-five years she had watched over him and managed all the household affairs. Now it was his responsibility to watch over her and to take over as many as possible of her former duties. He shopped, cleaned, cooked, did his utmost to understand her needs, even when she could not express them in words. In particular he tried to guard and respect her almost fiercely independent spirit. She had always resisted attempts to help her if, for example, she slipped or fell. Now in her almost helpless condition she must still be allowed to make every possible effort on her own. He would not intervene when she was trying to speak and finding it hard to express herself. When she had recovered sufficiently to make a journey to Cambridge he allowed her to pour tea for visitors at the hotel, though it was still hazardous for her to do so. He was utterly patient and understanding and with the help of a Pakistani (John Terry's ex-bearer) managed to keep the household going.

However, the respite was not to be for long. In February 1968 she died, and an ideally happy marriage came to an end. There were strong contrasts in their respective characters: a quiet, unassuming scholar, utterly dedicated to research and wanting nothing more than to be left undisturbed with his books: a charming, artistic home-maker who at the same time was deeply interested in people and happy to take part in social activities. By her sensitive understanding of her husband's needs and in certain respects, perhaps, inadequacies, Phyllis brought immeasurable enrichment to his life.

By a most fortunate coincidence the Heatons were now living in a substantial college house in Blackhall Road. The top floor was readily convertible into a small apartment for Dodd's occupancy and later a similar arrangement was made when the Heatons moved to a very attractive house in a small close on the west side of St. Giles'. Here, Dodd claimed, he had found his ideal study, better than any other of the various rooms in which he had worked. And, of course, he scarcely slackened at all in his regular regimen of study, even though his lecturing and writing grew less. There was one more book in process of maturing and its appearance brought him once more into the public eye.

During the sixties Mansfield College became the home of a flourishing summer school. It met each year in July and was specially arranged for transatlantic visitors who wished to combine refresher courses of a theological kind with opportunities to travel in England and sample its cultural facilities. At this school Dodd lectured regularly, with great acceptance, on the life of Jesus within the Gospel story, and a strong desire was expressed that the talks might find their way into print. He hesitated a long time but, as the nucleus had originally been presented at the University College of Wales, Aberystwyth, on a foundation which required the lectures to be published, he ultimately brought together the nucleus and the expansion into a volume entitled *The Founder of Christianity*.

The book was an immediate success. Within a short time there were four reprintings, and soon it became available in paperback. The crowning recognition of his attempt to present the story of Jesus in such a manner as to be faithful to the tested results of New Testament literary criticism and historical research and at the same time to be within the range of the average reader unfamiliar with the vocabulary of advanced biblical studies, was the award of the £1,000 prize given biennially by Collins the publishers for the best religious book of the past two years combining scholarly competence with popular presentation. In the autumn of 1971 Dodd, now in his eighty-eighth year, fully enjoyed the visit to London to receive his award from the Archbishop of York, chairman of the panel of judges, at a party arranged by the donors for the occasion.

However, the reactions were not all so favourable. The attempted reconstruction of the career of the Founder of Christianity did not by any means command universal assent from other New Testament scholars, though Dodd's intimate knowledge of the text and of the history of the ancient world was fully recognised. It was his confident attempt to recount 'what actually happened'—the stages of Jesus' 'historical' career, the details of His teaching, the exact form of His actions—that seemed to be open to serious question. Dodd would never indeed have claimed to have *solved* the problem of history. But he believed that, after weighing probabilities, the balance was in favour of a sequence of events such as he had set forth in this his final book. Others, however, remained unconvinced. The debate about the 'Jesus of History' still continues.[3]

Notes

1. *Gospel and Law*, pp. 60f.
2. After the death of Mrs. Dodd, he made one more journey to the East, this time to India. Mark, his son, was for a period the representative of the B.B.C. in India, and arranged for his father to stay with him and his family in New Delhi over Christmas 1966. Dodd delighted in his daily walks, which took him to the gardens and ancient buildings of the city. The highlight of the visit was the period spent with his son exploring the glories of Agra.
3. See Appendix I.

PART 6

Wider Ministries

16

'A First-rate Broadcaster'

DURING A PERIOD OF NEARLY FORTY YEARS DODD WAS CONSTANTLY involved in the preparation of scripts for broadcasting. Probably no British biblical scholar or theologian has thus far enjoyed so long an association with the B.B.C. In the spring of 1931, between 5 o'clock and 5.15 on six Sunday afternoons, he gave talks on the history of the Bible, the first from Savoy Hill in London, the remainder from a Manchester studio. His last talk was given in the Home Service on 12 March, 1968, under the title 'Religion in its Contemporary Context'.

In some respects his relationship with B.B.C. producers and officials was an embarrassing one. From beginning to end it was entirely cordial, but at times their patience must have been strained almost to breaking point. Programmes have to be planned well in advance and a strict time-schedule has to be observed. But this was a pattern to which Dodd had seldom been accustomed. In ordinary affairs—except perhaps in catching trains and giving lectures—a little lateness or slight deviations from schedule could be tolerated. Within the total network of the B.B.C., however, failure to produce on time could throw the whole system out of gear.

I doubt if any file of correspondence in the B.B.C. archives more consistently opens with apologies than that of Dodd's letters. Constant reminders were sent to him pleading that his script was due; that no reply had been received to an invitation to participate in some new series; that he had failed to return a contract; that even when he did return it some necessary detail had been omitted. Two extracts reveal his own distress and at the same time prompt the reflexion that our ancient universities might well have provided adequate secretarial help for their professors.

I am so sorry to have been silent in face of your repeated appeals for my script. The fact is that I seem to have mislaid it. I keep hoping it will turn up—as indeed it must, sooner or later—but so far I have not been able to find it. I shall keep up the search—if you can wait.

Again he writes:

I am afraid I am a most careless person with money and it is only too possible that I received the cheque and tore it up with the envelope. I have made search for the missing cheque everywhere I can think of.

On still another occasion he had to confess the discovery of a letter which he had written but which had lain unposted for a fortnight.

Sometimes, of course, delays had been understandable. An attack of flu 'had left my brain like a jelly and I simply couldn't get the stuff out. I feel it is still very stodgy.' Or the pressure of examining and absence from home had prevented him from producing a script just when it was needed. But the fact is that he never found it easy to change over from the kind of deployment of time appropriate to careful and detailed examination of documents to that required for the compression of material into the exact dimensions of a slot in an ongoing machine. The wonder is that he achieved success so often and over so long a period. In spite of all that producers must have felt, there is no record of his having actually failed them, even if the script did arrive at the last minute. What is clear is that the finished product rarely needed any emendation or alteration. It was so exactly what was required that officials were prepared to be patient and persevere and to make every allowance for a performer who always tried to be co-operative and whose material was so consistently first-rate.

II

In January 1931, soon after his move to Manchester, a letter came informing him that on all sides his name had been commended as the right person to undertake a series on the Bible. Something was needed to bring the critical approach to biblical literature within the grasp of ordinary listeners. In due course he sent in six scripts for inspection and these were examined not only by the regional producer but also by the Director-General (later Lord Reith) himself. The former liked them but found them 'too scholastic': he urged the writer to address himself *personally* to each listener. The latter commented on details of content: in particular he disliked the use of the term 'legends' in a biblical context and preferred 'traditions'.

Dodd was entirely ready to accept advice, remarking how 'incredibly difficult' he found it to write 'simply and colloquially in cold blood' with no audience in view. He also would feel inhibited if tied completely to his prepared script. 'Do you mind if I occasionally deviate in little asides on the spur of the moment? I can speak much more naturally if I do not feel entirely tied to my MS. I have no practice in operating from MS since I never write out anything in full except papers to learned societies.'

Whatever the uncertainties may have been beforehand (the North Regional Director had wondered about the 'nasal quality' of his voice), the series, which was subsequently printed, established his reputation immediately as eminently suited to the new medium. The musical variations of his voice, the slightly staccato manner of delivery, the clarity of his language, the obvious enthusiasm for his subject all combined to make him a key figure in the new process of popular education which the radio made possible. And within this process one of the most important features was that designed for schools. Here also Dodd proved to be very much the man for the hour.

As a regular feature of the Sunday morning service in Warwick, he had given a special address to children, a practice he continued when visiting churches as guest-preacher during the 1920s.[1] This perhaps made him the more ready to attempt the difficult task of speaking over the radio to school audiences. His first attempt was made in June 1933 in the Sunday afternoon programme 'For the Children' in which he spoke on what at first sight might appear a not very exciting theme—The Exile. But his opening sentences immediately lifted his listeners into a seat in an aeroplane journeying from Palestine to Babylon. He imagined them looking down on the wide, level plains, with their shapeless mounds where once there were cities. Then came a vivid description of recent excavations and of treasures now in the British Museum—'a child's doll—but how many thousands of years is it since the doll was put to bed?' With the stage thus set he went on to describe the drama of the king returning to Babylon from his military expedition, bringing prisoners of war in his train. 'At home every day when they woke, they looked up to the mountains that were round about Jerusalem. Here in these hot, endless plains their eyes ached for a sight of the hills.' And so to the exiles weeping by the rivers of Babylon, yet comforted by the man of faith who declared that God was as near in Babylon as in Jerusalem. 'Centuries have passed. But we keep in everlasting remembrance these men who in exile learned the lesson and taught it to us all that the whole world is God's house and His children can be at home with Him wherever they may be.'

By 1937 the broadcasts for schools had become a regular feature, and over the next twenty years Dodd was constantly in demand as a contributor. His series of four in 1938 was described by a grateful producer as 'by far the best we have ever had in the series', setting a standard which it would be very difficult for anyone else to follow. He never talked down to sixth formers but, however complex the subject, found ways of making it interesting. He spurned any tendency to thrust religion down his hearers' throats and adopted what he himself called a 'secular' approach. This, in fact, meant that he tried on every occasion to give a lively account, based on the best available evidence, either of the Hellenistic world within which Christianity first appeared or of the Christian movement itself, its origins, its distinctive teaching and its practices. He criticised any script which was 'too theological' and had a horror of the 'pulpit voice'. 'I know myself,' he once wrote to a producer, 'how if one turns on the Radio one can tell within two seconds whether it is a "religious" broadcast.'

So in his own preparation for schools broadcasts he took immense care not to be too theological or too sermon-like. And the response was remarkable. In the spring of 1958 a series on 'The Meaning of the Cross' (which he found unexpectedly difficult), drew from a grammar school in the north of England a letter in which the girls affirmed that he had explained their doubts and difficulties 'in such a way that they felt he had answered each one personally'. When his responsibilities as director of the New English Bible became too pressing, he had reluctantly to refuse a number of requests to speak to schools. Yet it is hard to think that any activity in which he engaged had greater potential for good.

III

Though travel to studios in London or Bristol was often exceedingly difficult in wartime, he somehow contrived to fulfil all his engagements on time. Just before his long illness he played a major part in a series on 'Everyman's Book' and after his recovery conducted three notable services in German for transmission to continental listeners.[2] In Lent 1945 a fruitful association with the Overseas Service of the B.B.C. began and, still more significantly, the inauguration of the Third Programme in September 1946 provided an ideal medium to convey the best results of New Testament scholarship to intelligent lay men and women.

Some indication of the regard in which he was held in B.B.C. circles can be gained from a memo submitted by a producer in 1940 to his superior: 'Dodd is the outstanding New Testament scholar in this country, is a first-rate broadcaster and sees the point of presenting the subject to an intelligent audience that is neither technically qualified in New Testament work nor initially interested in the Bible.' The memo was written in support of a proposal to repeat substantially on the Third Programme a series of public lectures given at Bedford College in the University of London on recent developments in the study of the New Testament. These were in fact relayed in four successive weeks in the summer of 1951 and subsequently printed in the *Listener*.

This carefully constructed series throws a great deal of light on Dodd's own dominant interests at the time. First came a beautifully balanced account of the environment of early Christianity with special attention to Hermetic writings and Rabbinic literature. Christianity[3]

> was sensitively aware of its environment and received influences from many sides, but by some inherent force shaped all it received into something quite new. While all that we are learning shows us the Christian movement as organically related to the most vital spiritual tendencies of the age, it is also true that when we come out of the first-century world to the New Testament and read it, in some measure, as an intelligent and interested contemporary might have read it, we are struck most powerfully by its difference from anything else in that world; by its distinctive quality; and that quality is to be felt in all its writings and gives unity to them in their diversity.

Few men had a more intimate knowledge of the life and literature of the Hellenistic world than Dodd: few could speak with greater authority on the literature of the New Testament. His testimony, therefore, to the *distinctive* quality of the writings is exceedingly impressive. But in what did the distinctiveness consist? The other lectures were concerned with this question, and Dodd was not prepared to settle for any trite or facile answer. After a rigorous examination of the current position of New Testament criticism and a survey of the fresh recognition of the importance of oral tradition, he came finally to what he regarded as the altogether distinctive element—the picture of Jesus Himself:[4]

> You will see [he concluded] that all this new work on the Gospels supplies a fresh perspective for the perennial problem of their value and credibility as sources for the life of Jesus. The immediate aim of the most active historical criticism of the New Testament at the present time is to reconstruct as faithfully, as scientifically, as possible, the Church's central and primitive tradition about that which is held to be

most vital to its own existence and its mission in the world. This tradition is found to take varied forms, related to the changing situations in a lively and progressive community. In all forms it is found to be orientated towards certain central affirmations about Jesus Christ—what He did, what He said and what happened to Him. These affirmations are seldom by way of plain items of information. The facts are communicated to us laden with meaning. All through, fact and meaning are integrated into a single but complex, picture. The problem of the 'quest of the historical Jesus' (to use a long familiar phrase) might be put in these terms: Granted this tradition, firm, central, and primitive, what manner of person, what kind of career in history, and what events as the climax of that career, are required to account credibly for the tradition, and for the character of the community which stands behind it? So conceived, the 'quest' appears to have good prospect of valuable results.

The *tradition* and the *community*—the first distinctive within the thought patterns of the first-century world, the second distinctive within its behaviour patterns. And behind tradition and community? What manner of person could have inspired such a tradition, could have supplied the dynamic for the creation of such a community? Dodd could not believe that this crucial question had to be left completely open. He believed that there was sufficiently firm and persuasive evidence to enable us to construct a true likeness of the historical Jesus, founder both of the tradition and the community of witnesses to the tradition. His own quest for the Jesus of history, whose distinctive features he could discern for himself and in turn unveil to others, never ceased.

IV

In the period immediately after his retirement invitations to give radio talks came in thick and fast. Home Service, Overseas Service, Third Programme, Sixth Forms Programme—all wanted his services. People began to be interested in the New English Bible and he was the obvious man to give information about what was going on. The first of many talks on this subject was given by him in November 1950. In 1960 he made his first appearance on television in connection with the same subject—with some apprehension for, as he wrote, T.V. is 'terra incognita to me' and he would much have preferred to stay with sound.

By 1960, when the New Testament was ready for publication, he was in his seventy-seventh year and, although the authorities recognised that he was the key man to publicise the new translation through the media, they did not wish to overtax his strength. In an advisory memo the following direction was given: Be sure that Dr. Dodd 'is used rightly and we do not impose too much on him. His continued life is more important than any programme we may do.' Nevertheless, he was called upon frequently in 1961 to explain the aims of the translators and the distinctive characteristics of the new translation. This he did with his usual warmth and lucidity and thereby showed himself to be a successful promoter as well as director of the new venture.

Of his broadcasts which subsequently found their way into print, probably the most widely acclaimed was the series entitled 'The Coming of Christ'. Originally given through the Home Service on the four Sundays of Advent 1950 they were repeated on the Overseas Service and then printed virtually as delivered. Edwin Robertson, at that time working in the department of religious broadcasting, has recalled that it was over tea one afternoon that he challenged Dodd to develop in a comprehensive way the theory which had come to be known as 'realised eschatology'. The challenge was accepted and four talks were produced, striking in their simplicity yet dealing with the profoundest mysteries of life and death.

In characteristic fashion Dodd directed his hearers to the two vast unknowns—the dimly envisaged past and the scarcely imaginable future. In between is the stretch of recorded history, culminating in the now, our present, but with a particular section highlighted for those who have committed themselves to Christian faith. That section is determinative for our understanding of the progress of events up to the present: it is also determinative for any vision we may entertain of that which is yet to come. In Christ, God's victory over evil was already won: yet it was not complete, there were many battles still to fight before the final victory, the 'unimaginable fullness' of the coming of Christ in glory.

Hanging upon what he called 'two fixed points'—the coming of Christ in history and the disclosure of Christ as Lord of history—we gain the assurance that Christ comes to us in our present situation. Every advent season reminds us that this is so. Still more vividly, the actual experience of eucharistic worship constantly re-enacts in symbolic form the coming of Christ—in the past in Bethlehem, in Galilee and on Golgotha: in the present wherever men celebrate the Supper together: in the future when the Kingdom of God is perfectly revealed. It was a serene exposition of the author's own intellectual conviction and religious faith, the former centred in the Jesus of history, the latter directed towards the Lord of history. Nowhere, I think, did he more succinctly express his own deepest and most cherished convictions than in *The Coming of Christ*.[5]

V

Looking back over his many broadcasts, a critic could urge that his range was very limited—the Bible, early Christianity, the Passion narrative, New Testament criticism—and that his presentation tended to be restricted to a well-defined historical framework: there were few direct references to our contemporary world and few divergences from principles of interpretation which he had accepted as early as the 1920s. Yet there can be no question about the success of his contributions to radio when measured by the standards both of producers and of listeners. He prepared his scripts with meticulous attention to balance and rhythm and clarity of expression. He tried to avoid statements that were abstract or hortatory, and there was never a trace of sentimentality. He never underestimated the intelligence of his listeners and never hesitated to invite them to face difficulties. Nevertheless, he was positive and constructive, and strengthened the assurance of many by the very firmness of his own conviction. He was content to make his main subject of discourse the history of the ancient world (including the early Christian movement) which he knew so intimately, and, although at times he might seem to have been repeating the same things, no broadcast that I have read seems stale or commonplace. He kept a remarkable freshness of touch which transported his hearers back into the situation about which he was speaking: it was then up to them to judge whether what had been said and done in the past could shed light upon their own problems and give them inspiration to pursue their respective ways with courage and hope.

One of the last, if not the last, of his broadcasts to schools was within a series entitled *Portrait of Jesus*. There were contributions from art and history and imaginative literature—what Dodd called 'an almost bewildering variety'. Then came his own assignment: 'Jesus: Good Man or God Incarnate?'. He invited his hearers to look again at the Gospels. For some speakers this would have meant a fairly conventional attempt to draw a composite picture out of the Gospel records but for Dodd it meant the working out of a deceptively simple but quite fascinating account of the most recent developments in New Testament scholarship so far as they bore on the Person of Jesus. The two stances from which he viewed the portrait were *matter-of-factness* and *mystery*. Once it would have been said that the first was characteristic of the Synoptic writers, the second of the Fourth Evangelist. But Dodd had little difficulty in showing that this was far too easy a contrast. However far back a New Testament critic tries to penetrate, he still finds the distinction recognised, without any attempt to separate the one element from the other. It is impossible to strip away the mysterious aspect and to find only a matter-of-fact man and vice versa. The angels of God ascend and descend upon the Son of Man.

The combination of matter-of-factness and mystery is most clearly displayed in the New Testament accounts of the Resurrection of Jesus. Few would deny today that it was the conviction that Christ had risen from the dead that brought the Church into being: this was the 'working centre' of the Christian faith. Yet the Gospels never attempt to *describe* the Resurrection. Rather they give varying accounts of the way in which disciples of Jesus—not only the Apostles—*recognised* the One who appeared to them. Now recognition implies *memory*.

For the first witnesses of Jesus the memory of Jesus was quite fresh. For the generation that gave us written Gospels it was already a corporate memory—what we call a tradition—continuous with the memory of the first witnesses. This corporate memory, or tradition, appears gathered about a rite, or sacrament, which was constantly repeated, so that the memory was never allowed to lapse. They broke bread 'in remembrance of him' and 'he was known of them in the breaking of the bread'.

So the New Testament scholar, now in his eightieth year, commended the faith to his young hearers. The Gospel story, he concluded, 'at every point has its feet firmly on the soil of first-century Palestine, and at every point also sets us in the presence of the eternal—the question which stands over this talk, "Good man or God incarnate?" offers no true alternative. The answer is "Both" '.

Notes

1. Sir H. J. Habakkuk, Vice-Chancellor of Oxford University 1973-7, has written in a letter to Professor W. D. Davies:

   Though I only met him on a few occasions, Dodd played a part in my life. When I was about nine years old, he came to preach at the chapel which my parents attended at Barry, where the minister was a former pupil of his at Mansfield. In the afternoon he gave a talk to our Sunday school on the seven (?) keys of heaven illustrated by seven drawings on an old cloth blackboard of the kind which had several 'leaves'. At that time my father was in charge of the Sunday school and Dodd came to the house afterwards. Even after half a century I can still remember his drawings, and what you wrote about his 'vital freshness' brings back very vividly his appearance as he spoke to us so long ago. He was, I suppose, the first distinguished teacher to whom I listened.

2. From 1937 onwards an increasing number of German refugees came to reside in Cambridge. Joint German–English services were arranged in Holy Trinity Church, and sermons in German were preached by Lutheran pastors. But in 1940 most of the men in the German community were taken to the Isle of Man and interned. Dodd agreed to preach in German as occasion required. Once 'in the middle of the sermon a lady not unknown for eccentricity got up and left the church, slamming the door. A letter appeared in the Cambridge local press protesting at a German being allowed to preach in "that language" at such a critical moment in the war. . . . I had the utmost joy of writing to the paper to advise the readers that the horrible German language had been spoken by one of the most distinguished English theologians alive, none other than Dr. C. H. Dodd.' Max Warren, *Crowded Canvas*, p. 103.

3. The *Listener*, 19 July, 1951, p. 105.

4. The *Listener*, 2 August, 1951, p. 185.

5. It is interesting to find a recent reference to *The Coming of Christ* in a notable book which is in no way directly related to theological themes. George Steiner, in the third chapter of *After Babel*, takes up the question of time and the word and refers to our uncertainty about mutations in time-sense when studying 'the grammars of temporal statement' used by early Christians. He recapitulates, as Dodd does, the change from the expectancy of an imminent return to a millenary calendar and then to a combination of pastness and present in sacramental experience. 'Even the most lucid of modern Christologists,' he writes, 'can do little more than state the paradox.' By illustrative quotations from *The Coming of Christ* he shows how Dodd first affirms the paradox and then declares that in each celebration of the Supper there is bodied forth a 'coming of Christ which is past, present and future all in one'. G. Steiner, *After Babel*, p. 151.

17

The Friend of Reunion

THE PROCLAMATION OF THE GOOD NEWS (*kerygma*) AND ITS APPLICATION to the life-style of those who accepted it (*didache*) were, Dodd believed, twin concerns of the early Apostles and continuing responsibilities of Christians everywhere today. But these responsibilities could not be fulfilled by isolated individuals. Those who proclaimed the Gospel were themselves members of a *community*: those who undertook the teaching did so within the context of a *community*. He never forgot what he owed to the supportive community within which he himself had been reared. He never ceased to value the tradition into which he himself had been initiated and which, he was convinced, stretched back without break to the apostolic age. *Koinonia*—a term constantly used in the Johannine Epistles to denote joint participation—became for him a word with the most sacred associations and the Body (*soma*—a term frequently employed by Paul) the most appropriate image to represent the church in its variety-in-unity.

I

The particular denomination to which Dodd's family belonged, of which he became an ordained minister and of which he remained a loyal member to the end of his life, has often been regarded as a collection of autonomous units where every congregation is free to do that which seems right in its own eyes. But Dodd did not so regard it. Every congregation, in fact, had its existence under the Word of God and owed its continuing life to the tradition out of which it sprang. He firmly believed that Congregationalism reflected the image of true catholicity and was happy to accept as his definition of the Church the words from the 55th Canon of the Church of England—'Christ's Holy Catholic Church, that is, the whole congregation of Christian people dispersed throughout the whole world'. He was prepared to strive to the utmost for the unity of Christendom, but did not believe that any existing Church possessed already the pattern of faith and order to which all should ultimately be led to conform. Though not uncritical of his own denomination, he saw no reason to withdraw from it and seek membership of another.

The pull to do otherwise must at times have been exceedingly strong. The Oxford to which he came in 1902 was dominantly Anglican— in its college chapels, in the University Church, in its parish churches, in its Divinity Faculty, in its associations with the Oxford Movement, in its theological colleges, in the nominal membership of the vast majority of its undergraduates in the Church of England. Probably the sense of loyalty to his home and to the congregation at Pen-y-bryn would have held him fast within his own tradition even if Mansfield College had not existed, but there can be little doubt that the worship and fellowship and intellectual stimulus of that institution played a major part in keeping him within the Congregational fold.

But a far more intimate and personal factor began to operate when he met and married Phyllis Terry. Through Fearon Halliday's ministry she had become familiar with Presbyterianism, but she remained a regular communicant of the Church of England. It was in a sense a 'mixed marriage' and although each was completely devoted to the other and in most respects shared the other's interests, neither accepted full membership within the other's denomination. In the early years of their marriage Phyllis would often accompany her husband to a preaching service while he, in the Manchester period, often went with her to a service of Holy Communion at the Parish Church of St. Nicholas, Burnage. In Cambridge he sometimes went to college chapel, sometimes to Emmanuel Congregational Church and sometimes with the family to St. Benet's or later to St. Edward's. After retirement and the return to Oxford, the dual arrangement continued with periodic attendance at St. Giles's Church with Phyllis and maintenance of his Congregational affiliation either at Mansfield College or at Summertown Congregational Church.[1]

What may appear a division of loyalties corresponded very closely to his own combination of ideals for public worship. In the tradition which had been familiar to him since boyhood days the preaching of the Word occupied a central place. The minister bore a solemn mediatorial responsibility: the people responded in prayer and praise. But partly perhaps because of his growing recognition of the importance of symbolic action, partly because of his early New Testament studies which revealed the centrality of the Lord's Supper in the life of the primitive Church, he became increasingly desirous of participating in regular eucharistic worship. Moreover, in sacramental worship he valued order and traditional ritual and the Order of Holy Communion, contained in the Book of Common Prayer, seems to have given him complete satisfaction.

No one who reads his writings comprehensively can fail to be impressed by the prominence given to the Eucharist in his theology and his devotion. His very first theological article accepted for publication was on the Eucharist. The opening chapter of his last book focuses attention on the Eucharist as the most obvious link with the past in contemporary Christian practice. 'The church—every gathering of the church, everywhere, under every form—*remembers* that on a certain night its Founder said and did certain definite things, briefly reported . . . The memory of the church thus takes us back to . . . the moment of the foundation of the church, when its Founder "suffered under Pontius Pilate".'[2] Nowhere, and at no time, did Dodd *feel* himself to be so contemporary with the Founder and the crucial events associated with that Founder as when he joined with others in the celebration of the Lord's Supper.

His most extensive treatment of this Sacrament may be found in a book which occupies a notable place in the history of Mansfield College. To celebrate its jubilee in 1936 a series of essays, written by former students or teachers, was collected and dedicated to Dr. Selbie, the retired Principal. The book had 'Public Worship' as its unifying theme, and at a time when in many of the Christian denominations fresh thought was being given to possible future development in this sphere, it set forth with considerable authority the best thinking within the Free Churches. But what the book made abundantly clear was that this way of thinking was amply shared by many belonging to the more 'established' traditions. Dodd's essay on the historical origins of the Sacrament as recorded in the New Testament would have commanded wide agreement, and his interpretation in terms of remembrance, communion and sacrifice would have provoked little criticism or dissent. His positive conclusions, which have won increasing acceptance over the past forty years, exemplify that drawing together of theology and worship which has been one of the most encouraging outcomes of the ecumenical movement.[3]

In the Sacrament [he writes] we accept that which God gives, become that which He makes of us (by grace, not by merit) and render it up to Him . . . Indeed, in this Sacrament the whole of what our religion means is expressed. That which otherwise we apprehend piecemeal is integrated in a rite which presents it all as the sheer gift of God. On any one occasion we may be conscious only of this or that element in the meaning; but it is all there, because God in Christ is there. In dependence on Him for everything, we render it all back to Him in thankful adoration.

II

In a book which followed *Christian Worship* two years later, Dodd confidently declared, 'The Church enters history with the apostolic *kerygma* as the expression of its life outwardly to the world, and the communion of 'the breaking of the bread' as the expression of the same life inwardly among its members.'[4] This, I think, was the constraining conviction which motivated him in all his efforts to promote unity among the churches in Britain and to support the ecumenical movement which received its symbolic expression with the establishment of the World Council of Churches at Amsterdam in 1948. He played little part in discussions about church organisation or problems of ministry. The endless claims and counter-claims about episcopacy passed him by. His concern was always to discover the positive elements within the Christian tradition on which agreement already existed. If these could be distinguished and understood more deeply a fuller experience of unity could be achieved, whatever differences in Church government and liturgical practice might still remain. It is significant that his three major contributions to international ecumenical conferences—Oxford in 1937, Amsterdam in 1948, and Evanston in 1954—were all concerned with biblical exposition. The Kingdom of God, the Covenant, the Christian Hope—these were significant biblical themes which needed to be re-examined and their implications recognised for the life of the Church in the world today. Only, he believed, by getting back to the beginnings of Christianity could the Churches find their common resources and responsibilities adequately portrayed.

Nearer home his chief activities were channelled into and through the Friends of Reunion. He attended a meeting in London in December 1932 when a progress report was presented on developments since the idea of such a movement was first mooted and a statement of aims was agreed. In May of the following year a conference of representatives from various denominations agreed to form 'a society of those who seek the unity of the Church of Christ, and who promise to further that end in any way that may be open to them'. To Dodd was entrusted the task of delivering the main address to the conference on 'The Basis of Reunion' and this was subsequently issued in pamphlet form. In substance it was an application to the British scene of principles agreed upon at the Lausanne Conference in 1927.

Three propositions concerning Faith and Order had received general acceptance, not as determining the *esse* of the Church, but as defining the grounds on which a conceivable visible unity might be established. First came the faith as proclaimed in the Scriptures and safeguarded in the Apostles' and Nicene Creeds: second, the Sacraments of Baptism and Holy Communion as expressing the corporate life of the whole fellowship in and with Christ: third, the ministry, exercised in history in varying forms but potentially capable of becoming acknowledged by the whole Church as possessing not only the inward call of the Spirit but also the outward commission of Christ. Dodd knew that there were many differences of opinion about creeds and sacraments and ministries amongst the churches in Britain. Yet he urged his hearers and readers to recognise that we all (except for fringe groups) use confessions of faith, observe sacraments and acknowledge some form of ministry. Can we not on the basis of these commonly accepted forms seek to understand each other's differing interpretations and convictions? Are we so completely satisfied with our own expressions of faith and worship that we could not entertain any suggestion of modification? He looked for a Church of the future which would incorporate the good from each tradition while rejecting the inessential or the false.

Dodd was elected to the executive committee of the Friends of Reunion and was present at their annual conferences in 1934 and 1935. At the former the proposals for a united Church of South India were examined in detail, with Dodd declaring that if only such a scheme had been put forward in the England of the seventeenth century there would be no nonconformity today. As he thought more about the scheme and its relation to the situation in England, he seems to have felt increasingly that there were no longer any serious *theological* disagreements between representatives of the different churches but rather that what he called 'non-theological factors' were the real obstacles on the path towards unity.

At the annual conference of the Friends of Reunion in 1937 he spoke of social and economic conditions, political sympathies, differences in educational background, as having been barriers between the Free Churches and the Church of England. The instinctive response to identical terms was often quite different in the one context from what it would be in the other. He appealed to his fellow Free Churchmen to seek constantly for an understanding of their own position deeper than of that of others. When there seemed to be irreducible differences, that was the time for an act of faith. A commitment to reunion could become the way towards a fuller understanding of the wholeness of truth and of the reconciliation of contraries.

III

As the movement slowed down and few concrete results appeared, he became even more concerned about non-theological factors. When asked for comment in 1945 on certain proposals for co-operation between the churches in ministerial training he replied, 'Our denominational differences are now largely extra-theological and theological differences cut sharply across denominational distinctions. For both reasons theology stands to gain by being pursued interdenominationally.' Amsterdam 1948 seemed to strengthen this conviction and at the meeting of the Faith and Order Commission (of which he was a member) held at Chichester in the following July a letter was read in which he had expressed his views at some length. This letter subsequently gained a wide circulation through being printed both in the *Ecumenical Review* and in a small booklet entitled *Social and Cultural Factors in Church Divisions*.

In this he began by remarking that in the course of nearly forty years of participation in conferences and discussions having reunion as their ultimate aim, he had often been puzzled by a recurring phenomenon. When the participants had come within sight of some real agreement, suddenly the ground of debate shifted and they found themselves back again at the very beginning. Shying away from taking the steps which seemed logically to follow, they would search around for new reasons why those steps should not be taken. But the real reasons, in Dodd's judgment, were unavowed or subconscious.

First, he instanced the almost compelling constraint of confessional loyalties to 'sacred tradition' or 'historic principles'. Let every man ask himself searchingly, 'Am I opposing the proposed action because of being grounded in some profound universal truth to deny which would argue the "lie in the soul"?' Or because of my pride (which may be legitimate) in the tradition to which I belong and my desire to save the face of my denomination at all costs? Secondly, so far as England was concerned, he claimed that the division between Anglicanism and Nonconformity stretched back at least to the Civil War of the seventeenth century. Ideals, habits, convictions, prejudices all combined to establish a distinctive mentality which made it very hard for the one side to understand the viewpoint of the other. Only by patient attempts to bring unavowed motives out into the open could the cause of reunion be substantially advanced.

Dodd was by no means the first to emphasise the importance of sociological factors in church divisions, but undoubtedly his letter prompted a new line of enquiry which has gained increasing attention since 1950. Yet even if what Richard Niebuhr in a famous book called *The Social Sources of Denominationalism* had gained due recognition, Dodd would not have been fully satisfied. He longed for the emergence of a new attitude, a readiness, adapting Cromwell's never-to-be-forgotten words, to admit that we all may have been mistaken. In a letter to the *Mansfield College Magazine*, written in March 1951, he pleaded with his fellow Independents to look afresh at key issues such as laxity regarding baptism and lay administration of the sacrament of the Lord's Supper, to see if what has been allowed can be defended by New Testament standards. In a frank conclusion he contended that certain practices among Independents had been contrary to the customs both of the early Church and of those who framed the Savoy Declaration. 'I submit that this is no case for politic concessions with an eye to corresponding concessions from the other side but of that "reformation by the word of God" which we like to think is the organizing principle of our church-order—without such reformation I doubt whether we shall make much progress towards re-union.'

Happily he did live to see one concrete example of reunion in England which embraced his own denomination: in 1972 the Presbyterian Church of England and the Congregational Union joined together within one body—the United Reformed Church. In a letter written to his own minister, Dodd expressed his satisfaction that such a union had been achieved and his regret that he could not be present at the service celebrating its inauguration.

I only wish it were possible for me to be present at so significant and indeed historic an occasion. It is the consummation of an ideal which I cherished for years before it was talked of. I have long felt it to be a nonsense that our churches should remain apart. We have long ago 'taken Presbyterianism into our system' (to use Archbishop Fisher's phrase). I suppose the present generation is hardly aware of it as I am for I grew up in the old Independency and lived through the whole process of Presbyterianizing and I know that the Congregationalism of to-day, centralized and bureaucratic, is as different from the Independent Congregationalism of old days as chalk from cheese and it is quite certainly more like Presbyterianism as I now know it. So the union, apart from all the considerations elaborately and solemnly set forth in our pamphlet and elsewhere, is to my mind plain horse-sense and I am glad of it. I need not say that there are deeper and more cogent reasons of which I am fully aware, having to do with the infinite priority of the interests of the Gospel and the Kingdom of Christ.

IV

Dodd was appointed a member of the Faith and Order Commission at Amsterdam in 1948 and took an active part in preparing the agenda for the Assembly at Evanston in 1954, when the theme was 'Christ—The Hope of the World'. In a broadcast before the Assembly met he told how, in discussions, he had become aware of the sharply contrasting views of hope for the future entertained by continental churchmen, Asiatic nationals, American social reformers and British moderates. They had been driven back again to the New Testament to get their bearings and had thereby made some progress towards a common mind.[5]

Back to the Bible, to the primitive Church, to the theological foundations of Christianity—this was Dodd's overmastering concern in all his labours for reunion. This did not mean, as I hope I have shown, that he was indifferent to what had happened in twenty centuries of history or to twentieth-century cultural and social differences. But he wanted to stand with others of whatever denomination and listen afresh to the Word of God in Christ: he wanted to kneel with others of whatever denomination and receive God's gift of the Body and Blood of Christ through the sacramental elements.[6] He had worshipped in the great churches of Rome and Berlin and New York as well as in the modest chapels of Wales and England. He had worked in closest harmony with Anglicans, Baptists, Presbyterians, Lutherans and Methodists and before the end of his life was to find himself reviewing with enthusiasm the Jesuit Raymond Brown's notable commentary on the Fourth Gospel for the Benedictine periodical the *Ampleforth Journal*.

In one sense he transcended denominational barriers; in another sense he undermined the barriers by his constant appeal to the New Testament, the book acknowledged by all as authoritative in matters of faith and conduct. Of few men of this century could it more truly be said that his praise was in all the churches. Even though his contribution to ecumenical assemblies and ecclesiastical diplomacy may have been slight, his writings, which were for ever celebrating the one Lord, the one Gospel and the one continuing eucharistic means of grace, may have done more to promote the unity of Christendom than the large and often dramatic meetings that have captured public attention and been hailed as evidence of the dawning of a new age.

As a tail-piece to this chapter it is pleasant to record that Hensley
Henson, when Bishop of Durham, said one day to Dodd, 'If things
continue at their present pace we may live to see you installed as Dean of
Durham.' Though such a prospect was never realised by the one to whom
the words were addressed, his son-in-law was in fact appointed to this
high office in 1973 and his daughter now has her home in the Deanery
which stands on the great rock above the River Weir.[7]

Notes

1. His position has been aptly described as 'occasional conformity'.
2. *The Founder of Christianity*, p. 14.
3. *Christian Worship*, ed. N. Micklem, p. 82.
4. *History and the Gospel*, p. 161.
5. In 1953 Dodd was stricken by flu and therefore unable to go to the preparatory meeting in Geneva. He arranged for Professor Owen Chadwick to
   go as his substitute and summoned him to his house for briefing. This was
   the outcome as described by Professor Chadwick:
   > He bounced up and down in bed as he talked. 'There is a conference of
   > theologians at Geneva. Its satirical duty is to draft a message which the
   > Churches will deliver to the world at their meeting in Evanston. The
   > meeting is all about Hope—that means, apocalyptic'. But, I said, I am not
   > a theologian and know nothing at all about apocalyptic. 'Exactly,' he said,
   > beaming and bouncing still higher. 'Just what I want. A typical Anglican!—
   > and a typical Englishman.' What will be my duty? I asked. 'Your duty,' he
   > said, 'will be to make Karl Barth roar as softly as any sucking dove.' So I
   > went; and after long, long fights in the day, late in the evening Barth would
   > take all the meeting to the pub, light an enormous pipe and discourse on
   > Schleiermacher till midnight. So to Dodd I owe a memorable experience.
6. Dr. Max Warren recalls a moving occasion in the winter of 1939-40 when
   in Holy Trinity Church, Cambridge, he found himself administering the
   Sacrament to Dodd (Congregationalist), Mrs. Dodd (Anglican) and Franz
   Hildebrandt (Lutheran) who were kneeling side by side.
7. In 1963 Dodd contributed the introduction to a volume of essays by members
   of Jesus College, Cambridge, entitled *The Roads Converge*. In it he surveyed the
   progress towards reunion in this century, with particular reference to the
   Lambeth Conference of 1920 and the initiative of Pope John XXIII in the
   months while the essay was being written. He followed the Pope in defining
   three stages on the way to reunion. The first, *rapprochement*, and this has been
   one of the most encouraging features of the century; the second, mutual
   interchange and understanding, which has increased particularly in the field
   of biblical scholarship; the third complete unity, which is yet to come. Dodd
   gives an impressive summary of the way in which co-operation in biblical
   studies has promoted the unity of the Church. He insists however that it is a

matter of unity in diversity—not uniformity. (*The Roads Converge*, ed. P.
Gardner-Smith, pp. 1ff.) He was delighted that some of his own books had
been translated into French and were being read by French Catholics: he
would surely have been even more delighted to learn that his last book, *The
Founder of Christianity*, had been adopted as a textbook in the Gregorian
University in Rome.

18

Director of the Translation
of the New English Bible

I

Dr. F. D. COGGAN, NOW ARCHBISHOP OF CANTERBURY, WHO WAS
Chairman of the Joint Committee on the New Translation of the Bible
from 1968 until the work was complete, has written in his book *Word and
World*:

> Though the names of those responsible for the work are not printed in
> the Preface to the New English Bible . . . it would hardly be an
> exaggeration to say that the presiding genius from start to finish was
> Professor C. H. Dodd, whose biblical scholarship and sensitiveness to
> the nuances of theology and language are known all over the world
> (p. 18).

This tribute would unquestioningly have been echoed by all who
worked with him on the panels and in the Committee, for at the conclusion of their labours they recorded a memorandum, parts of which
deserve to be quoted at length:

> From the beginning of the enterprise of New Translation, C. H. Dodd
> was given a prominent position. It would be truer to say that he
> marched unchallenged into the leading role. Here was someone who
> had no rival in the field of biblical scholarship: here was someone who
> was able to make himself available. So for more than two decades he
> exercised a dominant influence on a project in which his deep interest
> was engaged and his unequalled ability unstintingly employed.

Belonging to the Panels on both New Testament and Apocrypha, he engaged directly in the work of translation. As convener of the New Testament Panel he put at the service of the Literary Panel that fine sense of English style which imparted to his own writings such distinction of form and such lucidity of substance. A master of the written word, he excelled in popular exposition through radio and television; and of this the New English Bible was more than once the beneficiary.

His absences from the Joint Committee were very rare. When called to preside in the absence of the Chairman, he delighted members with the precision of his judgments and the firmness of his rulings, as also with that elfin humour so characteristically his own.

As rightly as the recipient of the laudation, he deserves to be called *doctor evangelicus et arca testamenti.*

In a very real sense Dodd was the leader and pioneer of the whole project. As early as the second preliminary meeting of the Joint Committee he was invited to prepare specimen translations and when these were submitted they were recognised immediately as setting a pattern which the Committee hoped that others would follow. Soon after came his official appointment as General Director and this gave him the authority to circulate for the guidance of all concerned a memorandum on the *Purpose and Intention of the Project.*

First he defined 'the public in view' for whom the translation was being made. He envisaged three major groups—the large section of the population which has no effective contact with the Church, for whom the language of the current versions is often unintelligible or has an air of unreality; young people who need a key to the meaning of the Authorised Version through language which can be regarded as 'contemporary'; highly intelligent people who still attend Church but for whom traditional language has become so familiar that 'Its phrases slide over their minds almost without stirring a ripple.'

For this 'tripartite public' what kind of version was needed? Primarily, Dodd wrote, the aim was for a version which should be as intelligible to contemporary readers as the original was to its first readers. He hoped that it would be dignified enough to be on occasion suitable for public reading but his whole emphasis was on meaning, intelligibility, reality. He wanted modern readers to be transported back in imagination to the situation of those who first heard or read the words recorded in the Bible and then to enter with them into the meaning of the message. Ideally the English used in translation should be 'timeless', avoiding both archaisms and transient modernisms.

Having established these guiding principles he proceeded to work out more detailed recommendations on such matters as text, idiom, and methods of work. Books were to be assigned to individual translators who would then submit a first draft for criticism by the whole panel. After revision it would be scrutinised by the literary panel and finally presented to the Joint Committee for approval.

Such a procedure naturally meant that a steady succession of meetings had to be organised for the panels and for the Joint Committee and Dodd was expected to be present at them all. In fact he was rarely absent. Meetings took place in Jesus College and Clare College, Cambridge: in the Queen's College and Mansfield College, Oxford; in a London Retreat House and in Fife, and in other centres convenient to the panels concerned. Each panel had its own convener and chairman and Dodd held this particular responsibility for the translators of the New Testament. I owe memories of the way he fulfilled this task to two of those who served under him on the team.

He always opened a session by reciting a prayer of St. Thomas Aquinas in Latin:[1]

> Domine Deus ac Deus noster, qui vere fons luminis
> diceris, in fundere digneri super animi nostri
> tenebras tuae radium claritatis, duplicas a nobis
> removens tenebras, peccati scilicet et ignorantiae,
> in qua nati sumus. Da nobis intellegendi acumen,
> interpretandi subtilitatem, eloquendi gratiam.
> Ingressus instituas, progressus dirigas, egressus
> compleas, per Jesum Christum Dominum nostrum.
>
> Amen

After the prayer the panel proceeded to business with the Chairman always alert, his mind never flagging, never losing interest even in the most minute details of debate. Though he never imposed himself and was always patient and courteous, he never lost control. If the discussion began to wander into irrelevancies, he would drum with his feet, speak a few sharp sentences and get things moving again on the right track. When there was an obvious division of opinion he would bow to the majority, except when some personal prejudice or some attachment to dogma seemed to be affecting a judgment. Then he would state his own position firmly while recognising that the final responsibility rested with the Joint Committee.

His promptness in dealing with letters relating to questions about translation was unlike his delays in coping with other correspondence, and at the meetings he was careful to keep a balance between work and relaxation, sometimes allowing a day off and always taking time for his own afternoon nap or for the reading of a detective novel. One famous occasion is remembered when tea had been provided at Jesus College, Cambridge, and Dodd was aware that an unusually large amount of cake crumbs had been distributed on the floor. Still, he knew where the cleaners' room was and when the others had gone he found the Hoover and brought it into the room. When one of his colleagues returned, however, it was to find him using the machine as a kind of carpet-sweeper, quite unaware that it needed to be plugged in and switched on!

The New Testament panel's task was smaller both in size and in difficulty than that of the Old and its work was virtually complete in 1959. Publication date was 14 March, 1961, and Dodd became heavily involved in the attendant publicity—broadcasting, writing, giving interviews. All this he did with a freshness of touch remarkable in one who had lived with the project almost day and night for more than ten years. He rarely repeated himself, a danger he avoided by drawing attention to varied examples from the new version, either by direct quotation or by some comment on the way a particular passage illustrated the aims of the revisers. Perhaps the most enthusiastic response to his personal commendation of the new translation was given him when he spoke at the Annual Assembly of the Congregational Union in England and Wales. Though his own denomination had numbered among its members many distinguished scholars and preachers, none, it is fair to say, had attained such universal recognition for his learning and powers of communication as had the man whom John Huxtable, when secretary of the Congregational Union, referred to affectionately as 'our Venerable Dodd'.

II

When the first stage of the great enterprise had been completed, Dodd did not relax. He began at once to collect comments and criticisms, with the result that when the whole volume was published nine years later, the New Testament appeared with approximately three hundred alterations.[2] Furthermore he remained in close touch with the other panels and in particular took his responsibilities as Vice-Chairman of the Joint Committee very seriously. He worked in closest harmony with the successive chairmen, the longest association of this kind being with Dr. A. T. P. Williams who presided over the Committee from 1950–68.[3] A tribute paid by Dodd to his Chairman is so revealing of the relations between the two men and of some of the problems they faced together, that it seems worth quoting at length. (So many of the characteristics which he attributes to Dr. Williams might well have been written of himself.)[4]

The committee was not an altogether easy team to lead. Its members represented various traditions and sometimes betrayed differences of attitude and approach to the work, and even their conception of the scope and intention of the work itself. In the main it is remarkable how well they combined, and increasingly so with growing experience of co-operation. In welding it into unity of purpose and direction the wisdom and judgment of the Chairman, and the irenic spirit which he diffused, played a chief part. At the time when he took over, the enterprise was passing through what I suppose might be called 'teething troubles'. Relations between the Joint Committee and the panels were not free from misunderstanding (and scholars are a touchy breed!). Cross-purposes began to reveal themselves. There were murmurs of doubt whether the project could ever be carried through, whether indeed it was worth all the effort; and there were even threats of resignation. Dr. Williams took the measure of the situation and 'played it cool' (one of his great assets was his refusal ever to be fussed or flustered). The difficulties were surmounted and committee and panels, understanding better their respective roles, settled down to what everyone now recognized would be a long grind . . .

In my own work as director, which was not always plain sailing, since I was in some sort a buffer between the committee and the panels, I came to rely more and more on the Bishop for counsel and support, and I found him a tower of strength. He was always accessible, and never minded (or at least never showed it!) being pestered with often trivial matters on which I sought advice or, it might be, a ruling from the chair. It was in the course of such consultations that we were drawn into more intimate personal relations, and I came to appreciate his warmth and friendliness and his inexhaustible store of human kindness. To respect and admiration was added a genuine affection, and our affection and our friendship is a deeply treasured memory.

Dr. Coggan, who was then Archbishop of York, succeeded Dr. Williams in the Chair, and again relations between Dodd and the Chairman became in every way cordial. At the time when Dodd was professor at Manchester, Dr. Coggan had come to the university from Cambridge as Assistant Lecturer in Semitic Languages and Literature. Now they found themselves, after very different careers, working together in the common cause of rendering the Scriptures more intelligible to those prepared to read them in a new translation. Dodd sat on the Chairman's right hand and in spite of his increasing deafness seemed always aware of points at issue and ready to speak about them with the authority of his unparalleled experience.

III

At length the complete Bible was published on 16 March, 1970. It was the signal for excitement, congratulation—and criticism. In fact there have been scores of critical reactions since the New Testament appeared in 1961, one of the most searching having been made in 1973 by Ian Robinson in his book *The Survival of English*. He had written unfavourably about the translation of the New Testament in a letter to the *Guardian* in 1961. It seemed to him then a 'sign of the times' and he set to work to gather material from many sources to illustrate what he believed to be a disastrous decline in the general use of English. In a chapter entitled 'Religious Language' he pilloried revisions of the Scriptures and of the Prayer Book as causing a diminution of our whole language.

The crux of the matter is the relation between language and meaning. Throughout his teaching career Dodd had a profound concern for *meaning*— not 'bare facts', not literal equivalencies, but understanding, significance, an imaginative entry into the mind of the author who originally wrote the words. History for him was occurrence plus meaning; somehow—and ultimately there was divine mystery in the process—somehow, words interpreting events conveyed meaning to hearers or readers. And once the *meaning* of a passage had been apprehended it became possible to act or react positively to the message which the words conveyed.

Dodd had been engaged in the business of translating ever since he became consciously aware that there were two languages in use in the town where he was born. Soon he was wrestling with Latin and Greek, within a discipline whose basic standards were accuracy and clarity—the overriding aims of the translators of the New English Bible. But there can be accuracy of spelling and grammar and even idiom, and still not certainty of grasping or conveying meaning. And there can be clarity of expression without the certainty that what stands out clearly conveys the true meaning of the original. There are also mysterious elements of style and rhythm and usage within a particular social group at a particular time. A wealth of scholarship was encapsulated within the several panels set up to interpret the languages of the ancient world but this did not mean that the members were necessarily equipped to render those ancient languages 'into the English of the present day'.

Dodd had no illusions about the difficulties of the translator's art:[5]

Translation is an art in which complete success is impossible [he wrote] since it is rarely that corresponding words in different languages cover precisely the same range of meaning.

Even more categorically he declared:[6]

Translation is an impossible art. Besides philological differences in the words themselves, there are differences in the associations which the words have acquired in different contexts of thought and experience.

In a letter responding to a B.B.C. producer's request for illustrations of changes of meaning derived from a study of non-literary papyri he pointed out that, although the papyri had brought about a new realisation of the nature of background and a more lively appreciation of subtle matters of idiom, these could not be illustrated through simple translations—even in a class-room the task was difficult. In other words, translation is interpretation and interpretation is a task which is never complete. The notion of 'timeless' English which Dodd put forward seemed an attractive ideal, but language cannot be abstracted from the time-process. His own brilliant success in the use of English was in no small measure due to his sense of timing, of rhythmic movement, of variation, of appropriateness to a particular context—not to a smooth timelessness which, to use one of his own metaphors, slides over the mind, producing scarcely a ripple.

Whether or not the New English Bible has proved its worth is still a matter of opinion. That no one could have done a more efficient and more devoted job as Director than Dodd would be questioned by few. But was it 'an impossible task'? If a biographer may be allowed to express a personal opinion, I could have devoutly wished that instead of directing the complex organisation he could have given some at least of the years which he spent self-effacingly in its service to making his own translation of the New Testament. Often in the course of his expositions or essays he decided to give his own translations. To me these seem without exception to be lively, often dramatic in the use of a particular word or expression, and bearing the note of authority gained from his intimate acquaintance with the Hellenistic world.

However, this is a vain wish. For all that he contributed to the New English Bible his name is honoured, his fame is assured. As his friend Dr. G. B. Caird has written in the fine memoir prepared for the British Academy (of which Dodd had become a Fellow in 1946):[7]

The climax of Dodd's career came on 16 March, 1970 when he stood in the centre of the sanctuary steps in Westminister Abbey, amid a fanfare of trumpets, to receive the copies of *The New English Bible* carried up the nave in procession by the Queen's Scholars of Westminster School, and to hand them to the representatives of the sponsoring churches and societies. Those present who did not know him could hardly have guessed from his erect carriage, his bright eye, his firm resonant voice, and his quick, bird-like movements that he was less than a month away from his eighty-sixth birthday.

It was a great occasion, and by general consent the voice that sounded out most clearly through the breadth and length of the Abbey was that of the Director himself, when, with word-perfect precision, he presented to the Queen Mother the product of the labours of himself and his colleagues over a period of more than twenty years.

IV

With the translation of the New Testament completed, Dodd might well have relaxed and turned his attention to other things. But his work as General Director continued, and his responsibility for considering criticisms and possible emendations of the new version brought further demands on his time. Yet this did not prevent him from giving his enthusiastic support to yet another attempt to bring the New Testament within the range of contemporary readers—this time, in particular, young people in secondary schools.

In 1964 Mr. Alan T. Dale, a lecturer at Dudley College of Education, sent Dodd the first section of a new translation he was in process of making for this type of reader, and, during the following year, the final and most difficult part—the writings of Paul and John. Dodd expressed warm approval of the first sample: 'You have been most ingenious in finding language for your young readers which conveys the meaning of the original.' But Paul and John would be a 'tougher proposition'. 'If you have succeeded in making Romans intelligible to young people, that will be a real *tour de force*.'

However, when 'Paul and John' arrived, Dodd became genuinely excited by what had been achieved:

> Your rendering brings out the essential meaning of the original in language which is straightforward and vivid, and often really moving . . . you have done the job of 'introduction' skilfully, explaining a thoroughly 'critical' view of the Fourth Gospel in a way which should offend none, should make the position intelligible, and should ease the way for any of the children who may go further with bible study in later years; it

should leave them with questions still to be asked, but with nothing to unlearn.

Not only did he send this message of encouragement: he also found time to examine critically the whole section on Paul and John and to offer more than fifty detailed comments for the author's consideration. Some of these illustrate the liveliness of the author's reflections and language:

I don't believe Paul had any interest in villages: he was a thoroughly urban character.

'outer space' for *bathos* and *hupsos* makes it really 'contemporary': I like it.

I have sometimes been tempted to translate (the phrase from Romans 12: 2) 'Don't try to be with it'—which is exactly what it means—but I don't recommend this!

'Apostles and prophets' are the 'official' and the 'charismatic' ministries representing the channels of authority and fresh inspiration in the Church.

I just don't believe what the commentators say about this [the translation 'mattress' in John 5: 9. In Dodd's judgment the word means light bed or stretcher].

[A long note on the amount of money suggested by Philip as still insufficient to purchase what was needed for the multitude]: A denarius is the normal day's wage. I suppose nowadays £1 a day would be considered fairly normal (on the skimpy side!) and so 200 denarii= £200. But when we were translating I wrote to our college manciple and said: 'I want to find how much I should have to spend on bread for a snack lunch for 5000 people—say a couple of sandwiches each. Can you give me an estimate?' The next day the estimate arrived, all set out in due form: £20. 17. 2. So I thought £20 was good enough. On the other hand . . . what with exchange and inflation and purchasing power the whole business is an insoluble riddle. But I suspect that if Philip had blown £200 on bread there would have been more than twelve basketfulls left over!

John 8: 6–9 sounds rather like: 'You do as you like: I am not going to be hustled by anybody.'

'scarlet cloak'. Why not 'purple'? Isn't royal purple still quite a familiar idea? They are making him look as much like a caricature of an emperor as they can. (Matthew makes it scarlet and misses the point.)

I have quoted these few examples to illustrate Dodd's unceasing concern for the exact meaning of Greek words and phrases in their New Testament context, his independence of judgment and yet his eager readiness to welcome fresh light and to revise an opinion if the evidence seemed sufficiently strong. David Daube once declared that, of all the scholars he had known, Dodd was the one most ready to admit an error or a possible error, and to change; in similar vein Geza Vermes, another Jewish scholar, noted in his book *Jesus the Jew*, that 'the first leading New Testament scholar to rethink his whole approach to the son of man problem in the light of the new Aramaic data was that youthful and indefatigable octogenarian, C. H. Dodd' (p. 191).

So the book *New World: The Heart of the New Testament in Plain English* was published, with due acknowledgement of the 'invaluable criticisms and suggestions' given by Dodd[8] and with a sparkling introductory commendation by Dodd's friend and successor as leader of the Cambridge New Testament Seminar, Professor C. F. D. Moule. In a final letter to the author Dodd wrote, 'It is a particular gratification to me to think that your work is helping to bring the New Testament home to children in the Schools—a job I should be quite unequal to myself.' Perhaps there was no objective about which he cared more than that of making the Scriptures come alive with meaning to those about to face the problems or uncertainties of our contemporary world.

Notes

1. Fortunately we have Dodd's own translation of the prayer: it may be found near the conclusion of the sermon preached in Westminster Abbey and printed as Appendix II.
2. Perhaps the most interesting change is to be found in Luke 1: 34. The 1961 version has: 'How can this be,' said Mary, 'when *I have no husband?*' Mr. T. S. Eliot strongly objected to this translation and wrote in protest to the *Times Literary Supplement*. He also entered into a friendly correspondence with Dodd but at the time the latter defended what the revisers (presumably with his own concurrence) had accepted. However, the 1970 edition gives the translation for which Mr. Eliot himself had pleaded with the minor addition of the word 'still': '*I am still a virgin.*' Here is a striking example of Dodd's openness to other points of view.
3. Dr. Williams was Bishop of Durham 1939–52, of Winchester 1952–61.
4. Quoted in *Bishop A. T. P. Williams* by C. H. G. Hopkins, pp. 116f.
5. *The Bible To-day*, p. 80.
6. *The Bible and the Greeks*, p. xi.
7. In a letter dated 18 March Dodd wrote, 'The presentation of the complete NEB in the Abbey on Monday was a moving occasion and for me in particular. When I realized some years ago what a long job it was going to be I scarcely expected to live to see it finished, and I felt deeply thankful that I had been spared.'
8. Of the ten books named as the scholarly works to which Mr. Dale owed greatest indebtedness, four were by Dodd.

PART 7

The Interpreter

19

'There and Back Again'

Home is where one starts from. As we grow older
The world becomes stranger, the pattern more complicated . . .

Only by the form, the pattern,
Can words or music reach
The stillness . . .

T. S. Eliot, *Four Quartets*

'PATTERN' IS A WORD WHICH ECHOES AND RE-ECHOES THROUGH
Mr. T. S. Eliot's poem *Four Quartets*. To discern *patterns* in nature and in
history is essential if life is to have purpose and meaning. Yet no exercise
is more complex, just because 'the detail of the pattern is movement'. No
pattern is eternally fixed.

Dodd, who was born four years before Eliot, shared his intense concern
for the discerning of *patterns*. In the sciences this interest scarcely extended
beyond geology and meteorology. But in history and in literature, pattern-
recognition became a steady aim. He loved the phrase used in Romans 6:
17: 'You have yielded whole-hearted obedience to the *pattern* of
teaching (Gk. *tupos didaches*), and although he was always suspicious of
elaborate schemes of typology, he was ever on the look-out for types,
patterns, forms, creating a sense of order both in literature and in life.

I

Is it possible to discern a dominant *pattern* in Dodd's own life? Of his
many writings the only non-theological book bore an intriguing title:

215

There and Back Again. It was for children, and the stories moved between two worlds—the familiar and the unfamiliar, the seen and the unseen, the immediate and the unexpected. But the latter of these two worlds is sometimes *religious*, sometimes *magical*: its characteristics are derived sometimes from biblical stories, sometimes from folk-tales. The author's imaginative excursions, in fact, are sometimes into biblical territory, sometimes into the lands where fables and legends of many peoples have been handed down and preserved. I suggest that *There and Back Again* was a controlling pattern of his life from start to finish, but that 'There' was not homogeneous or uniform. Starting from home ('Home is where one starts from'), he constantly went out to explore. He might have concentrated his whole attention and effort upon one limited area of human experience. Instead, if I read his career aright, he went sometimes in one direction, sometimes in another. Regularly he returned to base and shared the results of his explorations with others. But these results were never monochrome: they were the product of an intelligence and imagination which drew upon the inexhaustible riches of *two* cultural traditions and wove them into patterns which, like those of a Persian carpet, revealed ever fresh possibilities even though the basic materials remained almost unchanged.

The obvious prototype of this pattern was his daily walk. As I have shown by reference to his diaries, there was scarcely a day when he did not set out, purposefully and vigorously, to traverse some part of the countryside. Usually it was a roughly circular route—there and then back again by a different track. However many times he pursued the same paths or roads around Wrexham and Oxford, he seemed never to grow tired of them. There were always small variations in the scenes. And there was always the satisfaction of returning to the home and the family and the community, in some way enriched by what he had experienced on his walk, a bonus which often he could share with others.

Yet the base, the anchor, the foundation—whatever metaphor is most apt—was the home and the family. When he first left home to take up residence in Oxford, it was to go there at the beginning of term and come back again for vacations: rarely did he stay away beyond the necessary eight weeks. So too when he travelled farther afield—to Berlin, to Rome, to Aberdeen—his normal practice was to return to Wrexham as soon as the particular assignment had been fulfilled. And even during the time of the Warwick pastorate the return home for a brief visit was still part of the regular pattern of life. A constantly recurring theme in his biblical theology is that of the people of God, the family, the divine commonwealth, the fellowship, the social unit which retained its continuity through all vicissitudes. This aspect of God's purpose for mankind had been fulfilled abundantly in his own experience. The 'supportive community' in Wrexham provided a pattern of Christian living from which, in fact and in imagination, he could draw constant strength and inspiration and to which he could bring back from time to time some at least of the fruits of his own labours.

The occasion which most openly and dramatically symbolised the intimacy of his relationship with family and community in Wrexham was the admission of himself and his youngest brother A. H. Dodd as honorary freemen of the borough on 11 November, 1963. At the ceremonies the memory of their father, 'a much revered Headmaster', was recalled and the achievements of the one son in the field of biblical scholarship, those of the other in the field of Welsh history (including the *History of Wrexham*), were celebrated. The people of Wrexham, it was declared, could say of Dodd with pride and affection 'he is one of us' and he in reply told the assembly that his parents and four grandparents were Wrexham-born and so were six of the eight great-grandparents. He treasured the continuity of his family tradition. Still more, he would doubtless have affirmed, he treasured the Christian tradition into which he had been initiated and in which he had been nurtured in his parents' home and in the chapel at Pen-y-bryn.

II

Yet however deep is the attachment to the home in which he grows up, a man's urge is towards the attainment of at least a relative independence, the creation of a family and home of his own. The most strained and unsettled and unhappy period of Dodd's life was in his late thirties when disappointment in love was followed by the painful uncertainty whether his hopes would ever be realised. Then came the experience which Eliot describes so beautifully:

> See, now they vanish,
> The faces and places, with the self which, as it could, loved them,
> To become renewed, transfigured, in another pattern.

When he and Phyllis (I quote D. H. Lawrence) 'joined hands, the house was finished, and the Lord took up his abode. And they were glad.'

The home which Phyllis helped him to create was very different from the Wrexham original, but it provided the new base, the fresh pattern of security from which he could go 'there and back again', whether the physical location was in Manchester or Cambridge or Oxford. Perhaps Oxford held pride of *place*, but no house was more the family home than 3 Park Terrace in Cambridge. And, in the home, it was Phyllis who rescued him from lapses of attention to what seemed to him inessential things and who guarded him from those who might have exploited his generosity to anyone seeking information on this or that unimportant detail. He knew that he could always rely on her support, her encouragement and her balanced judgment. The foundations of daily living were secure. What this all meant to him he tried to express in the prefatory dedication of his greatest book:[1]

Phyllidi coniugi carissimae amantissimae hoc opus quod ipsa semper suadebat fovebat exspectabat quinto peracto lustro D.D. auctor.

Phyllis's death meant the break-up of the Oxford home, but he was not left alone and bereft. Until the last few months of his life he shared the Heatons' home and rejoiced to be near his grandchildren. Still he could go *there*—to Mansfield College; the university church; to his sister-in-law every Sunday afternoon for tea; to the occasional meeting or lecture—and back again to his study and books. In 1964 he even went farther afield, celebrating his eightieth birthday by taking his daughter to Greece and enjoying with her the sights which had become familiar to them both in imagination through their study of Greek literature. He also on occasion went with his grandchildren to Stratford, dazzling them *en route* by his detailed knowledge of Shakespeare's plays. But always it was back again, to add something to the body of knowledge which he had accumulated over the years and to think out fresh ways of sharing with others what had been so abundantly granted to himself.

III

I have suggested that the dominant characteristic of his experiences of life and his explorations of literature was that they took him into dipolar or complementary areas rather than along a single path of progress. A famous autobiography of this century by one of Dodd's contemporaries, Paul Tillich, was entitled *On the Boundary*, and this described, in turn, a whole series of border-line situations where the author felt that he had been compelled 'to stand between alternative possibilities of existence, to be completely at home in neither, to take no definitive stand against either'. This, he granted, had been fruitful for thought, but 'to stand on many border lines means to experience in many forms the unrest, insecurity, and inner limitation of existence, and to know the inability of attaining serenity, security and perfection'.[2] This progress of a dialectical kind, beset by dangers and punctuated by existential decisions, is the background of Tillich's interpretation of history and of man's relationship with God.

Yet although Dodd often found himself between two alternative possibilities of cultural and religious life, his constant aim was not to decide between the two but to embrace the two and bring them into a potentially harmonious and fruitful relationship. Where it was a question of right and wrong in matters of ethics or of aesthetics (especially in language-forms) he was firm in deciding for or against. But his ideal, as his knowledge of the varieties of human thought and experience expanded, was to appreciate goodness and truth wherever found and, having integrated them within his own consciousness, to essay the task of expressing them in forms appropriate to the age in which he lived.

The most obvious example of his dual experience may be found in the Welsh-English environment in which his earliest years were spent. He came from a family that for generations had lived in Wales: the Welsh language was constantly heard in the streets of Wrexham. Yet because this language had not been designated as a medium of education in the 1870 Education Act, his own schooling was entirely in English, and even at home and in the chapel to which the family belonged no place was found for the Welsh tongue. This is understandable in a context where the pursuit of learning was of paramount importance, but it meant that Dodd was deprived of that early easy familiarity with the language of his fathers which might have made him at a later stage an interpreter of the poetry and religious sensibility of his own people.

Be that as it may, he picked up a working knowledge of Welsh in his schooldays and nothing could deprive him of the love of music and song which was endemic to the Welsh valleys.[3] Moreover, he had music in his voice and an ample endowment of that fervour usually associated with the Celtic tradition. Fervour and imagination begat the sense of awe in the presence of mysteries beyond the ordinary canons of explanation. Dodd never deliberately played upon the emotions of any of his audiences, and indeed had his reservations about Welsh oratory and rhetoric. But when, for example, in his open lectures at Cambridge, in an academic setting and with a very mixed audience, he quoted the opening verses of the sixth chapter of Isaiah, the effect upon his hearers was electric. He himself was profoundly conscious of the majesty and the mystery: there was no need to do more than recite the words and allow them to transmit the vision to those who had eyes to see.

Wrexham, however, was near the Border, and the inroads of England's industrial life were already, in Dodd's boyhood days, bringing change. By and large, his was an *English* education, stressing numeracy and literacy, accuracy and memory-recall; it was designed to prepare children for a life which was becoming increasingly mechanical and commercial and in which the ability to understand the communications-system of the new industrial age became ever more important. Whether through heredity or through training he developed an astonishing memory; he gained a reasonable competence in elementary mathematics; above all he learned the basic disciplines of language, with the result that the native rhythm of his Welsh heritage was forever controlled by a concern for clarity of expression and attention to the rules which make inter-communication possible.

The Welsh-English polarity was soon followed by a still more significant interplay. Until he entered secondary school, the book which held an unrivalled place in his religious and cultural development was the Bible. Its stories, its standards of life, became increasingly familiar through home-reading, through Sunday-school teaching, through the regular diet of two Sunday sermons. The religious culture of the ancient Hebrews was like a fountain from which he drank ever more deeply. The conviction that God's purpose for mankind had been revealed through the whole progress of events recorded in the Bible became ever stronger as he understood more of the meaning of the sacred narrative.

Then came the opening of a door into a second world. At Grove Park Secondary School there was a master steeped in classical culture. He quickly conveyed to the boy, who already had some knowledge of Latin, his own enthusiasm for the heritage from Greece and Rome. Dodd became more than competent in the use of Latin: he read Latin texts with ease and ultimately gained an expert knowledge of inscriptions and epigraphs. But it was the Greek language and Greek literature which laid its spell upon him. This may well have been partly due to his excitement at being able to read the New Testament in the original. But probably this was not all. As he grew more familiar with Greek literature he found himself attracted by the Platonic vision of the two worlds—the realm of ultimate reality and the realm of phenomena which are symbols of the real—while his dramatic sense responded to the imperishable creations of the Greek theatre.

Greek language and literature could easily have become his life interest and the restricted field for his specialised study. But once he began his theological course in preparation for the work of the ministry he found that Hebrew was required of him as well as Greek. Fortunately for him, Mansfield possessed an outstanding teacher of Hebrew, and soon the splendour of the Greek heritage was counter-balanced by the glory of the

Hebrew. Dodd was devoted to Alexander Souter, a leading authority on New Testament Greek; he was equally devoted to George Buchanan Gray, who taught him Hebrew and Syriac. Until he left Oxford in 1931 he remained in constant touch with men who, like himself, had progressed through the rigorous discipline of Mods and Greats to a concentration of interest upon the New Testament and the literature of the Hellenistic world within which its writers lived: later in Cambridge he had as a regular member of his seminar Wilfred Knox, whose books on Christianity and Hellenism were amongst the most distinguished of his time. But his association with colleagues such as these did not lead him to neglect the Hebraic tradition. His friendship with H. Wheeler Robinson in Oxford stimulated his interest in prophetic symbolism, while his collaboration with David Daube in Cambridge greatly advanced his knowledge of Rabbinic Judaism. For him Judaism and Hellenism were adjacent fields in which he laboured alternately, and from which he brought home a succession of harvests. The Bible was his first love and to a certain extent, therefore, the Hebraic tradition retained a natural priority in all his studies. Yet the Greek New Testament became so much a part of his very being (when asked if it was true that if all written texts of the Greek New Testament were lost or destroyed he could reproduce it completely from memory, he replied quite simply that, having lived with it for so long, he was sure that he could), that when the total fruit of his labours is surveyed it seems that the Hellenistic tradition assumes the greater prominence. At least it can be said that few men have woven together the strands of the two traditions in such a masterly way.

IV

As his autobiographical reflections so vividly show, the population of Wrexham was sharply divided between Anglicans and Dissenters, and until he reached Oxford Dodd's experience of organised church life was almost completely confined to the latter camp. Even then, the strength of the Mansfield College community still held him firmly within what may be called Orthodox Dissent. Yet inevitably he began to view Anglicanism at closer quarters and with a more sympathetic understanding. Some of his closest undergraduate friends were Anglicans: he felt a kinship with Anglican Evangelicals in their concern for the Gospel, and denominational barriers were easily transcended within the fellowship of college or university Christian societies.

There is no sign that he wavered in his high regard for Independency, but gradually, as he gave more serious study to the doctrine of the Church and Sacraments, he came to an increasing recognition of its dependence upon a full-orbed theology. His own tradition, particularly in its Welsh expression, owed much to Calvin and in the *Institutes* a very high doctrine of Church and Sacraments is upheld. But within local autonomous congregations, this regard for the one great Church of Christ and its sacramental life did not always receive due recognition. When Dodd's own New Testament research revealed to him the extraordinary prominence of the concept of the Church as the Body of Christ and the obvious centrality of the Lord's Supper in early Christian practice, he could hardly fail to recognise that these elements of faith and order often gained fuller recognition within the Church of England than within his own denomination.

Whether he is more rightly termed an 'Occasional Conformist' or a 'High Church Dissenter' may be open to question. That he consistently upheld an exalted view of the whole Church as the Body of Christ, as a living organism indwelt by the one Spirit, and that he never ceased to lay stress on the Eucharist as the central outward expression of the Church's life are matters hardly open to doubt. He used liturgical forms within his own private devotions. He found refreshment for his own spirit within the fellowship both of Reformed and Anglican communions. To draw nearer to the New Testament pattern of life and thought is what he would have earnestly wished for both.

His experience of church organisation, however, was not confined to Reformed and Anglican. There were also Lutherans with whom he first came into close relationship during the summer term in Berlin in 1908. Here indeed for the first time the contrast between the British and the German traditions became clear to him. As I have already indicated, he gained an immense respect for German scholarship—in the theological field for Harnack in particular—and in later years his first advice to graduate students was to equip themselves with a sound knowledge of the German language and then to immerse themselves in the literature. Moreover, he played a notable part in the first theological discussions between British and German scholars after the First World War and in the setting up of the Society for New Testament Studies which drew together British and continental researchers in this field after the war of 1939–45. Yet with all his admiration for the achievements of German New Testament scholars in this century, he steadily refused to admit that they had said the last word or that it was necessary to undervalue the less trumpeted but often more solidly based contributions of his British or American contemporaries.

He greatly admired Schweitzer, but could not believe that his attempt

to enclose Jesus and his actions within a consistent eschatological programme did justice to the New Testament evidence as a whole. It is true
that Dodd could have been described as allergic to apocalyptic in general
(he makes scanty reference in his published work to the Revelation of St.
John the Divine), and therefore as unsympathetic to Schweitzer's radical
theory. Yet he did not deny the importance of eschatology as framework
or context so long as it was recognised that Jesus' own interpretation of
the eschatological hope was different from anything conceived in Judaism
before or during his time. The possibility of realising the blessings of the
End-time in the present experience of believers in Christ, at least in some
measure, was a notion more in harmony with the traditions of British
scholarship, even though it has never gained universal acceptance. His
profound concern for eschatology constitutes a striking example of Dodd's
willingness to draw upon the brilliant insight of a German scholar in
regard to the importance of a particular *instrument* of interpretation—but
then to adopt and adapt that instrument in his own distinctive way in
accordance with his own distinctive tradition.

Much the same might be said of his relation to Bultmann. Dodd's early
indebtedness for an awareness of the importance of form-criticism was to
Martin Dibelius, but he recognised Bultmann as the arch-practitioner in
this field, whose use of the method had led him to the most radical
conclusions. In particular, Bultmann had decided that little or nothing
can be said with confidence about the career and personality of Jesus: all
that we have is His teaching and even that must be shorn of every
accretion which could have originated in Hellenistic Christianity. Dodd's
answer in effect was to say:

> I recognise that form-critical methods are valid and useful. I will use
> them to the best of my ability. But they are not the only methods which
> can legitimately be employed for the task of New Testament inter-
> pretation. I shall still study the written sources with the utmost care, I
> shall still employ the comparative method by examining other forms of
> literature which belong to the first century of the Christian era, and I
> shall still leave open the possibility that an authentic portrait of the
> Jesus of history may be the reward of a patient and wide-ranging
> scrutiny of all the traditions which converge upon that one Figure.

For Bultmann there is a radical distinction between *a view of history* and
an encounter with history. In the former, he has had little or no interest. The
latter in his judgment, is not only important: it also constitutes a matter
of life or death for every man. His very existence is at stake as he finds
himself confronted by the Christ-event proclaimed in the death-resurrec-

tion Word which comes out of the past into his present. Dodd, on the other hand, felt an abiding need for an overall *view of history*. He did not believe that there could be a real encounter except within the context of such a view. Only as he saw the age-long working out of the purpose of God coming to its climax and its fullness of earthly expression in the whole career of Jesus could he experience the impact of the encounter. Not simply word-events nor the records of apostles bearing witness to Jesus' death-resurrection were sufficient of themselves, however important as media. Behind all traditions and testimonies Dodd looked for the lineaments of a *Person*, a Person who was himself the image of the invisible God, a Person who brought to fulfilment all that could otherwise be known of the activity of God in the whole process of history. The concern for *forms* he shared to the full. But whereas Bultmann wished to operate dialectically, separating the authentic from the inauthentic by a continuous exclusion of alternatives, Dodd wished to proceed organically, detecting the life-substance in each tradition and pointing to the way in which each element contributed to the process of integration into a living whole.

Notes

1. 'To Phyllis, dearest and most loving wife, this work, which she herself always encouraged, cherished, and waited for, was given by the author at the end of the fifth lustrum (i.e. twenty-five years) in the year of Salvation, 1950.'
2. P. Tillich, *The Interpretation of History*, pp. 3, 72.
3. 'The valley where I was born was one vast choral impulse.' Gwyn Thomas.

20

The Artist

I

I HAVE SELECTED SEVERAL PAIRS OF INFLUENCES WHICH SEEM TO ME TO have played a not inconsiderable part in the development of Dodd's pattern of life and thought. I could readily suggest others. There were dual constraints within his undergraduate studies: logic over against aesthetics, ethics over against metaphysics. Again there was the double responsibility of being on the one hand preacher and evangelist and on the other hand teacher and pastor, a duality which is symbolised by his constant emphasis upon *kerygma* (proclamation) and *didache* (teaching), and which is eloquently expressed at the conclusion of his book *The Apostolic Preaching*. In all these matters his aim was to strive, as far as possible, for integration—to hold together, in a constructive inter-relationship, the dualities which could easily become contrasts or contraries.[1]

This was particularly evident in his approach to the nature of the historian's task. One of his chief ambitions was to be a reliable *historian*, and what this meant to him became very clear in an article which was perhaps the most outspoken and severely critical that he ever wrote. It was a review of *The Rise of Christianity* by Bishop E. W. Barnes, and it appeared in the *London Quarterly and Holborn Review* in 1947. As always, Dodd tried to be fair to the book, acknowledging its constructive features. But in the main he found the Bishop's method of writing the history of the ancient world hasty and shallow. He likened it to a possible way of doing a jig-saw puzzle. 'The separate pieces of a jig-saw puzzle may look entirely meaningless, but it is unwise either hastily to discard a piece because you cannot think so queer a shape will fit anywhere, or to trim it to a better shape.' Patience, he claimed, would gradually bring the pattern of the whole to view. The historian, in his opinion, needs 'accurate information, command of critical method, patience, sobriety of judgment, and the historical judgment which includes the power to enter with sympathy into the minds of men of another age'. Because these qualities seemed to be deficient in Bishop Barnes's incursion into the writing of history (his qualifications as mathematician were of the highest order), the results could not be taken seriously.

Dodd's own special area of study was the Hellenistic world in the period when Christianity was born and began its living growth. He equipped himself in every possible way for a proper understanding of men's hopes and fears, their words and actions in this particular section of human history, but he was aware that no period could be viewed in isolation. He studied the antecedents of New Testament Christianity and to some degree its later developments in the patristic age: he tried to set the Hellenism of the first century A.D. within a comparable wider context. Then came the key question: how could the present be rightly related to the past, the past to the present? This was the polarity, more crucial than any others that I have mentioned, within which he laboured for upwards of fifty years. How could he be faithful to the past without divorcing himself from the present, and vice versa? There were those amongst his contemporaries who tried to identify themselves completely with the past: there were others who remained remote from it, as they judged everything by standards which obviously belonged to the present. How could past and present become integrated within a unified framework of meaning?

The principle which, I think, mattered most of all to Dodd was that of *continuity*. He saw as clearly as anyone that there are crises or critical junctures in human history but not, he believed, radical breaks or discontinuities. His own life-story (and who amongst us is not influenced by his own experience?) had revealed an amazing continuity, and he saw his own story stretching back through family traditions and through an unbroken Christian fellowship to the world of the first century. A favourite word he used again and again was *tradition*. If the tradition of Word and Sacrament was unbroken, if the same interpreting Spirit was guiding God's people today as in centuries long ago, then past and present became proximate: the events interpreted as saving events in the experience of first-century Christians could equally be regarded as instruments of salvation for people today. In spite of changes in language and circumstance, the fundamental needs of men in relation to their neighbours and to God remained unchanged. Using a striking image, he once declared, 'The more you read history the more you come to feel that it is in some queer way a mirror of your own life.'

What then did he see in the mirror? He saw, as he went on to affirm, *a pattern of events and a meaning lying behind them*. Here, probably, is the place where Dodd has been subjected to the most searching criticism. It is just conceivable that there is a certain *pattern* in the life of societies and of individuals which is reproduced from age to age and that it is possible to discern the essential features of this pattern. But how is the *meaning* within or behind the pattern to be discerned and transmitted? Dodd constantly affirmed that the meaning was not separate from the events, but was given with the events; the prophets of the Old Testament were held up as outstanding examples of men who were themselves involved in the events and at the same time were interpreters of their meaning. This is an affirmation but not an explanation, and in the last resort it was an affirmation of faith that completed the edifice which he so laboriously built. He tried to detect a recurring pattern in the movement of history; he tried to understand the meaning which men of vision and faith read out of the pattern; finally, by his own act of faith, he identified himself with the long succession of men of faith down through the centuries, above all with the One 'on whom faith depends from start to finish' (Hebrews 12: 1, N.E.B.), and with them saw in and through the pattern of events the revelation of the purpose and activity of the living God.

So he laboured patiently, day by day, with his documents. Earlier in life he had taken part in a few organised 'digs' and always retained a lively interest in archaeological discoveries.[2] But his chief aim was to get back to the original texts, to the writings of men who had lived through events and then interpreted them for their contemporaries and their successors. These writings fascinated him. His highest ambition was to enter into their atmosphere, to become sensitive to the ways of thinking which lay behind the words, at length to *understand* the message of the texts and so be in a position to transfer it from the faraway past into the language of his own contemporaries. He was never an antiquarian, escaping from the present into the past. He was never a 'de-mythologiser', in the sense of wanting to make a clean break with the imagery and symbolism of a former age. He believed in the one God working continuously in the history of mankind: he believed, too, in the essential unity of mankind, at all times and in all places; he believed that there was one Gospel for the salvation of mankind. If he failed, it was in thinking that modern methods of historical investigation could enable him to penetrate farther into the forest of man's past than was actually the case. He desperately wanted to get to the 'fountain-head' and to share its life-giving water with his fellow-men. But even history can take us only so far. There is no final certainty.[3] We walk by faith and not by sight.

II

In retrospect, Dodd's fame as a scholar rests, I think, more upon his work in the realm of philology than in that of history. From the time when he began his theological studies he recognised how serious was the challenge of modern historical methods of investigation to many of the assumptions about past events still entertained in Christian circles. He was determined to test all things, even those that seemed most sacred. On the other hand, he was resolved to pursue further the quest for the historical Jesus and not to rest content with Schweitzer's radical conclusion.

Yet, however valuable his historical researches have been for Christian apologists, it is as philologist that he stands supreme among New Testament scholars of this century. Words written by the distinguished musicologist Charles Rosen could be applied almost exactly to Dodd's work.[4]

> 'Philology' has been given vague and even contradictory meanings, but throughout the nineteenth century it generally meant the study of old texts and their humane critical interpretation in the light of the culture that produced them. The texts were documents of civilization to be deciphered, purified of the corruptions of time and incompetent scribes, and interpreted by the historical understanding. In this sense archaeology, history and literary criticism were necessary parts of philology. The philologist is interested not in language in general (a linguist) but in its evidence of a culture that has disappeared. The philologist, unlike the antiquarian, treasures a sense of distance from the past: he does not wish to revive it or transform it for modern use, but to comprehend its continuity with the present.

And the philology prepared the way for exegesis. A tribute richly deserved and often quoted is that Dodd was 'a prince among exegetes'.

Such was his chief title to fame as scholar. Surveying his work as a whole, however, I dare to suggest that he deserves equally to be remembered as a superb *artist*. Constantly, when reading his books, I have been struck by his appeal to the realm of art for language to describe the nature of the work he is examining as well as the task on which he is himself engaged. He notes the *dramatic* form of a narrative. He strives to produce an authentic *portrait* of a particular figure. 'Revelation', he declares, 'is not what the cinema trade (I believe) calls a "still"; it is a moving picture. It is a drama. Or, if you will, it is a musical symphony. The film, the drama, the symphony, conveys its meaning and value by movement. The movement is essential to it, even though in the end movement is transcended in a unity of apprehension. So with the Bible.'[5]

Here speaks the artist and the art-historian. The dramatic and musical imagery is attractive and illuminating. The general conception of a movement of dramatic action or of musical performance being transcended in a unity of apprehension is highly suggestive and penetrates to the very heart of Dodd's own experience. He delighted in the movement of the novel, the drama, the symphony (on a more mundane level he gained great satisfaction in the movement of his daily walk). Yet the movement was the 'instrument', a necessary instrument but not an *invariably* effective instrument. There might or might not be the unity of apprehension when listening to the Mass in B Minor; there might or might not be the unity of apprehension in witnessing the drama of the Passion story in its original setting or in reading it in written form. Yet this unity of apprehension is the goal of the artist which he in turn tries to communicate to his hearers or viewers. The final mystery of faith or unfaith remains, however, unsolved.

Every great artist is likely, at some time in his career, to 'attempt the infinite': to present, through the particular art-form which he practises, the vision of ultimate reality which he has at least dimly seen. For Dodd, it goes without saying, the ultimate reality was the living personal God: again and again he draws vivid sketches of God in action in the affairs of men. But long before his own efforts took shape, a supreme Artist had unveiled the nature and character of God through the dramatic actions of His earthly career and through the dramatic quality of His words. To re-enact, through his own spoken and written words, the drama of that central career was Dodd's highest aim.

It is significant that his conception of this task differed markedly from that of his fellow artist-theologian, Paul Tillich. At an early stage of his academic career, the latter abandoned any hope of reconstructing the outlines of the life story of Jesus of Nazareth. He decided that it was inessential to Christian faith whether the events recorded in the Gospels actually happened or not. What was essential was *the biblical picture of the Christ*. 'The picture of the New Being in Jesus the Christ' became Tillich's watchword. In the picture of the crucified Christ he saw the highest human religious possibility assumed and annulled at one and the same time. To stand or sit in sustained contemplation of a Crucifixion, whether by an ancient or a modern painter, was for Tillich the way to the depths of religious experience. In so far as there was *movement* it was in the stillness. And the same was true of his meditations upon the words and events of the Gospels.

But Dodd's conception was different. Drama, movement, a pattern of action, a story with beginning and middle and end—this seemed to him to be the nature of the Gospel-portrait and it was this portrait that he consistently sought to recover. Nowhere did he find the portrait more appealingly set forth than in the parables of the Synoptics and the 'Signs' of the Fourth Gospel. A beautiful summary is to be found in his American Bampton Lectures.

The parables of Jesus, he suggests, are the best starting-place for envisaging the teaching of Jesus as a whole.[6]

Practically everybody is agreed that the parables taken as a whole bear an unmistakable individual stamp. It is possible that one or two of them may be what is called in art-criticism 'studio-pieces', where pupils have worked on the master's design; but, just as the possibility that a few pictures ascribed to Rubens (let us say), are really studio pieces does not in the least shake our confidence that in general we know a Rubens when we see it, so we may say with confidence that a parable in the gospels is a work of art whose author can rarely be in doubt. They show perfectly definite recognizable characteristics.

What are these characteristics? First, a poetical and imaginative quality which is quite distinctive. Secondly, a realism and close observation of the pictures which they draw, even in a few strokes. The parables taken together constitute a picture of life in the *petite bourgeoisie* and working classes of a Roman province to which there is scarcely a parallel in the whole literature of the period. Thirdly, there is that dramatic quality, by which I mean the way in which the idea, whatever it may be, is expressed in action, concretely; recognizable human action in a realistic setting.

As regards the parables I believe everyone will agree that this is so. What is not always sufficiently recognized is that these same qualities, this same poetical, imaginative quality, this same realism, and this same dramatic power pervade virtually the whole of the teaching of Jesus as we have it in the Gospels.

Dramatic pictures of action in concrete situations: through these, Dodd believed, Jesus conveyed to men's imagination the vivid sense that God is here, not remote but near at hand, not an abstract conception but a living presence. And this same sense was conveyed even more powerfully by the drama which sealed His earthly career, a drama which Dodd himself reconstructed in a series of five acts with subsidiary scenes in the introduction to *Historical Tradition in the Fourth Gospel*. The drama of the Passion, in which the plot moves inexorably forward, in which the tension at times seems almost unbearable, stirs the human imagination to accept the story, either as the unveiling of the ultimate mystery of grace which lives at the heart of things, or as the portrayal of a good man tragically destroyed by the machinations of the powers of evil. Dodd tried by every artistic device known to him to produce an authentic portrait of the Jesus who lived, taught, suffered and died in Palestine, being convinced that it was through a *particular movement of events* that both message and meaning were conveyed. The three concluding chapters of his final work of literary art were devoted to a last attempt to portray for his own time what the Fourth Evangelist had portrayed for his—the glory such as befits the Father's only Son, full of grace and truth.

At the end of a long and highly appreciative review of *The Interpretation of the Fourth Gospel*, Professor S. H. Hooke once quoted a section from T. S. Eliot's poem whose central theme, as was the case in Dodd's *magnum opus*, was the Incarnation. He suggested that these lines provided a fitting commentary on Dodd's truly great achievement.[7]

> Men's curiosity searches past and future
> And clings to that dimension. But to apprehend
> The point of intersection of the timeless
> With time, is an occupation for the saint—
> No occupation either, but something given
> And taken, in a lifetime's death in love,
> Ardour and selflessness and self-surrender.

Notes

1. An intersting illustration of this aim is to be found in some of his book titles: *The Bible and the Greeks*; *History and the Gospel*; *Gospel and Law*.
2. He was fascinated by old buildings. His son writes, 'No walk, or later, car drive, was complete without visits to several country churches and very likely a ploughed field suspected of being the site of a Roman villa . . . He loved maps and the $\frac{1}{2}$-inch Bartholomew went everywhere with him. My mother would say he looked more at the map than the countryside.'
3. As Dodd himself fully recognised. Both his outline and his interpretation of Jesus' historical career were 'to some extent conjectural'. 'For the result I do not claim more than a degree—as it seems to me a high degree—of probability.' *The Founder of Christianity*, p. 179.
4. *New York Review of Books*, 6 February, 1975, p. 32.
5. *The Bible To-day*, p. 27.
6. *Gospel and Law*, pp. 53f.
7. To this I would add two sentences from a review in the *Times Literary Supplement*: 'The saint when he tries to express himself is no saint unless he is an artist. He must be ascetic in words no less than in life.'

21

The Last Frontier Post

I

ONLY WITHIN HIS INTIMATE FAMILY CIRCLE WAS DODD ADDRESSED AS Harold, and even there his brothers always referred to him as H. Students and colleagues might talk informally about C.H. or C.H.D., but in general he preserved the Victorian and Edwardian convention of using the surname in correspondence or in ordinary speech.

This practice, however, was not, in his case, entirely a matter of convention. There was always an element of reserve in Dodd's relations with his acquaintances and friends. He was not in the least cold or withdrawn but he never wore his heart on his sleeve. He never invaded another's private territory and 'Dodd' became the door which guarded the entrance to the inner sanctum of Christian names reserved for family use. Correspondingly, his custom of addressing even the best known of his students or colleagues by their surnames was a mark of respect for the other's private domain.

At a time when limericks were much in vogue, the name Dodd seemed fair prey for the rhymester's efforts. One verse became widely known and was ultimately inscribed on a glass tumbler now in the family's possession:

> I think it extremely odd
> That a little professor named Dodd
> Should spell, if you please,
> His name with three D's
> When one is sufficient for God.

But his brother, Professor A. H. Dodd, claimed that there was an earlier version and that its author was no less a person than Professor J. B. S. Haldane. Enlivened by a bump supper one evening and hearing the name Dodd, he straightaway (in about the year 1913) produced the verse:

> There once was a fellow named Dodd
> Whose name was exceedingly odd
> He said, if you please
> Spell my name with three D's
> Though one is sufficient for God.

At a later stage the name gained attention not so much because of its spelling but because of the way in which its letters were matched by its appendices; D.D. and C.H. The honorary doctorate was granted by a number of colleges and universities, but what Dodd doubtless valued most was the fact that each of England's ancient universities honoured him in this way—a distinction granted to very few. During Encaenia week in 1936, just before he assumed his new responsibilities at Cambridge, the Oxford doctorate was conferred: this of all his honours was the one most treasured by his wife, though to her great disappointment the splendour of the robes could never be displayed in Cambridge. Cambridge, on its part, made his retirement the occasion for the award at the June Congregation in 1949.

The Orator's speech in presenting him at Cambridge was imaginative and charming (in contrast to the Oxford presentation which had been little more than a *curriculum vitae*). No one, he claimed, had done more towards the accomplishment of that task which is the central concern of the Reformed Church—placing the Word of God in the hands of the people and causing it to be understood by their minds. He had done this in two ways: first, to the interpretation of the New Testament he had applied his talents to such effect that it would be impossible to find in his field of study anyone 'richer in learning, wiser in judgment or weightier in authority': secondly, he had effected this interpretation in so lucid and so elegant a manner that all who wished to investigate the foundations of their faith could receive through his books and lectures both knowledge and spiritual strength. Though the laws of the university decreed that he must be retired, the assembled Congregation had determined instead to honour a man who had made so brilliant a contribution to the whole cause of sacred learning.

There was one outstanding honour yet to come and this would, in a strange way, complete the 'oddness' celebrated in the limerick. In 1963, after the publication of the translation of the New Testament in the New English Bible, Dodd was created a Companion of Honour and went to Buckingham Palace to be invested by the Queen. Now his full title was

C. H. DODD, C.H., D.D.

In his British Academy memoir, Dr. Caird comments, 'It was Nathaniel Micklem who remarked that he spelt his name D-O-D-D recurring and he must have been one of the very few men entitled to wear his initials behind as well as in front of his name.'[1]

II

In the last years of his life Dodd suffered the handicap of increasing deafness. This often made conversations with others quite difficult. But his eyesight remained unimpaired and, until one day he was knocked down in Parks Road, his walking seemed as sprightly as ever. Former students visited him and sometimes reported on the projects in which they were engaged: 'His eyes sparkled,' wrote one afterwards, 'as he examined the work and quickly grasped its meaning and all the technical aspects of its construction.' He was surrounded by his books and never at a loss for new adventures in his own specialised field.

This was indeed the characteristic of his final years which provoked wonder and admiration amongst his friends—his complete openness to possible new interpretations of familiar material. For example, Professor W. R. Farmer of Dallas, Texas, studied with Dodd when he was professor in Cambridge and then visited him in Oxford when he was already in his eighties.

> I see him now [he wrote] with his short cropped grey wavy hair, his firm but interesting face, and I can hear his somewhat high pitched but vibrant voice, as he deftly, with authority but without being dogmatic, conveys his mind on the subject under discussion—which invariably when I was present turned to some matter of import for New Testament studies. In his presence it almost seemed unthinkable that conversation would wander aimlessly over matters of weather or general politics. No doubt he may have been quite different with close friends and members of his family. But this is something of how I remember him. A very human and business-like saint. Serious but not too serious. A giant of a man.

Or again, both Professor C. F. D. Moule and Bishop J. A. T. Robinson had occasion to correspond with him within two years of his death, the first in November 1971, the second in June 1972. Each found the veteran quick to respond to any suggestion of new insights or new perspectives in the exegesis of the New Testament.

His earlier letter reads in part:

I shall look forward with interest to seeing your views on *Son of Man*. I can't say that my own view is held with complete confidence and I am ready enough for fresh light.

Several times I had thought of writing you on a matter which I have been milling over in my own mind—ever since all the brou-ha-ha in the papers about the new translation of the Lord's Prayer, 'Do not bring us to the test'. I don't think we were exactly enamoured of that rendering but felt it was the best we could do. I am sure we were right in giving the general sense of 'test' rather than 'temptation' which has troubled so many people. But what I ask myself is whether we were really justified in insisting that the reference *must* be primarily to the eschatological tribulation. The only passage in the N.T. so far as I can see, where such a reference is quite certain is Revelation 3: 10, and there it not only has the article but it is most exactly defined. Everywhere, it seems, *peirasmos* is the kind of experience that may befall anyone, the sense, of course, including both 'test' and 'temptation' with the one or the other predominating. I don't know that such considerations would prompt any modification of our rendering but I do feel that when I kept on pressing the Literary Panel to reject *any* proposed different rendering which was *not* capable of primary reference to the eschatological tribulation, I may unwarrantably have ruled out some more acceptable way of translating the petition—several such were suggested. What do you think?

The second letter has been reproduced in full by Dr. Robinson in his book *Re-dating the New Testament*. I give extracts:

I have been through a rather rough patch, when I was not much in the way of serious letter-writing. I had to go into hospital for an operation, and came out to lead a semi-invalid existence. That however had not prevented me from thinking much about the challenging views on the Fourth Gospel which you put forward.—Your *volte face* takes one's breath away. For myself, with every motive for assigning an early date, I found this encountered too many difficulties for me to get over. However, I am open to conviction. You are certainly justified in questioning the whole structure of the accepted 'critical' chronology of the N.T. writings, which avoids putting anything earlier than 70, so that none of them are available for anything like first-generation testimony. I should agree with you that much of this late dating is quite arbitrary, even wanton, the off-spring not of any argument that can be presented but rather of the critic's prejudice that if he appears to assent to the traditional position of the early church he will be thought no better than a stick-in-the-mud. The whole business is due for radical re-examination. . . . I hope I have not darkened counsel by words without knowledge, or wearied you with the product of muddled thinking (for I am conscious that I do get muddled nowadays).

The brisk walker's aversion to the 'stick-in-the-mud' is interesting: it would be a bold man who claimed to have found examples of 'muddled thinking' in the writings of Professor Dodd!

III

For some months his daughter and her family were able still to look after him in his 'semi-invalid existence' but ultimately, in April 1973, he moved into a nursing-home at Goring-on-Thames. There he occupied a room with a lovely view over the river to the distant hills. Friends came to visit him and found him delighting either in the vision of the country-side where he had so often walked or in one or other of the versions of the Book which had been his companion throughout his life.

Dr. Coggan, then Archbishop of York, on the occasion of a visit to Oxford, took the opportunity to go out 'to thank him for all that he had been and all that he had done'. He seemed tinier than ever, bright but very deaf, with a Bible beside him which was clearly not the N.E.B. No, he said, he had found his copy of the N.E.B. too heavy to manage in bed. When the Archbishop reported this to the Press a special copy for his use was at once made available. Still later, John Robinson came, soon after a meeting of the New Testament Society, when affectionate greetings had been sent to their former president. His eyes lit up with pleasure. He bade his visitor go and stand at the window and look at the river and trees: then his eyes turned back to a copy of the Septuagint which was on the bedside table. The handiwork of God in Nature, the revelation of God in the Word—like the writer of the 19th Psalm he rejoiced in the double benediction of grace from the One who was eternally his strength and his redeemer.

His pastor from the Summertown Congregational Church went out to administer the Sacrament to him after each of the monthly services of Holy Communion in which he would normally have participated. But in the month when he moved to Goring, the Easter communion service was celebrated in his room by a friend who had been his student more than fifty years previously and who now lived at Benson, the scene of his own student-pastorate. Dr. Norman Goodall read to him the story of the walk to Emmaus—in the Authorised Version which he still preferred for liturgical use. Afterwards Dodd told his friend how glad he had been that this story had been selected. Lately, he said, he had read two passages from the New Testament more than any others: the story of the walk to Emmaus and the story of the meal by the lakeside in John 21. These, he believed, constituted the most self-authenticating testimonies to the Lord's Resurrection, and it was with the assurance of the reality of that Resurrection that he looked forward to the end of his own life.

He was realistic about death. On a visit to Cambridge when working on the New English Bible he met an old friend in Trinity Street. The latter, expressing pleasure at meeting him exclaimed, 'I only wish we saw more of you in Cambridge.' As the traffic rushed by, Dodd looked at his friend and with some intensity replied, 'There is so much I still want to do. *Erchetai nux*—' (Night cometh).

Yet he faced the future with what in an early comment on 1 Peter he had called 'strong serenity', and in a later comment on 1 John: 'serene certainty'.[2] Nowhere, I think, was this expressed more impressively than on the last occasion that he preached a university sermon in Cambridge. It was during Ascension Tide in 1963, when he was already in his eightieth year. Because the human Christ had 'ascended', he declared, He had become 'part of our present environment'. 'Christ has moved out of the remoteness of ancient history and become our contemporary.' Then, as the sermon reached its conclusion, he tried to draw out the implications for our own future of the fact that the risen Christ communicates to us 'His own divine humanity'.

As our days lengthen [he said] the inevitability and the finality of death are borne in upon us with increasing force. And then we recall that the earthly life of Christ also ended in death.—Few life-stories, perhaps, have been written in which the shadow of approaching death is so omnipresent; and the story of its ending has about it all, and more than all, that we should dread in contemplating our own death—all *except* finality. For His death was not final. There is One at least who has borne our common nature, who succeeded in carrying it unimpaired through death into endless life . . .

Once again, in the reading of the Gospels we contemplate Christ's victory over death as it was worked out in history and, once again, we appropriate it in the sacrament in which He comes to us. In that moment the two worlds are one. As we handle the simplest elements of our physical existence on earth—food and drink—we receive the Lord who is in heaven. We lift up our hearts to where Christ is on the right hand of God and He comes down to meet us here and to make us members of His Body. And as the Lord ascended to heaven, so shall His members ascend and with Him continually dwell. When for us this world has passed away, we shall possess in immediate reality that which we knew here in sign and sacrament. This is our sure ground for the blessed hope of everlasting life.

IV

Dodd died peacefully on 22 September, 1973. There was a simple funeral service at the Summertown Church conducted by the minister, the Rev. D. A. Tucker, and the Principal of Mansfield College, Dr. G. B. Caird. In the following months three services celebrated a life of devoted scholarship and gave thanks for one whose praise had been in all the Churches. In Cambridge the service was at Jesus College in February 1974: in Oxford at Mansfield College in the following June. These were in chapels with which Dodd had long and intimate associations.

The third of the services was a remarkable event which must surely be described as both historic and unique. A Free Church minister was honoured and acclaimed in Westminster Abbey on 25 January, 1974, in a service of thanksgiving in which the Dean recalled 'those loving and scholarly labours of his, centred upon the Jerusalem Chamber, which were fulfilled when the Scriptures of the Old and New Testaments, and of the Apocrypha, were newly translated into the English tongue'; in which lessons from this translation were read by the former Secretary of the Congregational Union and by the Moderator of the United Reformed Church; in which passages from Dodd's own writings were read by the Archbishop of York and by Dr. Caird: in which the memorial address was given by Professor J. K. S. Reid, a minister of the Church of Scotland; and in which the final blessing and commendation were said by the Archbishop of Canterbury. 'He belonged to all of us who bear the name of Christ. Every part of Christ's Church is a debtor to him.' These words, spoken by the Dean, summed up in simple terms the grateful feelings of as representative a company as has ever gathered in the Abbey to pay tribute to a distinguished Christian scholar. All recognised that through his labours the minds of countless readers and hearers had been illuminated by the new light breaking forth from God's Holy Word.

V

> With mercy and with judgment
> My web of time He wove.

To this 'fundamental pattern' of divine activity Dodd returned in imagination again and again. The absoluteness of divine judgment, the ultimacy of divine forgiveness were, he believed, manifested in the history both of nations and of individuals. 'The task of Christian living is the effort to work out that which is given us by sheer grace.'

Just as he conceived the pattern of divine activity in rhythmic form, so he spoke of man's response as a continuing 'rhythm of endeavour and renewal'. It could be imagined as a walk, a journey through many stages. The first sermon he ever preached was on the text, 'I am the way, the truth and the life.' Much later, in a valedictory address to Mansfield students about to begin their several ministries, he chose the image of the road. They would go out as disciples, followers of Him whose characteristic command was 'Up! Let us go forward'. Even when it had become abundantly clear that this way forward was the way of a cross, still in complete dependence upon the Father He refused to turn back. 'May His power,' Dodd concluded, 'rest upon those who are taking the road, His forgiving and renewing grace upon those who are travel-worn and His peace upon us all.' After his death the Chaplain of the Oxford College to which he came as an undergraduate wrote, 'If anyone walked with God, he did.'

He walked with God just because his memory and his imagination were constantly engrossed with the story of the One who, as God's representative, had walked on earth.

> To me, that story—ay that Life and Death
> Of which I wrote 'it was'—to me, it is;
> Is, here and now: I apprehend nought else.

Constantly the divine standard of judgment revealed in the life of the Christ spurred him to new endeavour: constantly the divine overflow of mercy mediated through the sacrifice of the Christ brought renewal of strength for the continuing task. It was a journey, he knew, with a beginning and an end. 'Birth and death,' he reminded his hearers in a notable broadcast on *The Lord of History*, 'are frontier-posts by which we enter and leave this limited realm; and the frontier control is strict.'

Yet is the boundary 'just a dead end'? When each individual reaches the frontier post of death, does he not step into the presence of the Eternal? The broadcast concluded with a perfectly simple yet deeply impressive confession of faith: 'From what Christ said and did, still more from what He was, we learn what it concerns us to know about the true and final relation between a man and his Maker; and that is in the last resort the key to everything. And finally, we learn from His earthly adventure and what came of it, the true nature of the last frontier-post and who it is that awaits us there. More than that we do not need to know.'[3]

Notes

1. In 1970 the Institute of Linguists awarded Dodd their Diamond Jubilee Medal for distinguished services to the profession, and after the completion of the New English Bible, Oxford University conferred upon him the honorary degree of Doctor of Letters.
2. 'The reserve which he [the author of I John] exercises about our future destiny, discouraging all fruitless speculation, combined with the serene certainty that we shall see our Lord and be like Him, is the model for all our thinking about the life to come.' *The Johannine Epistles*, p. 71.
3. *The Coming of Christ*, p. 32.

Appendix I

(From a letter written by Professor Langdon Gilkey of the
University of Chicago)

At Union Theological Seminary in 1950 'some of the graduate students
were invited to listen to a conversation between Tillich and Dodd, one
that we all knew was going to be very interesting—for the positions of
both of them were well-enough known to promise a major encounter.
Two more different species of the *genus theologicus* could hardly be
imagined: Tillich always reminded me in such conversations of a deliberate,
serene, quiet, rumbling lion—something (as I discovered later when I
read them to my son) like Aslan in the Narnia books of C. S. Lewis. This
was hardly Dodd; some form of very bright-eyed bird, perched on his
chair, continually moving about, looking everywhere—and very intelligent.
We all settled down for a significant listening—and we got it.

'The subject was the complex one of the relation of historical scholarship
to affirmations about the "Christ of faith", as we then called it, a subject
upon which Tillich's views were famous and very controversial. Martin
Kähler always poured out of Tillich on this subject: any "leaps" via
historical inquiry and its merely probable forms of certainty to the
Christ of faith—to the object of faith's affirmations—were for him far too
large to be possible. We are, he reiterated, *certain* of nothing here concerning the "historical Jesus"—i.e. certain via historical inquiry—and
faith cannot rest on such essential uncertainty. There is, said Tillich, only
one "risk" (that was the word he used) involved in the affirmation of faith,
namely that the *picture* of Jesus in the gospels is the picture of him who is
the Christ. Here Tillich felt there is *real* risk, and, moreover, it is a
theological or religious risk, appropriate to such a domain, namely one
involving our ultimate concerns. The risks involved in historical probability are, he maintained, incommensurate with religious "risks",
namely "preliminary" ones, not matters of ultimate concern. Besides, as
he always remarked in this connection, "I do not wish to be subject to a

phone call from my colleague in the N.T. field, telling me that some new data have been unearthed that compromise my ultimate affirmations concerning my being and non-being." He dealt with the problem of the relation of the "picture" in the N.T. to the "historical" referent thereof in a quite different way, namely *not* via historical inquiry, but as involved intrinsically in the affirmation of, or, better, the experience of faith itself.

'Since, he said that evening, the power of the new being grasped him *through* that picture, that "being-grasped" guaranteed (a) that the picture pointed to a *real* historical embodiment—for "unless essence had been united to existence (i.e. to a *historical* figure), the picture of that union could have had no power to transform our existence"; and (b) that, as the medium of that power of the new being, the picture in the N.T. was an "analogy" of its own ultimate historical referent. Thus faith does not guarantee any *historical* (i.e. historically reconstructed) picture or ground any historical assertions concerning this or that fact of the historical Jesus; but it does guarantee, out of itself so to speak, that there *was* a historical embodiment and that that historical embodiment was *analogous* to the picture. (I recall thinking, *Ja*, he is a real German: an idea to have power must be *real*; and the latter word, while having reference to "history", nevertheless is not just what an Anglo-Saxon means by that word).

'We were not surprised when Dodd replied that such a view did not satisfy the historian at all. No risk of faith is possible unless it has a historical ground—granted that it involves a "risk" about an affirmation concerning a historical figure. One cannot, he said, move from an inner *feeling* in the present to any sort of affirmation (via historical inquiry or not) about a past event. Thus while he agreed wholeheartedly that the *major* risk of faith had to do with the relation between Jesus (however known) and the act of God embodied in him: "the event of realized eschatology" (I suppose he said), still basic to the overcoming in faith of *that* risk, was the certainty that the witness of the N.T. to the eschatological event was based on a historical figure. Tillich then said, "Then there are *two* risks, a 'double risk', involved for the Christian: one that the witness of the NT refers to an actual historical figure, and the second that the figure so described is the Christ." Yes, said Dodd, there are two risks, one historical and the other religious—and a historical faith cannot escape either one. Tillich said he could not tolerate such a double indemnity, so to speak, and stuck to his "single risk" theory. They agreed that this divergence expressed accurately the differences between the two of them; and that to each of them the conversation had proved immensely clarifying and edifying—as it certainly was to all of us.

'Dodd then went on to maintain—and I don't think Tillich agreed with him—that the preliminary, historical risk was really not all that great. He clearly felt relatively comfortable with the "high level" of probability that was entailed in the assertions, via historical inquiry, that there was a historical Jesus and that the main characteristics of his life, relevant to his role as the Christ, could be known with great probability.

'I have tried to indicate, and it is important to do so, that this was an extremely amicable conversation with great respect on both sides, with no signs of irritation or polemics—but an effort by two very great men to understand the relation of their own thought to the thought of the other. I am sure each of them had a fairly clear notion of where precisely their major differences lay—but each was literally *delighted* to be enabled by conversation so clearly to isolate and define that difference. As far as I can remember, in all each of them subsequently said—and the patois of the students reflected this afterwards—the categories of "single risk" and of "double risk" now labelled what seemed to be the major options on this subject. Tillich then opened another bottle of wine—*only* done when the conversation had been really successful—and conversation turned to other things.

'As I remarked, I recall at the time thinking that while this was not precisely the conversation one would have heard between Hume and Hegel, nevertheless it was a reasonable facsimile thereof—and that we had had spread before us some of the major differences in the Anglo-Saxon and the German Guests. I am not sure that this issue they debated has been moved any further than this point, and certainly it has seldom been so clearly and precisely stated as by these two great men.'

Appendix II

A Sermon preached by Professor Dodd in Westminster Abbey to commemorate the 350th Anniversary of the Authorised Version and the inauguration of the New English Bible.

When your Advocate has come, whom I will send you from the Father—the Spirit of truth that issues from the Father—he will bear witness to me. And you also are my witnesses, because you have been with me from the first.

John 16: 26–7

In the Acts of the Apostles we are told how the incipient church set about filling a vacancy in the apostolate—a vacancy created by the defection of Judas Iscariot. The apostle Peter, acting as presiding officer, states the minimum essential qualification required in a candidate for the vacant post. This is what he says: 'One of those who bore us company all the while we had the Lord Jesus with us, coming and going, from John's ministry of baptism until the day when he was taken up from us—one of those must now join us as a witness to his resurrection.'

One might have expected that a candidate for so responsible an office in a new community, with its way still to make, would be required to show qualities of leadership, or of intellect, or of prophetic utterance, or the like. Such qualities were certainly to be found among early Christians, and they were highly prized; but apparently they were not thought indispensable for the office of an apostle. What *was* indispensable was that he should have personal acquaintance with the facts of the ministry of Jesus Christ from beginning to end, and out of such acquaintance should be able to give first-hand testimony to the fact of his resurrection.

So much we learn from the Acts of the Apostles. The passage I read for text takes us a step further: 'The Spirit of truth that issues from the Father—he will bear witness to me. And you also are my witnesses, because you have been with me from the first.' Here again, the apostles are to be witnesses: that is their special function. And the qualification is the same: they have been in the company of Jesus all through, and therefore know the facts about him. But we now learn that behind, and within, the witness of the apostles is the witness of the Spirit. Their testimony is inspired testimony. I take it you do not need special inspiration to give an honest report of events that happened under your eyes. But it did call for very special insight in these men to see what it all meant: what was the bearing of these disconcerting facts upon their personal problems and upon human life and destiny at large, what difference they made to the total relationship between God and man. This was the work of the Spirit of truth, interpreting to the apostles the things they had seen and heard. The facts were not less factual for being interpreted, not less historical. On the contrary, the meaning they were now seen to bear was that which made them a turning point in history. Fact and interpretation are one in the witness of the apostles.

And here it lies before us, in the scriptures of the New Testament. The first witnesses said their say; they spread the message abroad through the mouths of others; it was written down and bequeathed to the church as a permanent possession. Here in the New Testament—in gospels and epistles alike without distinction or separation—we have the final deposit of the witness borne in the earliest age, when the memory was still fresh. And that is the fundamental reason (whatever other good reasons there may be) why the public reading of the Bible, and the study of the Bible, must always keep its commanding position in the life of the Christian society.

Not that the apostolic testimony comes down to us in one channel alone: it filters through the whole common tradition of Christian belief and practice; it is heard in the preaching of the gospel from age to age; it is set forth in the unbroken ministration of the sacraments from the earliest times. But it is documented and certified by the written word of scripture, which remains unchanged, and is accessible to all. Not only Christian preaching and teaching, but Christian worship itself is what it is because of the special place it gives to the reading of the Bible. The language of devotion and praise, of contrition and aspiration, is not peculiar to the Christian religion; but in Christian worship such language receives a peculiar content because, through lesson, gospel and epistle, the worshipping congregation is continually brought back to the facts about Jesus Christ and the meaning of those facts.

For the presupposition of our whole approach to God is that the Word became flesh: the eternal and divine entered history and fell under human observation. This provides a point of reference for every act of worship. The Christ in whose name we pray, to whom we ascribe glory with the Father and the Holy Spirit, the Christ who gives himself to his people in sacrament, is the same who once worked and taught in Galilee and Jerusalem, and suffered under Pontius Pilate. And how are we to know what he taught and did and suffered except through the testimony of those who were there? And where can we go for that except to the New Testament? No speculative theology, and no mystical vision, could give us facts of history, and our faith is anchored to the gospel history in which it pleased almighty God to make Himself known to men. In the New Testament itself the boldest flights of theological speculation are still an effort to interpret the given facts. 'Our theme,' says one of the New Testament writers—certainly not one of the least theological of them— 'our theme is the word of life. This life was made visible; we have seen it and bear our testimony. . . . What we have seen and heard we declare to you.' And at every reading of the New Testament it is declared afresh. That is what gives the Bible its unique character. Here we renew our faith where it first began. And in this all Christians are at one.

All Christians are at one. That is something to think about when we are despondent about our continuing divisions. After all, we read the same Bible; we nourish our faith on the same testimony; and in this we already possess a real measure of unity. This great assembly of Christian people of different communions is (within its limits) a sign of such unity. Over a wider field in recent years the study of the Bible on a scholarly level has become a truly co-operative enterprise, in which Catholic and Orthodox, Lutheran and Reformed, Anglican and Nonconformist, find themselves drawn together across the barriers, to learn from one another and to discover afresh how close we are, in spite of everything, when we get down to the 'grass roots' of the faith. I say this as one whose privilege it has been during the past forty years to have some part in it, and I am persuaded that we have here one of the most promising channels through which the spirit of unity is making its way and preparing for the time (perhaps still distant) when the whole Christian people shall be visibly one.

This new translation of the Bible on which we are engaged is also a co-operative enterprise among members of various Christian communions. Our fellowship in the work has been a great experience. Ecclesiastical or denominational differences fell away as we became absorbed in our task: our one concern was to reach a common mind about the meaning of the text before us. For the purpose of our enterprise is the same as that which has governed the broad movement of return to the Bible all over Christendom. It is, quite simply, to find out just what the Bible means, resisting (to the best of our ability) the temptation to make it mean what we should like it to mean, or, alternatively to take refuge in a safe ambiguity. Of course the assumption behind it all is that the Bible (whatever other demands it makes of us) demands to be *understood*. Is that something that might go without saying? I think not. The Bible may serve various purposes which are served also by other religious books. It may kindle feelings of devotion, or supply language for such feelings when they are barely articulate; it may suggest elevated thoughts that might never visit us without such aid; it may provide the first step towards heights of contemplation. For such purposes much hangs upon the suggestive or evocative power of words; their exact meaning may for the time lie in the penumbra of consciousness. Thus the language of the Authorised Version, or of the Prayer-book version of the Psalter, often noble in itself, has acquired layer upon layer of hallowed association through the centuries; it has overtones which call forth an instinctive, almost an inherited response in those who were brought up within the tradition. But of how many in our society is this no longer even remotely true? And of those of whom it is true, is there not the danger that they may be so soothed by the flow of splendid words half understood that they escape the harsh challenge of the Bible to mind and conscience? If, as I have urged, the special quality of the New Testament is that of a testimony to intractable facts of history, and to the meaning the facts bore to people who stood directly under their impact, then it does demand to be understood. The more precisely we come to understand the words of the scripture, the more open we must be to the initial witness of the apostles and within it the witness of the Spirit of truth which gave them, and can give us, living knowledge of the Word made flesh.

It was this conviction that moved the early translators of the Bible into English—Wyclif, Tyndal, and Tyndal's successors whose work ultimately issued in the Authorised Version. It is the same conviction that has inspired those who are working on the New English Bible. Because we hold that conviction, we have thought no labour lost in trying to understand as precisely as possible what the Hebrew or Greek of the biblical writers means, and to bring that meaning to English readers in language as clear, and as comely, as we can make it. This has been our aim, and our ideal. That it should be realised completely is not to be expected of fallible mortals. But we trust the promise is not vain, and that our all too human infirmity has not left us altogether impervious to the illumination of the Spirit of truth that issues from the Father.

There is an ancient Latin prayer, attributed to St. Thomas Aquinas, which has often been used in our sessions for translation. In English it might run somewhat as follows:

Lord God, and our God, who art called the true Fountain of light and wisdom, be pleased to pour upon our dark minds the clear radiance of thy light, removing from us the twofold darkness, of sin and of ignorance, in which we were born. Give us keenness of understanding, subtlety of interpretation, and grace of expression. Shape our beginning, guide our progress, and make our ending complete; through Christ our Lord.

In the spirit of that prayer we have tried to handle our task, and in that spirit we now render up the first fruits of our labour to those from whom we received our commission.

Bibliography

A bibliography of Dodd's writings which he regarded as noteworthy up to 1954 was printed in the Festschrift entitled *The Background of the New Testament and its Eschatology*, ed. W. D. Davies and D. Daube (Cambridge University Press, 1954, reprinted 1964).

This was brought up to 1970 by the Rev. J. Tudno Williams as an appendix to the printed report of a lecture given to the Honourable Society of Cymmrodorion on 8 October, 1974, entitled *Aspects of the Life and Works of C. H. Dodd*. Mr. Williams has kindly given permission for his appendix to be reprinted below. A complete bibliography is available in the U.S.A. at Lexington, Ky. R. W. Graham, *Charles Harold Dodd 1884–1973. A Bibliography of his Published Writings*, Lexington Theological Seminary Library Occasional Studies, 27 pp.

1954
'Christ, the Hope of the World', in *We intend to stay together* (with G. K. A. Bell and others) (Four Broadcast Talks on Evanston): S.C.M. Press.

Editor: *Texts and Studies* (Contributions to Biblical and Patristic Literature) (New Series) (Cambridge).

1955
'Some Johannine "Herrenworte" with parallels in the Synoptic Gospels', *N.T.S.* ii.

'The Appearances of the Risen Christ: an essay in form-criticism of the Gospels', in *Studies in the Gospels: Essays in memory of R. H. Lightfoot*, ed. D. E. Nineham (Blackwell, Oxford).

'The Beatitudes: a form-critical study', in *Mélanges Bibliques rédigés en l'honneur de André Robert* (Bloud and Gay, Paris).

'The Life and Thought of St. Paul', in *The Teacher's Commentary* (Revised Edition), ed. G. Henton Davies and Alan Richardson (S.C.M. Press).

1957
'The Prologue to the Fourth Gospel and Christian Worship', in *Studies in the Fourth Gospel*, ed. F. L. Cross (Mowbray, London).

'A l'arrière plan d'un dialogue johannique', in *R.H.P.R.* xxxvii.

1959
'The "Primitive Catechism" and the Sayings of Jesus', in *New Testament Essays: Studies in Memory of T. W. Manson*, ed. A. J. B. Higgins (Manchester University Press).

1960
'The Translation of the Bible: some questions of principle', in *The Bible Translator* xi, no. 1 (reprinted from the *Times Literary Supplement*).
Das Gesetz der Freiheit. Glaube und Gehorsam nach dem Zeugnis des Neuen Testaments (Chr. Kaiser, Munich).

1961
Introduction, *The New English Bible: New Testament* (Oxford and Cambridge University Presses).
'Wilfred Lawrence Knox, 1886–1950', British Academy, *Proceedings*, 1961.
'Some Problems of New Testament Translation', *E.T.*, lxxii, no. 9.

1962
'The Prophecy of Caiaphas: John xi. 47–53', in *Neotestamentica et Patristica. (O. Cullmann Freundesgabe). Supplements to Novum Testamentum*, vi (Brill, Leiden).
'T. W. Manson and his Rylands lectures', in *E.T.*, lxxiii, no. 10.
'Eight English Versions of the New Testament', in *E.T.*, lxxiii, no. 12.
'Une parabole cachée dans le quatrième évangile', in *R.H.P.R.*, xlii.

1963
Historical tradition in the Fourth Gospel (Cambridge University Press).
Introduction to *The Roads Converge: A Contribution to the Question of Christian Reunion*, ed. P. Gardner-Smith (Edward Arnold, London).

1964
'Alan Richardson's *History, Sacred and Profane*', in *E.T.*, lxxv, no. 7.

1965
Christ and the New Humanity (Two Essays) (Fortress Press, Philadelphia).
A New Testament Triptych on Christ's Coming, His Gospel, His Passion (Forward Movement Publications, Cincinnati).

1967
'The portrait of Jesus in John and in the Synoptics', in *Christian History and Interpretation* (Studies Presented to John Knox), ed. W. R. Farmer, C. F. D. Moule, R. R. Niebuhr (Cambridge University Press).

1968
More New Testament Studies (Manchester University Press).

1970
The Founder of Christianity (Macmillan, New York).
Introduction, *The New English Bible with Apocrypha* (Oxford and Cambridge University Presses).

'Paul and his world' and 'The Thought of Paul', in *A Source Book of the Bible for Teachers*, ed. R. C. Walton (S.C.M. Press).

1972
'The Gospel According to John: a Review Article', in *The Ampleforth Journal*, lxxvii, Part 1 (1972).

1976
†Notes in *Technical Papers for the Bible Translator*, 27 (1976).

1977
†Notes in *Technical Papers for the Bible Translator*, 28 (1977).

Index

252